Engendering the Woman Question

Women and Gender in China Studies

VOLUME 12

The titles published in this series are listed at *brill.com/wgcs*

Engendering the Woman Question

Men, Women, and Writing in China's Early Periodical Press

By

ZHANG Yun

BRILL

LEIDEN | BOSTON

Cover illustration: *Funü shibao 9* (February 1913). Shanghai Library collection. Reprinted with permission.

The publication of this book is partially supported by the Harvard-Yenching Institute Alumni Publication Grant.

Library of Congress Cataloging-in-Publication Data

Name: Zhang, Yun, 1986-
Title: Engendering the woman question : men, women, and writing in China's early periodical press / by Zhang Yun.
Description: Leiden ; Boston : Brill, [2020] | Series: Women and gender in China studies, 1877-5772 ; volume 12 | Includes bibliographical references and index.
Identifiers: LCCN 2020027692 (print) | LCCN 2020027693 (ebook) | ISBN 9789004438538 (hardback) | ISBN 9789004438545 (ebook)
Subjects: LCSH: Women–China–History. | Periodicals–Publishing–China–History.
Classification: LCC HQ1767 .Z444 2020 (print) | LCC HQ1767 (ebook) | DDC 305.40951–dc23
LC record available at https://lccn.loc.gov/2020027692
LC ebook record available at https://lccn.loc.gov/2020027693

Typeface for the Latin, Greek, and Cyrillic scripts: "Brill". See and download: brill.com/brill-typeface.

ISSN 1877-5772
ISBN 978-90-04-43853-8 (hardback)
ISBN 978-90-04-43854-5 (e-book)

Contents

Acknowledgements

This book derives from the doctoral dissertation I completed at the University of Hong Kong in 2015. My first and deepest gratitude goes to my supervisor, Louise Edwards, for her unwavering support during the years of my graduate study and continued help and encouragement after I graduated. The time, patience, and care that she devoted to my research were remarkable: from having weekly writing sessions with me for the entire first year of my PhD to reading and commenting on every draft of the manuscript along the way. Her intellectual rigor, infectious energy, and indomitable spirit have taught me how to be a committed and resilient scholar.

I have also benefited from the generous support and guidance of other teachers and colleagues. Prof. Gail Hershatter provided invaluable comments for my book proposal and pushed me to articulate and reformulate my main argument. The challenging and important questions she raised helped make possible a radical rethinking and rewriting of the dissertation. My thesis committee members, Prof. Joan Judge, Dr. Binbin Yang, and Dr. Su Yun Kim, offered constructive comments and advice to help me improve the dissertation. Prof. David Der-wei Wang and Prof. Ellen Widmer provided insightful advice on the topic, content, and structure of the dissertation. Professor Clara Wing Chung Ho gave me useful information on finding sources. Dr. Loretta Kim shared her expertise and knowledge in Manchu studies and corrected my mistakes. Two anonymous reviewers for Brill offered perceptive comments that significantly transformed the manuscript.

I received generous financial support from the School of Modern Languages and Cultures at the University of Hong Kong. A Harvard-Yenching Visiting Fellowship from the Harvard-Yenching Institute funded my research at Harvard University for eighteen months. I am particularly thankful for the Harvard-Yenching Institute Alumni Publication Grant that I received for the publication of this book. The postdoctoral fellowship from the School of Humanities at Nanyang Technological University made the revision of the book a peaceful and pleasant experience. The librarians at the University of Hong Kong, Wuxi Library, Shanghai Library, Harvard-Yenching Library, and Nanyang Technological University provided able assistance and invaluable support. I am grateful to them.

There are many individuals I would like to thank for their support and friendship at different stages when I conducted this research: Prof. Kam Louie, Prof. Kendall Johnson, Selena Orly, Shirley Chen, and Selina Lai-Henderson at the University of Hong Kong; Sadie Rosenthal, Jooeun Noh, Yueyan Li, David

Dadui Yao, Masao Imamura, Yun Ge, Qian Yang, Ruohong Li, Susan Scott, Lindsay Strogatz, and Elaine Hall Witham at Harvard-Yenching Institute; Dr. Fang Xiaoping and Prof. Uganda Sze Pui Kwan at Nanyang Technological University. I would also like to express my gratitude to Qin Higley for her efficient work and professionalism and to Elizabeth You and the production team for helping turn the manuscript into a book. I also appreciate my copyeditor Debra Soled's thoughtful and meticulous editorial work.

I owe the deepest personal debt to my family. My parents have nurtured my intellectual interest from an early age and provided unconditional support and love all along. My sister and brother are my close friends and have offered constant emotional support. Finally, I thank Alex for the unfailing support and companionship and our daughter, Chloe, for bringing meaning to our life. This book is dedicated to them.

Chapter 2 has appeared as "Nationalism and Beyond: Writings on *Nüjie* and the Emergence of a New Gendered Collective Identity in Modern China," *Nan Nü: Men, Women and Gender in China* 17, no. 2 (2015): 245–275. An earlier version of Chapter 5 has appeared as "The Emerging Modern Woman: Representations of the 'Girl Student' in Early Twentieth-Century Urban China," *Harvard Asia Quarterly* 16, no. 3 (2014): 50–59. I am grateful to the publishers for giving reprint permission.

Figures

Introduction

Defining the early Chinese women's periodical press has been a thorny task not only because it was a multiauthored, multivocal, and heterogeneous print genre but, more significantly, because of its complex gendered character.[1] Although Chinese women's journals seem to be markedly gendered, as suggested by the terms *nü* 女, *nüzi* 女子, *nüjie* 女界, or *funü* 婦女 in their title, they were by no means designated for or designed by only women. Even in a women's journal edited and written by women, men exerted influence as financial sponsors, production managers, and even direct or imaginary interlocutors, let alone in women's journals for which men assumed prominent roles as editors, publishers, and contributing authors. At the same time, however, male-dominated women's journals also allowed space for women to make their discursive contributions, and in many instances, women pushed to enlarge their intellectual authority and scope for action in ways that men had not expected.

This book carves out new terrain in research on the Chinese women's press through a major shift in focus—that is, from a gendered site coded as either "feminine" or "masculine," depending on the gender imbalance in editorship and authorship in specific journals, to a mixed-gender public space in which men and women were both intellectually active and involved in dynamic interactions to determine the contours of their discursive encounters. This approach does not presume that male and female writers or editors always directly encountered or openly argued with one another in the pages of any specific women's journal. Rather, it suggests that a women's journal was an integral part of a wider intellectual and print context in which masculine cultural norms often dominated. It focuses on the dynamic interplay between men's and women's writing that took place both on the pages and in the broader historical and print culture of particular journals, highlighting that women consistently maneuvered to expand their discursive authority by modifying, challenging, or even defying these norms. It thus delineates what recent studies have advised in the study of Chinese women's journals—to "make the role of gender central

1 On the multiregister and heterogeneous nature of Chinese women's periodical press, see Joan Judge, Barbara Mittler, and Michel Hockx, "Introduction: Women's Journals as Multigeneric Artefacts," in *Women and the Periodical Press in China's Long Twentieth Century: A Space of Their Own?*, ed. Joan Judge, Barbara Mittler, and Michel Hockx (Cambridge: Cambridge University Press, 2018), 1–18; on the vexed question of gender in the women's press, see Margaret Beetham, "Preface: The Role of Gender in Defining 'Women's Magazine'," in ibid., xxv–xxix.

 DOI:10.1163/9789004438545_002

and explicit."[2] Most important, this approach foregrounds an analytical continuity in discussions about a wide range of prominent topics central to the woman question across different kinds of women's journals from the late Qing (1644–1911) to the early Republican period (1912–1949). It thus opens a window onto men's and women's gender-specific approaches to these topics, revealing their gendered visions of Chinese modernity in general and modern Chinese womanhood in particular.

1 The Mixed-Gender Public Space in the Women's Press during the Late Qing and Early Republican Period

The Chinese women's press was at once an important part of the rapidly expanding Chinese print media that bourgeoned in the late nineteenth century and a particular print genre of its own.[3] It thus afforded an unprecedented public space for discussions of a variety of topics that converged on an exclusive focus—women. The first Chinese women's journal, *Nü xuebao* 女學報 (*Journal of Women's Learning*; English title: *Chinese Girl's Progress*), appeared in the summer of 1898 at the height of the Hundred Days' Reform, a movement launched by the Qing government to drive systemic institutional, political, social, and educational change. Although the journal was forced to cease publication shortly after the coup d'état by the Empress Dowager Cixi 慈禧 (1835–1908) in September of that year, it was subsequently followed by a blossoming of various women's journals over the next few decades. Between 1898 and 1911, over forty women's journals were published, and by 1918 thirty more had appeared.[4] Although this number was modest compared with the overall

2 Beetham, "Preface,' " xxvi.

3 The first Chinese-language daily newspaper, *Shenbao* 申報, was founded in 1872 in Shanghai, and, according to one estimate, by 1937 over 1,500 newspapers had been published. See Judge, Mittler, and Hockx, "Introduction: Women's Journals as Multigeneric Artefacts," 2. For the seminal study on *Shenbao*, see Barbara Mittler, *A Newspaper for China? Power, Identity, and Change in Shanghai's News Media, 1872–1912* (Cambridge: Harvard University Asia Center, 2004).

4 Two Chinese scholars estimate that about fifty women's journals appeared between 1898 and 1918. See Xu Chuying 徐楚影 and Jiao Lizhi 焦立芝, "Zhongguo jindai funü qikan jianjie, 1898–1918 中國近代婦女期刊簡介（一八九八——一九一八年） [An Introduction to the Early Chinese Women's Periodical Press, 1898–1918]," in *Xinhai geming shiqi qikan jieshao di si ji* 辛亥革命時期期刊介紹第四集 [*An Introduction to the Periodicals during the Xinhai Revolution, Volume Four*], ed. Ding Shouhe 丁守和 (Beijing: Renmin chubanshe, Xinhua shudian faxing, 1982). Drawing on other data, some recent studies suggest the number should be over seventy. See Song Suhong 宋素紅, *Nüxing meijie: lishi*

number of periodicals and newspapers published during this period, by the late 1930s about 250 women's journals had begun publication.[5] Many women's journals founded before 1911 were short-lived and were available for a period from several months to a few years. The longest-lasting women's journal at this period was the revolutionary *Nüzi shijie* 女子世界 (*Women's World*), which lasted from 1904 to 1907. The women's journals produced during the early Republican period, particularly the commercial women's journals, were published longer and had higher circulation than the pre-1911 women's journals. For example, two of the most influential early Republican commercial women's journals, *Funü shibao* 婦女時報 (*Women's Eastern Times*) and *Funü zazhi* 婦女雜誌 (*Ladies' Journal*) were published from 1911 to 1917 and from 1915 to 1931, respectively. *Funü shibao* printed an estimated 6,000 to 7,000 copies per issue, and *Funü zazhi*'s circulation was as high as ten thousand. To determine the actual extent of readership, these numbers should be multiplied several times, as it was common for each issue to be shared among several people.[6]

These journals can be divided into different types, from reformist to revolutionary, from anti-Qing feminist to pro-Manchu, and from political to commercial. The journals were characterized by the sheer diversity in their contents, which comprised a rich reservoir of images, advertisements, and texts in a full range of genres, including poetry, polemical essays, public speeches, biographies, translations, and fiction.[7] A large number of these women's journals, which used to be difficult to get ahold of as they were housed in different libraries in or outside China, are now more accessible because of the large-scale reprinting and digitization projects in China and the online databases built through international collaborative projects.[8]

---

yu chuantong 女性媒介：歷史與傳統 [*Women's Media: History and Tradition*] (Beijing: Zhongguo chuanmei daxue chubanshe, 2006), 38–41; Liu Renfeng 劉人鋒, *Zhongguo funü baokan shi yanjiu* 中國婦女報刊史研究 [*A Study on the Chinese Women's Periodical Press*] (Beijing: Zhongguo shehui kexue chubanshe, 2012), 89–92, 125; Yuxin Ma, *Women Journalists and Feminism in China, 1898–1937* (Amherst, NY: Cambria Press, 2010), 58, 98, 151.

5 An estimated 450 periodicals were published before 1913. This number continued to rise in the Republican era. See Roswell S. Britton, *The Chinese Periodical Press, 1880–1912* (Shanghai: Kelly & Walsh, 1933), 127–128; for the number of women's journals by the 1930s, see also Judge, Mittler, and Hockx, "Introduction," 3.

6 Joan Judge, *Republican Lens: Gender, Visuality, and Experience in the Early Chinese Periodical Press* (Berkeley: University of California Press, 2015), 18; Jacqueline Nivard, "Women and the Women's Press: The Case of the Women's Journal (*Funü zazhi*) 1915–1931," *Republican China* 10, no. 1 (1984): 37.

7 For a recent collection exploring the wide range of genres in the women's periodical press, see Judge, Mittler, and Hockx, *Women and the Periodical Press*.

8 Shanghai Library has extensive holdings of pre-1949 Chinese women's periodicals and made most of them accessible through its two prominent digital archives: Wan-Qing qikan

The study of the early Chinese women's periodical press has emerged as a thriving research field and received increasing scholarly attention in recent years. Feminist and literary scholars have used feminist journals to illustrate the tangled relationship between nationalism and feminism in early twentieth-century China.[9] Scholars of media studies have revealed intriguing stories of women journalists as newly emerged professionals in the public sphere in modern China.[10] In the eyes of historians, women's journals have served as an invaluable lens with which to view the complexities of China's gendered past, as they abounded in texts and images about critical political, social, and cultural changes and shifting gender roles at particular historical moments.[11] In addition to the diverse perspectives presented in women's journals, new approaches and methodologies have also been developed by international collaborative research teams to examine the intricacies of women's journals as materials and historical objects. A recent edited volume on the Chinese women's periodical press by Joan Judge, Barbara Mittler, and Michel Hockx, for example, devised four modes for reading women's journals: "horizontal," "vertical," "integrated," and "situated." These new reading strategies not only enable fresh analyses of all the contents from a specific journal but also help to bring to light the connections between a women's journal and the wider print culture or other source materials that inform its broader historical context.[12]

Although much has been written about the materials in a specific women's journal and certain themes in particular types of women's journals, this book approaches the early Chinese women's press as a mixed-gender public space, which allows the investigation of distinct themes and topics as they emerged across different women's journals and historical moments. Without claiming to be an exhaustive study of all women's journals, this book assembles reformist,

quanwen shujuku 晚清期刊全文數據庫 [Late Qing Dynasty Periodical Full-Text Database, 1833–1911] and Minguo shiqi qikan quanwen shujuku 民國時期期刊全文數據庫 [Chinese Periodical Full-Text Database, 1911–1949]. Two scholars in China, Wang Changlin 王長林 and Tang Ying 唐瑩, led a reprinting project that includes the full text of seventy-nine women's periodicals from 1903 to 1949; see Wang and Tang, *Zhongguo jinxiandai nüxing qikan huibian* 中國近現代女性期刊匯編 [*Compilation of Women's Journals in Modern China*] (Beijing: Xianzhuang shuju, 2008); scholars in North America, Europe, and East Asia, have constructed a database with detailed information on four prominent women's journals (https://kjc-sv034.kjc.uni-heidelberg.de/frauenzeitschriften/).

9 Charlotte Beahan, "Feminism and Nationalism in the Chinese Women's Press, 1902–1911," *Modern China* 1, no. 4 (1975); Amy Dooling, *Women's Literary Feminism in Twentieth Century China* (New York: Palgrave Macmillan, 2005), 44–49.

10 Ma, *Women Journalists and Feminism in China*.

11 Judge, *Republican Lens*; Judge, Mittler, and Hockx, *Women and the Periodical Press*.

12 Judge, Mittler, and Hockx, *Women and the Periodical Press*, 8–10.

revolutionary, anti-Qing feminist, pro-Manchu, and commercial women's journals systematically and emphasizes the mixed-gender public space as their shared characteristic. Scholars have long noted the gender imbalance in women's journals in terms of editorship, authorship, and readership. For example, the overseas Chinese feminist journals that flourished in Japan in the first decade of the twentieth century were published, edited, and written almost solely by women, even if men constituted part of the readership. At the same time, the commercial women's journals that emerged in the early Republican period were overwhelmingly edited and staffed by men.[13] Even though women were active contributors to and engaged readers of these journals, men also comprised a robust, if not larger, percentage of the authors and readers.[14] Given the gender disparity in editorship and authorship in these two distinct types of women's journals, how can one suggest that they each afforded a mixed-gender public space of their own?

To address the complex and varied forms of mixed-gender public space in the women's press, it is crucial to integrate the feminist women's journals into the broader feminist print culture and place them within the larger context of Chinese feminism and nationalism.[15] An example of gendered writings about the concept *nüjie* 女界 (lit. "women's world/space/circles"), offers a glimpse into the unique mixed-gender public space afforded by the feminist women's journals. *Nüjie* was originally a term constructed by a male nationalist feminist to refer to Chinese women as a subjugated collectivity in the context of national salvation. The term, however, was soon appropriated by women in the overseas feminist journals to articulate essential feminist ideas, such as "female citizenship" and "absolute gender equality," which challenged men's definition. Although men did not contribute to the overseas women's feminist journals, women writing about *nüjie* used the masculine definition of it

13 Two of the most influential commercial women's journals *Funü shibao* and *Funü zazhi* were edited by men, and only one woman, Hu Binxia 胡彬夏, briefly served as the editor of *Funü zazhi*. But whether she actually fulfilled the role of an editor remains a question of scholarly debate. See Yung-chen Chiang, "Womanhood, Motherhood and Biology: The Early Phases of *The Ladies' Journal*, 1915–1925," *Gender & History*, 18, no. 3 (November 2006): 542, note 44.

14 For example, in the first commercial women's journal *Funü shibao*, the journal's male chief editor estimated that only 20 to 30 percent of the contributors were female. In her recent study of the journal, Joan Judge estimates it at around 50 percent (*Republican Lens*, 69).

15 This method of situating a women's journal in both its immediate print context and a wider cultural and historical context is inspired by the "integrated reading" and "situated reading" proposed in Judge, Mittler, and Hockx, *Women and the Periodical Press*.

as a potential object of critique or interrogation. In this sense, the feminist journals and the surrounding feminist print culture and context constituted a mixed-gender public space, which served as an ideal locus for us to discern the dynamic between men's and women's writings about *nüjie*.

The ideas of "male editorial agency" and "female authorial subjectivity" help us understand another form of mixed-gender public space in commercial women's journals. In contrast to the feminist journals, in commercial women's journals, it was primarily men who devised editorial strategies and exercised power in determining the agenda and contents of a publication, which was defined by a recent study on the commercial women's journals as "male editorial agency."[16] Although this "editorial agency" was influential, female contributing authors challenged this agency and demonstrated their authorial subjectivity through their encounters with the visual and textual contours largely mapped out by men. Like the women writers in the mixed-gender public space of the feminist press, female contributors to the commercial women's journals seldom publicly confronted or criticized men. Even the most subversive women's feminist writings that offered a radical rejection of masculine norms were not produced through women's direct argumentation with men. What marked the mixed-gender public space of the commercial women's journals was female contributors' active negotiation with and appropriation of dominant masculine discourses on women, which had the effect of "resignifying power discourse with subversive citations from within."[17]

In addition to these two prominent forms of mixed-gender public space, this book also examines two others that are noteworthy: the first, which was created by the first and foremost women's journal, the reformist 1898 *Nü xuebao;* and the second, which was manifested in two pro-Manchu women's journals. *Nü xuebao* constituted a mixed-gender public space in which men were not contributing authors to the journal and yet formed the journal's agenda. Before the journal was founded, male intellectuals and female contributors had participated in public gatherings, which greatly facilitated the birth of

---

16 Liying Sun, "Engendering a Journal: Editors and Nudes in Linloon Magazine and Its Global Context," in Judge, Mittler, and Hockx, *Women and the Periodical Press*, 57–73; for a study of the dynamic interplay between "male editorial agency" and "female authorial subjectivity" in two women's journals in the 1920s, see Rachel Hui-Chi Hsu, "Rebellious Yet Constrained: Dissenting Women's Views on Love and Sexual Morality in *The Ladies' Journal* and *The New Woman*," in Judge, Mittler, and Hockx, *Women and the Periodical Press*, 158–175.

17 Joan Judge and Hu Ying, ed., *Beyond Exemplar Tales: Women's Biography in Chinese History* (Berkeley: Global, Area, and International Archive/University of California Press, 2011), 285.

the publication. Men also actively engaged in writing treatises on the promotion of women's education, which became the stated objective of the journal. Moreover, men provided direct financial sponsorship and management for the journal. The pro-Manchu women's journals reveal a mixed-gender public space in which men and women offered distinct gendered approaches to and, in some instances, directly argued against one another in making sense of a Manchu woman's suicide and the issue of Manchu ethnicity.

2 The Mixed-Gender Public Space and the Woman Question

Recent studies of gender and modern Chinese history have noted the inextricable links between China's quest for independent nationhood and for modernity and the woman question. Gail Hershatter, for example, astutely observes, the Chinese modernity "sought by a heterogenous lot of reformers and revolutionaries ... was a shifting and receding target that encompassed economic and military strength but would also, many felt, require a thorough overhaul of cultural practices ... that could irreversibly consign semicolonialism to the past,"[18] and "women were figures through which national modernity was imagined."[19] Joan Judge also points out that the Chinese woman question was characterized by the convergent treatment of gender and national issues. Unlike in Western countries, where modern ideas of nationhood emerged almost a century before the issues of female emancipation were put forward, in China calls for gender and national reform emerged together and were addressed simultaneously.[20]

The Chinese woman question was first raised at the turn of the twentieth century, a tumultuous moment when China faced profound crises and challenges: tumultuous political and social reforms, constantly redrawn geographic borders, reconceptualization of deep-seated Confucian doctrines, and intellectual turmoil caused by interactions with Western notions and ideas. In their effort to address these crises, Chinese intellectuals regarded Chinese women's status as central to refashioning China into a modern nation. China was weak, they argued, because Chinese women were benighted, cloistered,

---

18 Gail Hershatter, *Dangerous Pleasures: Prostitution and Modernity in Twentieth-Century Shanghai* (Berkeley: University of California Press, 1997), 7–8.

19 Gail Hershatter, *Women in China's Long Twentieth Century* (Berkeley: University of California Press, 2007), 79.

20 Joan Judge, *The Precious Raft of History: The Past, the West, and the Woman Question in China* (Stanford: Stanford University Press, 2008), 8.

and oppressed; China would become a strong country only if Chinese women were liberated and their status raised. In short, conditions for Chinese women became a signifier of China's condition as a nation-state and of its place in the modern world—a symbol of China's lack of power, authority, and prestige as a civilized modern state, and this discourse defined the difference between China, a feeble, backward state, and the modern Western world.

Male intellectuals initiated public discussions about the causal links between the state of women and the state of the nation, but educated women also participated in the debates.[21] Scholars have noted that both male and female commentators identified women as a potent symbol of big debates about the overriding project of national strengthening, but little attention has been paid to the important gendered differences in reconfiguring the place of women in the country. Like their male counterparts, female intellectuals recognized the nation as the new meaningful context for prescribing new roles for women, but they were also important agents in imagining new womanhood on their own within and beyond the context of nationalism. This study shows that the mixed-gender public space in the women's press provides a prime site for seeing the gendered articulations of the woman question as it intersected with various prominent topics that first appeared during the 1890s and the 1910s, including women's literary capabilities, education, feminism, ethnicity, women's health and modern science, and women's public behavior.

Liang Qichao 梁啟超 (1873–1929), an influential late Qing scholar and journalist, was one of the first male reformers to articulate the woman question. He underscored the centrality of women in China's national survival by promulgating women's education in China. In 1897, in a sweeping critique of Chinese women as illiterate, physically inferior, and economically dependent, Liang made a passionate plea to develop women's education, which determined, in his words, "whether a nation will survive or be destroyed and whether it will prosper or languish in weakness."[22] However, as some recent scholars have

21 Western missionaries in China also portrayed Chinese women as ignorant and oppressed and saw women's status as a barometer of China's degree of civilization. See, e.g., an essay by an American missionary, Young J. Allen (Lin Lezhi 林樂知), "Quandi wudazhou nüsu tongkao xu qiyi 全地五大洲女俗通考序其一 [Preface to *Women in All Lands*]," *Wanguo gongbao* 萬國公報 29 (August 1903). Late Qing intellectuals drew upon these narratives of Chinese women, but they departed from the missionaries, as they believed that Chinese women could be saved by nationalistic reform, rather than Christianity. See Weikun Cheng, "Going Public through Education: Female Reformers and Girls' Schools in Late Qing Beijing," *Late Imperial China* 21, no. 1 (2000); Hershatter, *Women in China's Long Twentieth Century*, 82.

22 Liang Qichao 梁啟超, "Lun nüxue 論女學 [On Women's Education]," in *Jindai Zhongguo nüquan yundong shiliao* 近代中國女權運動史料 [*Historical Materials on*

pointed out, Liang's dismissal of all Chinese women as dependent and uneducated in effect overlooked the fact that Chinese women had a long tradition of contributing to the household economy and the market and that elite Chinese women had a long tradition of learning that could be traced back to the Han dynasty (206 BC–220 AD).[23] Liang's conception of the woman question resonated with many of his like-minded reformers but, at the same time, caused dissent among some female reformers. Although these elite women concurred with men that women should be educated for nationalist reasons, they strove to construct their own vision of new Chinese womanhood by relying on their writing tradition, which had been vehemently denounced by Liang.

Debates over the woman question became increasingly rigorous in the first years of the twentieth century, when Chinese nationalism was inextricably entangled with feminism. The association between women and the nation became even more explicit as Chinese women as a whole were construed by male nationalists as an oppressed group whose emancipation was subordinated to national salvation. Male thinkers envisioned women as mothers whose primary responsibility was to produce able-bodied citizens. Feminists and female revolutionaries, as exemplified by the female students who traveled to Japan, however, called for women's full participation in the modern nation as citizens in their own right. These female activists effectively used nationalism as their legitimizing and authorizing discourse to reposition women as independent national subjects and to articulate their own feminist agendas. Some radical revolutionaries even called for an end to the improvement of women's status for the sake of a modern Chinese nation and demanded absolute equality between men and women, which ruptured the causal link drawn between women and the nation.

In addition to Han nationalists and feminists, non-Han reformers also took on the woman question to articulate their own visions of ethnicity, identity,

---

Modern Chinese Women's Movements], ed. Li Youning 李又寧 and Zhang Yufa 張玉法 (Taipei: Longwen chubanshe gufen youxian gongsi, 1975), 1: 552. The translation is in *The Birth of Chinese Feminism: Essential Texts in Transnational Theory*, ed. Lydia H. Liu, Rebecca E. Karl, and Dorothy Ko (New York: Columbia University Press, 2013), 194.

23 Joan Judge, "Reforming the Feminine: Female Literacy and the Legacy of 1898," in *Rethinking the 1898 Reform Period: Political and Cultural Change in Late Qing China*, ed. Rebecca E. Karl and Peter Zarrow (Cambridge: Harvard University Asia Center, 2002), 158–179; Hu Ying, "Naming the First 'New Woman'," in Karl and Zarrow, *Rethinking the 1898 Reform Period*, 180–211; idem, *Tales of Translation: Composing the New Woman in China, 1899–1918* (Stanford: Stanford University Press, 2000); Nanxiu Qian, "Revitalizing the *Xianyuan* (Worthy Ladies) Tradition, Women in the 1898 Reforms," *Modern China* 29, no. 4 (2003).

and the nation. An example that best illustrates this "ethnicized" approach to the woman question was some Manchu reformers' effort to envision their own ideal of modern womanhood following a Manchu woman's suicide. In 1905, a Manchu woman killed herself to put a spotlight on women's education, and her death received widespread media coverage. But most national newspapers neglected or downplayed this woman's Manchu ethnicity, which aroused discontent among the Manchu communities. Some Manchu reformers then took pains to publicize this suicide and celebrate the woman as a Manchu heroine who willingly sacrificed herself for the sake of the Manchu nation. Their construction of a Manchu version of modern womanhood reflected an attempt to assert their Manchu racial identity, which was in question in the face of Han nationalism. Like their Han counterparts, these Manchu reformers deployed the figure of Woman in their debates over broader racial and national issues. At the same time, female Manchu reformers refused to see their ethnicity as a marker or mechanism of distinction in their conception of modern womanhood. In contrast to Manchu men, they allied themselves with all other subjugated Chinese women in gender terms, rather than ethnic terms.

The connection between new womanhood and a modern nation persisted well into the Republican period. As the new Republic was founded in 1912, calls for equal rights and women's suffrage were suppressed, and women's participation in national politics was prohibited by the government. Instead, women were called on to perform the role of wise mothers and good wives who possessed modern housekeeping and child-rearing skills. Using the newly introduced knowledge of Western medicine, male intellectuals envisioned women as practicing the science of hygiene for the well-being of the nation in general and the health of the modern family in particular. Some female intellectuals subscribed to this new ideal of womanhood and understood women's health as a linchpin in the epic, grand project of national strengthening. Others, however, incorporated the knowledge and language of feminine hygiene into the fabric of women's everyday life and emphasized their individual bodily experiences. For these female thinkers and writers, the cultivation of women's health was not only essential to the prosperity of the national body but empowered women to understand and publicly discuss their own gendered bodies.

Whereas reformist intellectuals declared that the most fundamental role for women in the new Republic was to be modern, educated, productive wives and mothers, they also approached the woman question by means of discursive regulation. They spilled a great deal of ink on the disciplining and public behavior of young female students, a new category of women who were often cited as the negative foil of the "wise mothers and good wives" ideal. They criticized the extravagant and outlandish clothes worn by these students and focused on the potential threats that they posed to public spaces and the social order. Some female commentators went along with men in trying to control the young female students, but they were more sympathetic and often aimed to correct the misconceptions about them by sharing their own personal experiences. In general, the effects of such regulatory efforts were limited because the number of female students rose quickly, and their public appearance was pervasive. But the practice of regulating modern gender practices persisted well into the 1920s and 1930s as the urban intellectuals designed the characteristics of the New Woman and the Modern Girl.

The results of women's participation in the debates over the woman question varied: some women succeeded in configuring a new womanhood distinct from the one conceptualized by men and subverted the ties between women and the nation; others, in most cases discreetly, modified new ideas about womanhood as laid out by men and understood them in their own way. But, as the following chapters show, it was their writing in the mixed-gender public space of the women's journals that produced a record of women's gendered approach to the woman question and their own conceptions of gender, the nation, and modern identity. In this newly carved out public space, they asserted themselves as active, engaged writing subjects of public discourse and deployed writing as a way to expand their discursive and intellectual authority.

3 Women's Writing as a Way to Enlarge Their Discursive Authority

The French Sinologist Jacqueline Nivard noted that the publication of a women's journal at the turn of the twentieth century constituted a "revolutionary act" in itself.[24] Women's journals not only served as an unprecedented mixed-gender public space in which women could engage in public debates with men but also opened up an important creative space for women to experiment with new textual modes and discuss politics, gender, and national issues in ways unknown to their predecessors. Existing scholarship has revealed two high tides in women's writing in Chinese history. The first was from the late Ming (1368–1644) to the early Qing and was marked by literary activities and productions by courtesans. The second one was from the High Qing to the late Qing, roughly from the mid-eighteenth century through the nineteenth century, in

24 Quoted in Paul J. Bailey, "Chinese Women Go Global: Discursive and Visual Representations of the Foreign 'Other' in the Early Chinese Women's Press and Media," *Nan Nü: Men, Women and Gender in China* 19, no. 2 (2017): 225; see also Jacqueline Nivard, "L'évolution de la press féminine 1898 à 1949," *Études Chinoises* 5, nos. 1–2 (1986): 160.

which gentry women from elite, scholarly families formed the majority of this new female literary collective.[25]

Despite the remarkable number of female writers and their cultural impact, their writing remained an activity in which women expressed their innermost feelings and emotions as well as their concern regarding family interests and social issues that were not intended for a broader reading public.[26] Even when a female writer's work was published or circulated within a broader circle, owing to the help of male patrons or family members, by no means did she intend to reveal her inner world to unknown readers or strangers. Further, women's writing in the late imperial period was rarely directed at criticizing the body politic or serving any true public/official purpose.[27] Although women wrote about social changes, dynastic falls, wars, and riots, these topics were seldom the focus of their writing, and their engagement with political and social issues remained indirect and peripheral.[28] It was even rarer for women to engage directly in discursive political writing the same way as their contemporary male counterparts did. Women's literary talents and creative activities were

25 In past decades, literary scholars and historians have compiled and edited women's writings over the course of Chinese history into collections and anthologies. Some notable collections were Ellen Widmer and Kang-I Sun Chang, ed., *Writing Women in Late Imperial China* (Stanford: Stanford University Press, 1997); Wilt Idema and Beata Grant, ed., *The Red Brush: Writing Women of Imperial China* (Cambridge: Harvard University Asia Center, 2004); Dorothy Ko, *Teachers of the Inner Chambers: Women and Culture in Seventeenth Century China* (Stanford: Stanford University Press, 1994); Susan Mann, *Precious Records: Women in China's Long Eighteenth Century* (Stanford: Stanford University Press, 1997).

26 According to Hu Wenkai 胡文楷, from the High Qing to the late Qing, there were around 3,600 women writers, a figure that exceeds the total number of women writers in previous ages. See Zhang Hongsheng 張宏生 and Shi Min 石旻, "Fulu: Gudai wenxue funü de yanjiu qidian jiqi tuozhan: Hu Wenkai *Lidai funü zhuzuo kao* de jiazhi he yiyi 附錄：古代文學婦女研究的現代起點及其拓展——胡文楷《歷代婦女著作考》的價值和意義 [Appendix: The Modern Starting Point and Developments on Studies of Women in Traditional Chinese Literature—the Value and Meaning of Hu Wenkai's *Research on Women's Works from All Dynasties*]," in *Lidai funü zhuzuo kao* 歷代婦女著作考 [*Research on Women's Works from All Dynasties*], ed. Hu Wenkai (Shanghai: Shanghai guji chubanshe, 2008), 1206. On the emergence of new reading publics and print culture in late imperial China, see Cynthia J. Brokaw and Kai-wing Chow, ed., *Printing and Book Culture in Late Imperial China* (Berkeley: University of California Press, 2005). See, in particular, Anne E. McLaren, "Constructing New Reading Publics in the Late Ming China," 152–183.

27 Grace Fong, "Radicalizing Poetics: Poetic Practice in Women's World, 1904–1907," in Judge, Mittler, and Hockx, *Women and the Periodical Press*, 104–120.

28 For a recent study on women's writing in the Ming-Qing dynastic transition, see Wai-Yee Li, *Women and National Trauma in Late Imperial Chinese Literature* (Cambridge: Harvard University Asia Center), 2013.

heralded as safe havens from the cold, heartless male intellectual world and distant from politics.[29]

In stark contrast to women's writing in the late imperial period, the women writing for women's journals consciously addressed a public audience and employed writing as a way to enlarge their intellectual authority in public discourse. A salient example that characterizes this public engagement was female journalists' frequent adoption of a new form of polemical writing, which often took the form of *lun* 論 (discursive essay) and *shuo* 說 (persuasive discussion). Originally modes that appeared in imperial male literati scholars' statecraft writings, *lun* and *shuo* carried new connotations and discursive power as they absorbed the meanings encapsulated in the Western journalistic genre of "leading article." Eventually, in late Qing journalism, *lun* and *shuo* developed into a powerful genre for public political discussion.[30] In the women's press, women used this genre not only to publicly engage in writing on national politics but also to discuss social concerns, gender relations, and other topical issues concerning the Chinese woman question. This very act of women adopting *lun* and *shuo* had a social effect: it granted women public visibility and authorial presence in an intellectual world from which they had been excluded. Just as male intellectuals' deployment of this new mode of writing manifested their "authoritative" voice in judging between right and wrong in the public sphere, women's active participation in *lun* or *shuo* writing testified to their effort to claim discursive authority in the public discussion of national and gender concerns.[31] This new polemical writing also enabled women to compete with men for authority in the mixed-gender public space of the women's journals. That women could write like men using the new writing mode did not mean that women wrote about things the same way that men did. Many women employed *lun* or *shuo*

29 Ellen Widmer points out that the vast majority of Ming-Qing women's poetry was devoid of political content, in large part because the publication and printing of many women's works were heavily dependent on gentry families' financial resources. See Ellen Widmer, "The Rhetoric of Retrospection: May Fourth Literary History and the Ming-Qing Woman Writer," in *The Appropriation of Cultural Capital: China's May Fourth Project,* ed. Milena Doleželová-Velingerová and Oldřich Král (Cambridge: Harvard University Asia Center, 2001), 195.

30 In her discussion of the editorials in *Shenbao* called *lun* or *shuo*, Barbara Mittler maintains that both forms served the function of political critique—"often from outside the established bureaucracy" (*A Newspaper for China?* 69–78).

31 On the power of *lun* or *shuo* writing to distinguish right from wrong, see Tan Sitong 谭嗣同, "Baozhang wenti shuo 報章文體說 [On Newspaper Styles]," *Shiwu bao* 時務報 29–30 (June 6–21, 1897).

writing to articulate their own ideas about the topical themes examined in this book.

In addition to writing *lun* or *shuo*, women journalists also actively experimented with other novel textual modes, including historical biography, public speech, and expository essays. Usually writing under the heading "Biography," they appropriated the form of biographical writing to translate and disseminate the life stories of exemplary and heroic Western women, offering Chinese women new visions of womanhood to emulate. Women were also among the first to adopt *baihua* 白話 (lit. "plain, unadorned speech"), a newly invented vernacular journalistic style at the turn of the twentieth century, to address female readers. *Baihua* writings often fell under the heading "Public Speech," a regular column that became a staple in most women's journals. It is noteworthy that *baihua* writing was originally created by male nationalist journalists as a medium to propagate nationalism among the lower classes. However, women appropriated this genre for their own public and progressive expression. For example, as some recent studies show, some female overseas Chinese students in the early twentieth-century feminist press developed this nationalist-inflected, class-based style as a new mode of vernacular writing aligned with progressiveness and their advocacy of feminism.[32]

Women also engaged in new forms of expository prose, among which the genre of *shiyantan* 實驗談 (discussing real-life or personal experience) was most prominent. According to Joan Judge, this genre was introduced from Japan to connote the notion of actual experience in the early twentieth century, and *shiyantan* articles were prevalent in the Chinese periodical press, particularly in early Republican commercial women's journals.[33] Both men and women wrote in this genre, but they took different approaches. Whereas *shiyantan* essays by men focused on empirically based science, women, as this book demonstrates, adopted this genre not only to draw on scientific expertise but also to provide candid accounts of their immediate experience on a variety of topics on women's health and bodies, such as menstruation and childbirth. Through this *shiyantan* genre, women wrote publicly and with scientific authority about their own gendered bodily experiences.

Poetry, one of the primary genres for women's self-expression throughout history, continued to play a role in women's writing practices in women's journals. Although Liang Qichao openly dismissed women's talent for poetry as trivial and useless when he espoused education for women that would be

32 Zhang Yun, "Feminism in the Vernacular: *Baihua* Writing, Gender, and Identity in Late Qing China," *Twentieth-Century China* 45, no. 1 (2020).

33 Judge, *Republican Lens*, 90.

instrumental in China's national strengthening, the majority of women's journals still reserved space for the publication of women's poetry.[34] Their poems were published in the section called "Wenyuan 文苑 (Literary Garden)," which was standard in late Qing and early Republican women's journals. As some recent studies show, the reason that poetry did not lose its vitality was that women used it to go beyond typical boudoir themes; they introduced a new lexicon and rhetoric to the poetic form to address social, political, and national concerns.[35]

Women's poetic practice and production in the women's press notwithstanding, prose writing was the most direct medium and the principal mode used for their public expression of ideas, opinions, and critiques in the mixed-gender public space of women's journals. For instance, some editors of the early Republican commercial women's journals explicitly called for submissions written in prose, rather than poetry. They contended that prose was a more effective medium for the expression and dissemination of practical and medical knowledge, one of the most valorized editorial objectives of these journals. Although a considerable number of women also contributed in poetic forms, prose writings by women gained public attention and prominence.[36] For these reasons, the writings selected in this book are mostly prose, including but not limited to *lun* or *shuo* essays, which often appeared as "Editorials," the most central venue for the discussion of a journal's topical theme, as well as translated biographies, vernacular journalistic writing, and expository articles. Women's writing in these genres not only testified to their public engagement in the discussion of pressing topics concerning the Chinese woman question but also reflected their persistent efforts to amplify their intellectual authority in the discursive space and public domain of the women's press.

4 The Chapters in the Book

This book is organized as a series of prominent themes that were key to the Chinese woman question as they emerged and were the most hotly discussed in the mixed-gender public space of the women's press from the late Qing to the early Republican period. At the same time, these chapters present different forms of mixed-gender public space in the various types of women's journals.

---

34 Liang, "Lun nüxue."

35 Fong, "Radicalizing Poetics."

36 On indirect and subtle social and political critiques in women's poetry in early Republican women's publications, Judge, *Republican Lens*, chaps. 2 and 5.

Chapter 1 examines the mixed-gender public space constituted by the first Chinese women's journal, *Nü xuebao*, and the public discussion in it of women's literary talent and women's education by both men and women. It focuses on how a cohort of genteel, reformist women responded to male intellectuals who advocated a civic female education that trivialized and rejected elite women's long-existing learning tradition and literary accomplishments. This rejection was most evident in men's virulent criticism of talented woman. Most reformist women concurred with men in promoting women's education for national prosperity, and some women even voiced men's criticism of female talent, but in practice they did not completely submit to men's total repudiation or break away from the literary tradition in which they had been trained. The editor-in-chief of *Nü xuebao*, for instance, served as a prime example of a gentry, reform-minded woman who publicly defended elite women's educational tradition and literary heritage. Moreover, women writing for the journal appropriated and developed practices that had been used to cultivate female talent to meet new nationalist demands, which is shown in their use of writing as a way to transcend the divide between inner and outer domains and expand their authorial influence in the public space, their effort to bring the late imperial epistolary tradition into the women's periodical press, and their linguistic choices. These strategies attested to the creative ways in which women offered their own conceptualizations of the woman question in the dynamic public discursive space of the first women's journal.

Chapter 2 examines the gendered articulations of *nüjie* in the mixed-gender public space of the feminist press. The neologism *nüjie* was initially coined by male nationalists to refer to Chinese women as an oppressed group and as an object of critique in the pressing calls for national strengthening. It was later used by female feminist writers as an analytical category to examine a wide range of questions concerning women and to signify women's agency within and beyond the context of nationalism. By examining writings on *nüjie* in three influential late Qing feminist journals—*Nüzi shijie* (1904–1907), *Zhongguo xin nüjie zazhi* 中國新女界雜誌 (*Magazine of New Women's World of China*, 1907), and *Tianyi* 天義 (*Natural Justice*, 1907–1908), this chapter shows that women writers used *nüjie* to construct feminist critiques within—and against—the nationalist discourse and ultimately to envision a new public identity for Chinese women. This new gendered identity redrew the connections between the Chinese nation and women, gendered social relations between men and women, and, more broadly, the relationship between Chinese women and the modernizing world.

Chapter 3 explores the way in which the woman question was understood by non-Han reformers through a case study of a Manchu woman's suicide, an event that best illustrated the entangled problematic of nationalism, gender, and ethnic identification in the late Qing context. It focuses on male Manchu reformers' concerted effort to foreground the Manchu ethnicity of the woman who committed suicide and establish her as a female Manchu martyr in two pro-Manchu women's journals. This construction reveals the Manchu reformist men's profound concerns over the impending erasure of their racial identity in the context of Han nationalism. They attempted to reclaim their recognizable Manchu identity through a Manchu nationalist heroine. While male Manchu reformers sought to assert their racial identity, Manchu women tended to identify themselves on a basis of sharing the same gender, rather than of ethnic difference. In the mixed-gender public space of the pro-Manchu women's journals, they openly argued against men in seeing their ethnicity as a marker of difference from Han women and conceived of themselves as part of the subordinated collectivity of "women," as did their elite Han sisters.

Chapters 4 and 5 turn to the mixed-gender public space of the early Republican commercial women's periodicals. Chapter 4 examines the emerging ideal of "wise mothers and good wives" in the early Republican period and both men's and women's writings on women's health and bodies through *weisheng* 衛生 (the science of hygiene) in two influential commercial women's journals, *Funü shibao* and *Funü zazhi*. Although both men and women contributors recognized the essential role of women's health in the building of a strong nation, they had different emphases. Whereas men used the *weisheng* discourse to design a new hygienic womanhood as tools of their vision of a hygienic modernity, women writers adopted the knowledge and language of feminine hygiene to create a new epistemology for women's reproductive health and bodies. For them, the science of female hygiene was just as much about preventing disease as it was about the ability of individual women to understand and engage with their own gendered bodies.

Chapter 5 examines how the young female student, the antithesis of the wise mother and good wife ideal, became the subject of public attention and social controversy in the commercial women's journals. The young female student was often represented as someone who lacked morality and virtue, devoted excessive attention to exterior trappings rather than cultivation of inner qualities, and possessed scant knowledge of domestic affairs. At the same time, however, she was portrayed as being consciously transgressive, gazing boldly back at herself and the public, and an avid consumer of modern material goods. Male and female intellectuals imposed regulatory discourse on young female students, but not in the same ways. Women held ambivalent attitudes toward the young female students, and their criticism tended to be empathetic because of their own previous experiences as students. The efforts to regulate the public visibility and behavior of young female students had a limited effect in real life. The way in which intellectuals disciplined the young female students, however, acquired resonance in subsequent discourses on the New Woman and the Modern Girl.

Taken together, this book reveals the various forms of mixed-gender public space constituted by the late Qing and early Republican women's periodical press and traces many important aspects of the Chinese woman question as they were discussed in this public space. The mixed-gender public space of the women's press not only served as a focal point for both men's and women's gendered articulation of prominent themes about the woman question but also attested to women's relentless efforts to push for larger discursive and intellectual authority. This book then offers insights gained from examining the previously unexplored gendered approaches to the imagined nexus of women, nation, and modernity in early twentieth-century China.

CHAPTER 1

Articulating the Woman Question: Women's Literary Heritage, Education, and the Nation

In his essay "Bianfa tongyi 變法通議 (A General Discussion of Reform)," which was published serially in 1896 and 1897, Liang Qichao devoted a special section to the centrality of women's education to China's national survival. In this section, called "Lun nüxue 論女學 (On Women's Education)," Liang dismissed all Chinese women as ignorant, enfeebled, and dependent. This sweeping critique of women's lack of education disregarded and rejected the long-standing tradition of learning and literary accomplishments among a minority of elite women known in Chinese history as *cainü* 才女 (talented women). Liang had no reservations about disparaging these talented women. He denigrated their achievements in writing as trivial, saying they were "nothing more than several stanzas of ditties upon the beauty of the wind and moon, verses describing the flowers and the grasses, or poems lamenting the passage of spring or the loss of a friend. These activities cannot be called learning."[1] Real learning, he suggested, would teach a woman pragmatic knowledge and skills to earn a livelihood. Liang further contended that modern education for women was fundamental for the protection of the nation and humanity.[2]

This instrumentalist and politicized conception of women's education was in line with Liang's broader reform-oriented nationalist agenda. The causal link he drew between reforming women's education and national prosperity was emblematic of the late Qing reformist discourses. In the early 1890s, reformist intellectuals had begun to argue for improving China's rate of female literacy in a new age of nationalism in a global context.[3] What distinguished Liang's rhetoric from that of his contemporaries was that he predicated his espousal of women's education on the denigration of "talented women." The existing scholarship notes that Liang's criticism was more reflective of his

1 Liang, "Lun nüxue," 1: 550–551; translation in Liu, Karl, and Ko, *The Birth of Chinese Feminism*, 192.

2 Liang, "Lun nüxue," 192–195.

3 Judge, "Reforming the Feminine," 160–161. Evelyn Rawski estimates that 30–45 percent of the men and 2–10 percent of the women knew how to read and write during the mid- and late nineteenth century. See Evelyn Sakakida Rawski, *Education and Popular Literacy in Ch'ing China* (Ann Arbor: The University of Michigan, 1979), 140.

 | DOI:10.1163/9789004438545_003

attempt to break with China's feminized cultural past as embodied by the image of *cainü* than it was of his actual views about them.[4] Indeed, as a cultural giant in the late Qing, Liang would have been aware of highly literate women and their remarkable literary and scholarly accomplishments in or before his time.[5] The monolithic and static representation of *cainü* as useless and self-indulgent was a reductive fiction that built on political necessity and rhetorical expediency, rather than an objective description of women's past cultural accomplishments. Recent studies on women and Chinese history illustrate the diversity of women's texts and their importance in providing new perspectives on women's lives within and beyond their domestic sphere.[6] It turns out that *cainü* played a far more vibrant role in literary practice and Chinese history than Liang's oversimplification would lead us to believe.

However, we cannot simply dismiss Liang's negative appraisal of *cainü*. In fact, Liang's criticism of *cainü* and their literary practice and production did have some evidential support. First of all, it was accurate to say that women were most active and accomplished in the poetic genre.[7] Second, in their poetic writing, women demonstrated relatively little concern for society and the state. They sometimes used poetry to comment on the body politic in Chinese history, but this body of political writing was small and limited.[8] Grace Fong notes that in Confucian patriarchal society, women's poetry was circumscribed from serving any true public or political function.[9] Moreover, Liang's attempt

4 For a discussion of the political concerns behind Liang's disdain of the *cainü* tradition, see Hu, *Tales of Translation*, 6–8.

5 In 1897, Liang Qichao published a biography of Kang Aide 康愛德, the first female Chinese doctor who graduated from the University of Michigan. In the biography, Liang celebrated Kang Aide as the first new Chinese woman by contrasting her with two *cainü* writers: Liang Duan 梁端 (1793–1825) and Wang Zhaoyuan 王照圓 (1763–1851). Both women were well versed in classical studies and traditional learning and published works that were available during Liang Qichao's time. For a well-documented study of Wang Zhaoyuan's achievements, see Harriet Zurndorfer, "Wang Zhaoyuan (1763–1851) and the Erasure of 'Talented Women' by Liang Qichao," in *Different Worlds of Discourse: Transformations of Gender and Genre in Late Qing and Early Republican China*, ed. Nanxiu Qian, Grace Fong, and Richard J. Smith (Leiden: E.J. Brill, 2008).

6 Seminal works in this field include Ko, *Teachers of the Inner Chambers*; Mann, *Precious Records*. More recent works include Grace Fong, *Herself an Author: Gender, Agency, and Writing in Late Imperial* China (Honolulu: University of Hawai'i Press, 2008); Xiaorong Li, *Women's Poetry of Late Imperial China: Transforming the Inner Chambers* (Seattle: University of Washington Press, 2012); and Binbin Yang, *Heroines of the Qing: Exemplary Women Tell Their Stories* (Seattle: University of Washington Press, 2016).

7 Li, *Women's Poetry of Late Imperial China.*

8 Guotong Li, *Migrating Fujianese: Ethnic, Family, and Gender Identities in an Early Modern Maritime World* (Leiden: E.J. Brill, 2016): 111.

9 Fong, "Radicalizing Poetics," 113.

to erase the *cainü* culture from Chinese history may have spread the narrative that Chinese women as a group were victimized and had no worthwhile past. This narrative became salient in the late Qing nationalist discourse and continued to characterize the May Fourth writings on gender.[10]

In examining the *cainü* legacy at the turn of the twentieth century, we should regard Liang's assessment with caution and take into account the changing historical context and gender politics underpinning his critique. During the last decades of the Qing dynasty, the economic and cultural factors that contributed to the flourishing of *cainü* culture were seriously undermined.[11] Women's literary talent and artistic skill, previously celebrated for their distance from the world of politics, now had to be reevaluated so that they could serve the new national politics. But *cainü* did not cease to exist overnight or present a radical break with the modern world, as might be inferred from Liang's dismissive view. In fact, the deepening political and cultural crisis and the perceived urgency of national strengthening not only propelled male reformist intellectuals to construct new conceptions of female learning but also engaged a small but significant segment of genteel, learned women in open debates on a wide range of issues, such as women's literary talent, education, and national reform. This cohort of women was highly privileged, well-educated daughters, wives, or relatives of the elite classes who had been exposed to politically progressive ideas circulating at the time in the literati circles. They fit the conventional category of "talented women" in terms of the education they had received and the versatile literary talent they demonstrated, but the ever-changing social and political circumstances in which these women lived made the scope, topics, and genres in their writing exceed those of other *cainü* in previous generations. They were simultaneously overt or covert inheritors of the *cainü* legacy and the creators of their own discourse in a refashioned form of female talent in response to the modern nationalist project.

Nü xuebao, which emerged during the 1898 reform period, was the first Chinese women's journal and it offered a unique and important perspective on

10 Judge, "Reforming the Feminine," 164; for the prevalent literary portraits of victimized women in the May Fourth–New Culture period (1915–1927), see Ko, *Teachers of the Inner Chambers*, 1–5.

11 A number of factors may have contributed to the decline of *cainü* culture in the Jiangnan area, such as the economic recession in the 1820s, the Opium Wars, and the Taiping Rebellion. See Susan Mann, *The Talented Women of the Zhang Family* (Berkeley: University of California Press, 2008); Hershatter, *Dangerous Pleasures*; Ono Kazuko, *Chinese Women in a Century of Revolution, 1850–1950*, trans. Kathryn Bernhardt et al.; ed. Joshua A. Fogel (Stanford: Stanford University Press, 1989); Tobie Meyer-Fong, *What Remains: Coming to Terms with Civil War in 19th Century China* (Stanford: Stanford University Press, 2013).

this unprecedented female participation in public culture. That year marked a critical historical moment when Chinese intellectuals made the first conscious attempt to transform China from a millennia-old imperial polity to a modern nation-state.[12] The call for including modern civic female literacy in the national project, as attested by Liang Qichao's tract, was a major theme of the 1898 reform agenda. Male intellectuals persistently advocated for female literacy to be more broadly based, utilitarian, and political and for their ideas to imbue with the goal of discrediting traditional, elitist female cultural literacy. The traditionally educated but reform-minded women who were involved in these debates as both objects of critique and expected advocates of the new female literacy, nonetheless, held far more complex attitudes.

This chapter explores how the woman question was first articulated in the 1898 reform period through discussions of female talent and women's education by both men and women in the mixed-gender public space afforded by *Nü xuebao*. Recent scholarship has noted the neglected but significant roles played by women in the 1898 reform movement and their agency in constructing their own visions of women's education and a new Chinese womanhood that differed from men's. For example, based on the activities and writing practices of reformist women, exemplified by Xue Shaohui 薛绍徽 (1866–1911), a renowned poet and essayist as well as the editor-in-chief of *Nü xuebao*, Nanxiu Qian argues that female participants in the reforms were active organizers and independent thinkers, who were by no means subordinated to male reformers' agendas and ideas. Qian notes that although men initiated the campaign for women's education for political purposes, female reformers used it as poetic inspiration in fulfilling their cultural ambition. Qian further illustrates that female reformers conceptualized a new Chinese womanhood through their conscious adoption and appropriation of the ideal of *xianyuan* 賢媛 (worthy ladies), which valorized women's talent, virtue, and intellectual independence.[13]

Drawing on Qian's insights, this chapter shows that women reformers in effect demonstrated complex and ambivalent attitudes toward male reformers' politicized conception of women's education and indictment of female talent.

12 Recent studies have reexamined the historical and historiographical significance of the 1898 period in modern Chinese history, interpreting 1898 as not only a watershed event, a historical conjuncture, but also an extended moment at which Chinese intellectuals and society began to confront the problematic of Chinese modernity at both local and global levels. For a systematic reexamination of the 1898 period, see Karl and Zarrow, *Rethinking the 1898 Reform Period*.

13 Qian, "Revitalizing the *Xianyuan* (Worthy Ladies) Tradition"; idem, *Politics, Poetics, and Gender in Late Qing China: Xue Shaohui and the Era of Reform* (Stanford: Stanford University Press, 2015), 123–158.

Women's pursuits were not purely cultural, devoid of any political aspirations, nor was their agenda diametrically opposed to men's. Like their male counterparts, female reformers assimilated the narrative about the assumed transparent connection between female literacy and national empowerment and recognized that they had to prioritize the nation as the new meaningful context in their writing and self-definition. But their approaches to and writing about this emerging woman question were distinguished from those of men. In some instances, female reformers even diverged from one another. Some women were particularly outspoken in refuting men's disparagement of the *cainü* legacy and proposed redefining female talent for the sake of national strengthening. The majority of them appropriated the literary practices that had been used to cultivate female talent in the imperial period to answer new nationalist calls, best illustrated by their use of writing to assert authorial publicity and authority, their effort to transpose the imperial epistolary practice into the new print medium, and their preference for literary and classical language in their writing. By examining their activities and writing in the mixed-gender public space afforded by *Nü xuebao*, this chapter reveals the complexity and dilemma of female reformers in the 1890s, when they strove to cope with their traditional cultural heritage and construct a gendered modern identity in relation to the nation and the modernizing world.

1 The Mixed-Gender Public Space in *Nü xuebao*

The publication of *Nüxue bao* was among the important initiatives in response to the 1898 reformists' passionate advocacy of modern women's education. Inspired by Liang Qichao's powerful tract on women's education, a group of reformist intellectuals gathered in Shanghai in the fall of 1897, proposing the establishment of the first Chinese-run girls' school. The initiative was spearheaded by Jing Yuanshan 經元善 (1841–1903), a prominent literatus-merchant and social activist, and several other influential intellectuals also took part in this collaborative effort, including Liang Qichao; Chen Jitong 陳季同 (1852–1907), a prominent diplomat-writer; and Kang Guangren 康廣仁 (1867–1898), the younger brother of Kang Youwei 康有為 (1858–1927) and one of the six reformist martyrs in the coup d'état by the empress dowager in 1898.[14] In

14 Jing Yuanshan 經元善, "Yuanqi 緣起 [Preface]," *Zhongguo jindai sixiangjia wenku: Jing Yuanshan juan* 中國近代思想家文庫·經元善卷 [*Works by Modern Chinese Thinkers, the Volume on Jing Yuanshan*] ed. Zhu Hu 朱滸 (Beijing: Zhongguo renmin daxue chubanshe, 2014), 68–71.

addition to this male participation, a cohort of learned gentry women was also involved in this new enterprise. Among those who played an active role were Kang Youwei's daughter 康同薇 (1878–1974), Chen Jitong's French wife Lai Mayi 賴媽懿 (Maria-Adèle Lardanchet, 1848–1921) and their two daughters. While actively seeking female supporters and promoters, the male reformers recognized the necessity of raising public awareness about the importance of establishing a new school. Several influential newspapers published announcements and regulations for the potential girls' school by leading figures such as Liang Qichao and Yan Fu 嚴復 (1854–1921). As a result, an ever-growing community consisting of government officials, reformist intellectuals, journalists, literati scholars, and Western missionaries formed to support this educational project.[15]

Although male reformers took the lead in initiating the plan and the associated preparatory work, the women involved in the project soon gained public visibility as they began to preside over steering committee meetings, after the first two run by men. These women went on to found the Women's Study Society (Nü xuehui 女學會), an organization to bring together more female supporters in order to discuss and promote the campaign for women's education. Unlike the study societies that were founded by scholar-officials as political groups to advocate reforms,[16] Women's Study Society to a certain extent resembled the late imperial gentry women's literary gatherings or poetry clubs.[17] For example, the society's first meeting was a public gathering marked by a considerable number of verses written by women attendees. Nevertheless, there was a fundamental distinction between the Women's Study Society and earlier forms of women's literary or poetic organizations in

---

15 Jing Yuanshan offered an exhaustive list of all the important participants and sponsors for the opening of the Chinese Girls' School, see his "Yuanqi," 68–69. Nanxiu Qian provides a detailed documentation of the impressively large number of people attracted to this project, in "Revitalizing the *Xianyuan* (Worthy Ladies) Tradition," 402–405.

16 One of these societies was the famous Qiang xuehui 強學會 [Society for the Study of Self-Strengthening] founded by Kang Youwei and other like-minded reformist scholars in 1895. On the eve of the Hundred Days of Reform, a group of study societies emerged across the country to call for scholar-officials' public engagement in the advocacy of reform. These study societies were often political in nature and played an important role in the 1898 reform movement. For a discussion of these political societies, see Richard Belsky, "Placing the Hundred Days: Native-Place Ties and Urban Space," in Karl and Zarrow, *Rethinking the 1898 Reform Period*, 141–146.

17 The most famous women's literary association of this kind was the Banana Garden poetry club established by a cohort of women poets in seventeenth-century Jiangnan. For an insightful discussion of its members, purposes, and activities, see Ko, *Teachers of the Inner Chambers*, 234–246.

history. Bound by a commitment to the social and political cause of advocating women's education, rather than the individual aspirations to learn or to teach among a small literary clique, Women's Study Society, which had more than a hundred members, did not have as its primary purpose the cultivation or advancement of members' poetic talents. Rather, this loosely formed group of women used poetic exchange as practical tool for promoting a new national cause.

However, composing poetry enabled the society's members to create a community that related to other well-versed gentry women at that moment and their literary predecessors in the past.[18] By referencing the female exemplars in ancient times and corresponding with one another in verse, these women not only used the poetic genre to address the particular nationalist demands around them but also created a unique intellectual network that nurtured a shared gendered identity. At the society's first gathering in December 1897, a female member named Jiang Wanfang 蔣畹芳, who was also a future faculty member of the Chinese Girls' School and contributor to *Nü xuebao*, composed two poems to celebrate the event and express her ambition to become versed in both Chinese and Western knowledge.[19] Jiang's poems immediately inspired several corresponding poems by other women, both members and nonmembers of the society, and sparked further enthusiasm.[20] The act of gathering, the energy generated by the occasion, the use of the poetic form, and the shared commitment to develop women's education were effective ways of forming solidarity and fellowship among these women and consolidating their cultural and political identity.

With the collective efforts by both men and women reformers, the Chinese Girls' School was officially established on 31 May, 1898. About two weeks before the opening of the school, the Women's Study Society decided to launch a new publication as its mouthpiece. The society published an announcement in *Xinwen bao* 新聞報 (*The News*), an influential and widely circulated Shanghai newspaper at the time, to recruit "worthy, virtuous, and renowned ladies"

18 For a discussion on the communal function of Chinese classical poetry, see Stephen Owen, "Poetry in the Chinese Tradition," in *Heritage of China: Contemporary Perspectives on Chinese Civilization,* ed. Paul S. Ropp (Berkeley: University of California Press, 1990) 296; Shengqing Wu, *Modern Archaics: Continuity and Innovation in the Chinese Lyric Tradition, 1900–1937* (Cambridge: Harvard University Asia Center, 2013), 37.

19 Jing Yuanshan, "Zhongguo nüxue jiyi chubian 中國女學集議初編 [Discussions on Women's Education, First Edition]," in Zhu, *Zhongguo jindai sixiangjia wenku*, 81.

20 Jing Yuanshan recorded that over twenty corresponding poems were composed after the gathering, in "Zhongguo nüxue jiyi chubian," 83, 97–99.

(*xianshu mingyuan* 賢淑名媛) to be desired contributors.[21] An immediate response was sent by Xue Shaohui, an eloquent advocate of women's education, who had written a constructive curriculum proposal for the founding of the Girls' School early in 1897. Xue was born to a declining (bordering on impoverished) scholar-official family in 1866 in Fuzhou and received an outstanding traditional education.[22] She grew up in the Min region (present-day Fujian Province), which had a long-standing culture of literate women, and displayed a gift for poetry from a very early age and a determination to build on Min women's scholarly and literary legacy.[23] At the age of fifteen, she married Chen Shoupeng 陳壽彭 (1857–c. 1928), the younger brother of Chen Jitong and a graduate of the famous Fuzhou Naval Academy. Xue spent most of her life before the late 1890s living in Fuzhou with her French sisters-in-law raising children, but she developed a growing awareness of the world beyond China, as reflected in her poetry, thanks to knowledge that her husband had brought back with him after sojourns in Europe and other areas in China.[24]

Xue was soon recruited as a principal contributor and became one of the main editorial members to prepare the publication of the potential journal. Many women in addition to Xue who had been active in journalism also joined as contributors. Qiu Yufang 裘毓芳 (1871–1904), for example, had been a regular contributor to *Wuxi baihua bao* 無錫白話報 (*Wuxi Vernacular Newspaper*), one of the earliest vernacular newspapers. She and her uncle Qiu Tingliang 裘廷梁 (1857–1943), a vocal supporter of the late Qing vernacular movement, founded the newspaper in May 1898. Qiu Yufang wrote a series of essays for *Wuxi baihua bao* and avidly engaged in vernacular writing on a variety of topics, including women's education, science, and reports on reforms in other countries.[25] Kang Tongwei was also an experienced journalist. Beginning in

21 Shen Ying 沈瑛, "Zhongguo Nüxue ni zengshe baoguan gaobai 中國女學擬增設報館告白 [Announcement of the Proposal of Establishing a Journal Affiliated with the Chinese Girls' School]," *Zhixin bao* 知新報 55 (June 9, 1898): 26b.

22 Qian, *Politics, Poetics, and Gender*, 1–20.

23 For Xue Shaohui's connections with the Min writing-women culture, see Qian, *Politics, Poetics, and Gender*, 23–58. For a discussion of the tradition of Fujian *guixiu*'s [genteel ladies] learning in the eighteenth century, see Li, *Migrating Fujianese*, 108–130.

24 For detailed account of how Xue's poetry recorded her companionship marriage to Chen Shoupeng and her acquisition of Western political knowledge, see Qian, *Politics, Poetics, and Gender*, 88–102.

25 In addition to her vernacular writing in the journal, Qiu Yufang established a society to promote the use of the vernacular language with Qiu Tingliang in August 1898. For a biographical account of Qiu Yufang, see Richard W.L. Guisso and Jun Fang, "Qiu Yufang," in *Biographical Dictionary of Chinese Women: The Qing Period, 1644–1911*, ed. Clara Wingchung Ho (Armnok, NY: M. E. Sharpe, 1998).

1897, Kang worked as a translator and reporter for the *Zhixin bao* 知新報 (*New Knowledge News*), a reformist newspaper published by Kang Youwei and Liang Qichao in Macao. She wrote several powerful polemics in the newspaper to encourage reforms to strengthen the Chinese nation and develop women's education.[26]

On July 24, 1898, *Nü xuebao* was published in Shanghai, with a list of eighteen women on the cover of the first issue as the main editors (Figure 1).[27] These women's names were all preceded by their native place and followed by *nüshi* 女史 (female historian), a revered title often used to designate highly educated and literate women.[28] This gender-specific appellation not only indicated the journal's all-female editorial board but also accentuated these women's intellectual authority within the public sphere.[29] At times, the journal also published or reprinted men's essays. For instance, in the inaugural issue of *Nü xuebao*, Liang Qichao's "Changshe nü xuetang qi 倡設女學堂啟 (Announcement of Establishing the Girls' School)," first published in *Shiwu bao* 時務報 (*Chinese Progress*) in 1897, was reprinted in its entirety.[30]

In the twelve issues of the journal, female writers published over twenty essays on a wide array of topics, such as women's education, women's rights,

26 One of these essays, titled "Nüxue libi shuo 女學利弊說 [On the Advantages and Disadvantages of Women's Education]," was later republished in *Nü xuebao*. For a discussion of Kang's journalistic activities and her advocacy for women's education, see Yu Lifen 余麗芬, "Kang Tongwei nüzi jiaoyu sixiang shuping 康同薇女子教育思想述評 [A Review of Kang Tongwei's Thought on Women's Education]," *Zhejiang shehui kexue* 浙江社會科學 4 (1995).

27 Some writers were in and out in the following issues, but major contributors such as Xue Shaohui and Qu Yufang were listed throughout the issues of the journal.

28 *Nüshi* first appeared in one of the earliest books of rites *Zhouli* 周禮 [*The Rites of Zhou*] and referred to the female officials who were in charge of etiquette and rites for the queen consort in the imperial palace. The term later became a common appellation for respectable and educated women. For the historical transformations in the meaning of *nüshi*, see Li Qinde 李勤德, "Nüshi kao 女史考 [An Investigation of the Term *Nüshi*]," *Xueshu yanjiu* 學術研究 1 (1992).

29 Men at times also adopted the appellation of *nüshi* as part of their pennames. For instance, the male journalist Shao Piaoping 邵飄萍 often wrote under the name Piaoping nüshi 飄萍女史 (see Chapter 5). But here in *Nü xuebao*, the suffix *nüshi* served as an unmistakable indicator of the biological reality of sex of these female contributors.

30 *Shiwu bao* was an influential newspaper edited by Liang Qichao during the 1898 reform period and it served as a prime source of information for reformist intellectuals interested in current social and political affairs and "new learning." Liang Qichao, "Changshe nü xuetang qi 倡設女學堂啟 [Announcement of Establishing the Girls' School]," *Shiwu bao* 時務報 45 (1897). The announcement was republished under the title "Zhongguo changshe nü xuetang qi 中國倡設女學堂啟 [Announcement of Establishing the Chinese Girls' School]" in the first issue of *Nü xuebao*, but with the author's name removed.

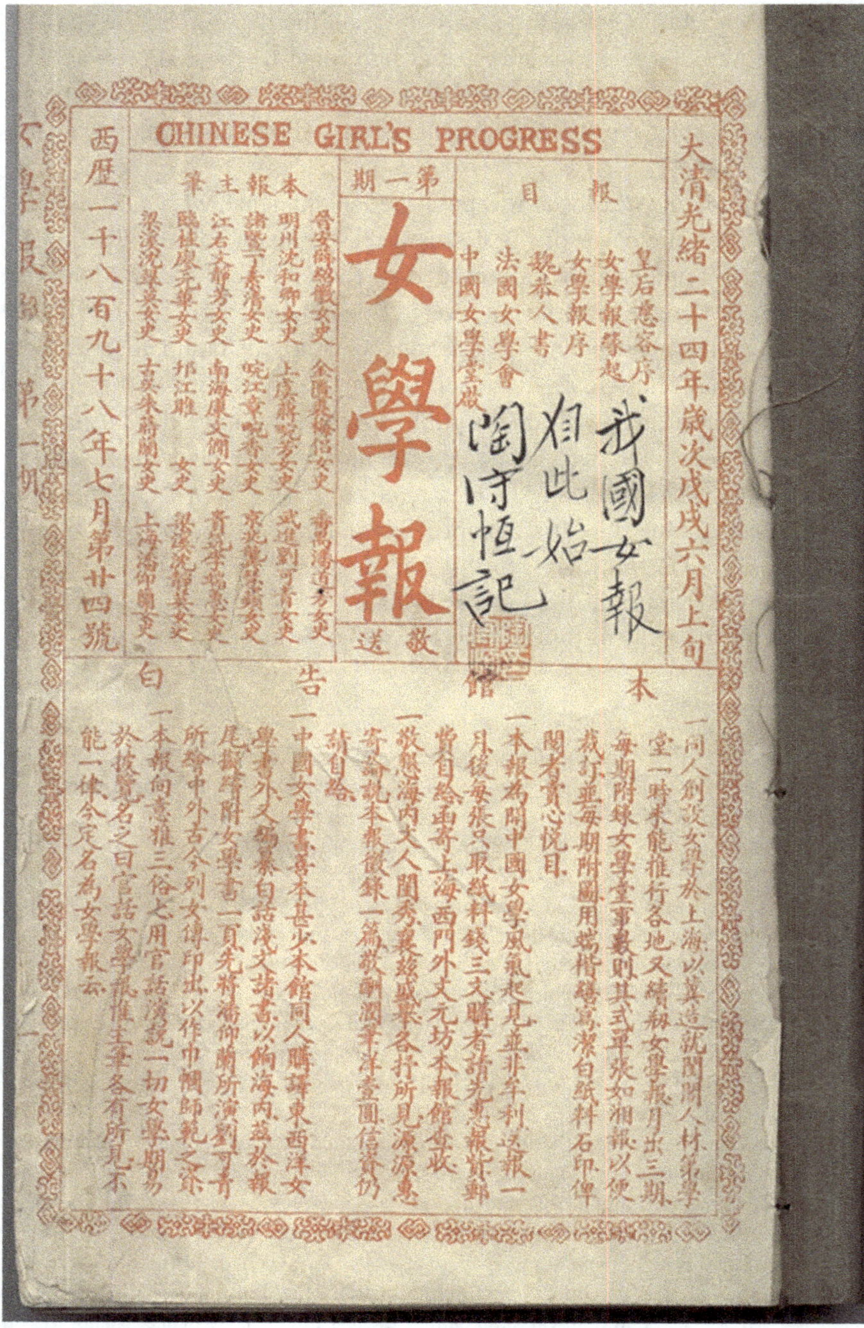

FIGURE 1 Cover page of the first issue of *Nü xuebao* (1898)
SOURCE: WUXI LIBRARY COLLECTION

and science and technology, together with illustrations—one in each issue—that portrayed women's participation in physical exercises, studying at the Girls' School, and other activities, such as sewing, weaving, embroidering, and breeding silkworm.[31] These activities were illustrated not just to show women's commitment to the traditional female virtues of domestic labor but to demonstrate the possibility of using modern technology to perform these tasks. An illustration in the eighth issue, for example, depicts a woman holding a microscope to examine a silkworm on a mulberry leaf (Figure 2). The microscope, with the word in English on its barrel indicating that it was a modern invention imported from the West, forms an interesting contrast to the woman holding it, who appeared to be a member of the gentry in traditional and elegant dress.

From its inception, *Nü xuebao* offered a mixed-gender public space for open discussion of women's education and national survival. Although the journal was characterized by an all-female editorial board and a high number of female contributors, men's participation and influence were palpable. For example, Jing Yuanshan served as a production manager and direct financial sponsor of the journal. His suggestion to design a curriculum for women that combined Chinese and Western knowledge had a direct impact on Xue Shaohui's curricular proposal and vision of women's education in *Nü xuebao*.[32] Although Liang Qichao did not directly contribute to *Nü xuebao*, his influential essay "Lun nüxue" often served as a frame of reference or a potential object of interrogation when female contributors wrote on the subject of women's education. For example, as discussed below, in her reexamination of women's traditional literary heritage and envisioning of modern women's education, Xue Shaohui persistently, albeit implicitly, made Liang Qichao's view of *cainü* the target of criticism. This cross-publication interaction was indicative of the existence of a mixed-gender public space in which men's and women's debates were not limited by or confined to the pages of *Nü xuebao*. Rather, they belonged to a bigger and immediate discursive context consisting of the journal and its writers. Only in this mixed-gender public space can we discern the dynamic and tension between men's and women's commentaries on the emergent woman question and see how women articulated and enacted their ideas about women and the nation.

Nü xuebao also affered an important creative space for female writers to experiment with a new type of political discursive prose writing in the form of *lun*

31 Only nine issues were extant, and the final three were missing, with titles preserved in Du Jikun's 杜繼琨, "Zai tan *Nü xuebao* 再談女學報 [A Continued Discussion of *Nü xuebao*]," *Tushuguan* 圖書館 4 (1963).

32 Qian, "Revitalizing the *Xianyuan* Tradition," 423.

FIGURE 2 Women tending silkworms, *Nü xuebao* 8 (1898)
SOURCE: WUXI LIBRARY COLLECTION

or *shuo*. This mode of writing had its most prominent origins in the statecraft writings by the male literati in imperial China, but it was in effect a novel genre developed under the strong influence of the Western journalistic "leading article" in the nineteenth century.[33] This type of essay writing was innovative in terms of publicity and the scope and breadth of debates it allowed. And more importantly, it was defined by discourse on China's national strengthening and thus attempted to draw social issues into political discussions from which they had been excluded.[34] Widely adopted by the Chinese-language newspapers beginning in the 1870s, this form of writing became a powerful medium for public political discussion. The women writing for the *Nü xuebao* used this new genre to engage in debate about women in a new national context and to justify their entry into the cultural public sphere.

2 Debates on the *Cainü* Legacy

As scholars such as Joan Judge and Paul Bailey have pointed out, Liang Qichao's "Lun nüxue" sparked heated debate and created a new, radical trope which would become pervasive in later reformist as well as revolutionary writings on women's education: the denigration of women as illiterate parasites in the national and family economy.[35] Building on the missionary Timothy Richard's theory of *shengli* 生利 (profit making) and *fenli* 分利 (profit sharing), Liang remarked that "the nation's two hundred million women, among whom all are consumers and none are producers."[36] The reason that women were treated by men as slaves and endured endless sufferings, Liang wrote, was that they had

33 For a discussion on how the translation of the Western "leading" or "editorial" article into the Chinese context in the late Qing drew inspiration from the imperial statecraft writing, see Andrea Janko, "Translating Genre: How the 'Leading Article' Became the *Shelun*," in *Mapping Meanings: The Field of New Learning in Late Qing China*, ed. Michael Lackner and Natascha Vittinghoff (Leiden: Brill, 2004), 331.

34 Janko, "Translating the Genre," 331–332.

35 Judge, "Reforming the Feminine"; idem, "Talent, Virtue and the Nation: Chinese Nationalisms and Female Subjectivities in the Early Twentieth Century," *American Historical Review* 106, no. 3 (2001); Paul J. Bailey, *Gender and Education in China: Gender Discourses and Women's Schooling in Early Twentieth-Century China* (London: Routledge, 2006).

36 Liang, "Lun nüxue," 191. Timothy Richard published two respective articles on *shengli* and *fenli* in the 1893 *Wanguo gongbao* 萬國公報, but it is worth pointing out that in both articles Timothy Richards did not categorize women as "unproductive." See Liu Huiying 劉慧英, "Shengli shuo de laiyuan ji yansheng yu funü wenti "生利" 說的來源及衍生於婦女問題 [The Origins and Developments of the Theory of "Profit Making" and Its Impact on the Woman Question]," *Nankai xuebao* 南開學報 6 (2009).

to live off men's labor and were economically dependent. Just as he seemed to willfully ignore the active role that *cainü* had played in Chinese cultural traditions, Liang elided Chinese women's productive activities taking place in the domestic realm and their significant contributions to the family economy. In her discussion of women's work and women's place in imperial China, Francesca Bray notes that the devaluation and marginalization of women's productive roles in the family could be attributed to the increasing urbanization and occupational specialization that began in the Song dynasty (960–1279). The growing demands for quality cloth in the bourgeoning Song commercial market facilitated the emergence of urban workshops where men were hired as labor. Specialized skills such as silk weaving gradually became a men's preserve and were more widely acknowledged, although the yarn used at the workshops was mostly produced by women working at home. By the late imperial period, as Bray points out, the changes in women's legal status and in kinship practices nurtured a growing emphasis on women as child bearers and household managers, rather than generators of household economy, which may have contributed to the popular—and often negative—view that women consumed without producing.[37]

This ethos gained unprecedented prevalence in the late Qing and provided the reformist intellectuals with solid ground on which they strove to link women's education and national strengthening. Yan Fu, a renowned translator and prominent advocate of women's education, reiterated women's lack of productive capacity and denounced them as mere parasites, stating that

> the fact that women have been illiterate for centuries is the reason why they are in their entire lives capable of nothing but powdering their faces, binding their feet, sitting idle and eating, and awaiting their deaths. … All the members in the family are completely reliant on the support of

37 For this detailed articulation, see Francesca Bray, *Technology and Gender: Fabrics of Power in Late Imperial China* (Berkeley: University of California Press, 1997), 173–272; idem, *Technology, Gender and History in Imperial China: Great Transformations Reconsidered* (London: Routledge, 2013), 91–120. For other discussions on *nügong* 女紅 [women's work] as a moral activity linked to feminine virtue and gendered identity rather than a subsidiary activity in the economic sense in the late imperial era, see Mann, *Precious Records*, 172–177; Ko, *Teachers of the Inner Chambers*, 143–178; Gail Hershatter examines how women's work in the domestic realm continued to be rendered invisible and unremunerated by the Party-state in 1950s China. See Gail Hershatter, *The Gender of Memory: Rural Women and China's Collective Past* (Berkeley: University of California Press, 2011), 182–209 and 236–266.

men, and women share not even an iota of responsibility in providing for the family.

Yan also echoed Liang's criticism of talented women and regarded their learning as nothing but the ability to "understand some proses or verses."[38]

Liang's and Yan's dismissal of women's economic roles and cultural legacy in Chinese history resonated with some female reformers. For example, in the fourth issue of *Nü xuebao*, Liu Renlan 劉紉蘭 offered a vehement critique of the talented women's poetic tradition and even went further to deconstruct the entire women's writing tradition established during the late imperial era. Her tone was evocative of Liang Qichao's but more radical.[39] Qiu Yufang and Kang Tongwei concurred with the view of their contemporary male counterparts that talented women's literary practices had no practical value.[40]

The most eloquent defender of female talent and women's position in history was Xue Shaohui, the chief editor of *Nü xuebao*. She first took issue with Liang's negative portrayal of Chinese women as "200 million wanderers and barbarians" (二萬萬之遊民吐番):[41]

> Is it true that the two hundred million Chinese women are all useless? Abiding by the former kings' precept of separating between the inner and outer boundaries, we have strictly guarded our virtue, purified our minds, and tenderly conformed to the natural course of the Way. The fact that we are committed to our domestic roles makes it seem that we are capable of nothing other than domestic duties.[42]

---

38 Yan Fu, "Lun Hushang chuangxing nü xuetang 論滬上創興女學堂 [On the Development of Girls' Schools in Shanghai]," in *Wan-Qing wenxuan* 晚清文選 [*Collected Works in the Late Qing*], ed. Zheng Zhenduo 鄭振鐸 (Shanghai: Shanghai shenghuo shuju, 1937).

39 Liu Renlan 劉紉蘭, "Quan xing nüxue qi 勸興女學啓 [Letter on Advancing Women's Education]," *Nü xuebao* 4 (1898), in *Zhongguo jindai funü yundong lishi ziliao, 1840–1918* 中國近代婦女運動歷史資料，1840–1918 [*Historical Materials on Modern Chinese Women's Movements, 1840–1918*], ed. Xu Huiqi 徐輝琪, Liu Jucai 劉巨才, and Xu Yuzhen 徐玉珍 (Beijing: Zhongguo funü chubanshe, 1991), 96–98.

40 Qiu Yufang, "Lun nü xuetang yu nan xuetang bingzhong 論女學堂與男學堂並重 [On the Equal Importance of Establishing Girls' and Boys' Schools]," *Nü xuebao* 7 (1898); Kang Tongwei, "Nüxue libi shuo," *Nü xuebao* 7 (1898).

41 Liang, "Changshe nü xuetang qi," 8.

42 夫中國婦女，數雖二萬萬，豈盡無用哉？特以先王內言外言之戒，操守彌堅，貞潔其心，柔順其道，故於中饋內助而外若無能為也者。Xue Shaohui, "Chuangshe Nü xuetang tiaoyi bing xu 創設女學堂條議並序 [Suggestions for Establishing the Girls' School, with a Preface]," *Qiushi bao* 9 (1897): 6a–6b.

To Xue Shaohui, Chinese women's utility lay in their faithful adherence to the womanly virtues outlined in the Confucian precepts. Calling attention to the significant role played by women in the domestic realm, she implicitly criticized the assertion that women were deplorable parasites on the family. But she also admitted that household responsibilities might restrain them from pursuing learning. Taking pride in her youthful experience in receiving instruction from her mother (*cheng mu xun* 承母訓)—a sign of her "family learning" (*jia xue* 家學)[43]—and in studying with other wise and learned scholars (*tongru* 通儒), she nonetheless lamented that this process had been interrupted by her household responsibilities as a housewife and mother. Referring to the burden of managing a household and raising children, along with occasional encounters with disease and hardship, Xue explained, "even tasks such as drawing water from the well and husking rice cannot be tended to at times, not to mention continuing learning!"[44]

In spite of these duties and distractions, she still contended that women were by no means devoid of other accomplishments outside the home. Citing the examples of Xie Daoyun 謝道韞, an eminent female poet in the Eastern Jin Dynasty (317–420) who was often invoked as the icon of literary talent,[45] and the less-known artist Wu Yingyun 吳靈蕓 in the Three Kingdoms period (220–280), Xue was convinced that the number of this kind of talented women in China was vast. She further commented,

> Although men and women are equally given the opportunity to receive education in Western countries, I do not know, however, among the virtuous women and gentle ladies from their past till now, how many are talented, and how many are skilled. Is the number of their talented and artistic women really larger than that of ours in China?[46]

---

43 A daughter who carried on the teachings of her natal family by instructing her daughters or sons was said to "pass on" or "inherit" family learning [*jiaxue*]. *Jiaxue* was inherited both matrilineally and patrilineally. From the Han to the Qing dynasty, women were the custodians and transmitters of family learning. A woman's display of family learning was often seen as a sign of her erudition and scholarly distinction. For discussions on women's role in family learning traditions across Chinese history, see Patricia Buckley Ebrey, *The Inner Quarters: Marriage and the Lives of Chinese Women in the Sung Period* (Berkeley: University of California Press, 1993), 185–186; Ko, *Teachers of the Inner Chambers*, 237–240; Mann, *Precious Records*, 86–108.

44 Xue, "Chuangshe Nü xuetang," 6b.

45 On the celebration of Xie Daoyun as the symbol of female talent and as the ideal of erudite womanhood in the High Qing, see Mann, *Precious Records*, 76–83.

46 西國雖男女並重，餘不知其自古迄今，名媛賢女，成才者幾何人？成藝者幾何人？其數果能昌盛於中國否耶？Xue, "Chuangshe Nü xuetang," 6b.

This passage could be read as a direct response to Liang's praise of Western educational systems for women in his essay "Lun nüxue." Liang argued that, in Western countries, men and women were the same because education could make them useful to the nation. He pointed out that in those countries men and women both succeeded in practical studies such as agriculture, handicrafts, medicine, business, science, and law.[47] While Liang established Western women's education as a model for China to emulate, Xue employed female talent as a yardstick to measure the accomplishments of women in Western countries. Her emphasis on the uniqueness of Chinese talented women in the global context thus was not merely a result of her own classical education but also a conscious refusal to sacrifice Chinese cultural differences in order to completely subscribe to the demands of imperialist Western modernity.

Xue's stress on the significance of Chinese traditional models of female education in general and female talent in particular received a positive response. In the curriculum proposal that she designed for the Girls' School, Xue incorporated both *cai* (literary talent) and *yi* 藝 (artistic talent) as indispensable components of a new educational agenda for women and believed that the development of female talent was not incompatible with the cultivation of women's virtue. She envisioned women's education in China combining both Chinese and Western knowledge and suggested that each could be studied in the light of the other.[48]

In her "*Nü xuebao* xu 女學報序 (Preface to *Nü xuebao*)," Xue asserted that women's learning was not in itself useless but, rather, that it was not properly recognized and used. Given opportunities, Xue argued, women could use the knowledge and skills they had mastered to run the family and thereby to serve the state. She also emphasized the necessity and urgency for women to gain new learning, but this understanding grew out of her astute historical and global consciousness, rather than the commonly held presumption of women's lack of literacy. She summed up the objectives of this new epistemology of women's learning as follows:

> In the present day, new learning (*xinxue*) from other countries is flourishing and has the tendency to go beyond the scope of the Hundred Schools of Thought [of the Zhou Dynasty]. If we women, staying in the inner quarters all day long, still adhere to the divide of inner words and outer

47 Liang, "Lun nüxue," 201–202.

48 Nanxiu Qian notes that Xue put the learning of poetry, prose, and lyrics as a prerequisite for the cultivation of womanly virtue [*fude* 婦德] and womanly speech [*fuyan* 婦言] through an account by Xue's daughter, in *Politics, Poetics, and Gender*, 149.

> words and limit the scope of our own learning, how is it possible to talk about acquiring knowledge suitable for [realizing] the idea of creating new people?[49]

In contrast to the male reformists' propagation of a civic women's education that radically broke away from the tradition of female literacy of the past, Xue Shaohui valorized female learning built on the cultural legacy of literate women, addressing the need to acquire knowledge in the new global context. In choosing such a modest and balanced approach, she demonstrated a conscious effort to preserve her cultural identity as an erudite, gentry woman who was conversant with the classical tradition, while adapting to the changing historical context and actively seeking to fashion a new womanhood. At the end of the "Preface," Xue expected this new kind of learned women to excel in assisting their husbands and instructing their children, to the point of using their knowledge about regulating the family to contribute to the enterprise of nation-building.

Xue went on to argue that Chinese women had been learned since ancient times: "In poetry they created poems such as 'Guanju 關雎 (Cry of the Ospreys)' in the *Shijing* 詩經 (*Book of Poetry*), and in ritual they compiled 'Nei ze 內則 (Inner Principles)' in the classic *Liji* 禮記 (*Book of Rites*)."[50] Although the question of whether these poems or classical texts were actually written by women remained a subject of scholarly debate, her claim for female authorship in canonical texts suggests an attempt to justify Chinese women's long-held history of learning.[51]

Other reformers also valorized learned women in remote antiquity or the idealized past as the embodiment of learning par excellence. For example, Jing Yuanshan stated that in ancient times not a single woman was illiterate, and half the poems in the *Shijing* were written and composed by women with a humble social background (*lüxiang furen* 閭巷婦人). Not until the Tang Dynasty, Jing claimed, did women descend to the dismal and irreversible state of illiteracy and benightedness.[52] Kang Tongwei also looked to the distant

49 第今日各國新學，燦然秀發，有出諸子百家外。吾輩日處閨閣，若仍守其內言外言之戒，自畫其學，安足以講致知而合於新民之旨耶？ Xue Shaohui, "*Nü xuebao* xu 女學報序 [Preface to *Nü xuebao*]," *Nü xuebao* 1 (July 24, 1898): 3a.

50 Xue, "*Nü xuebao* xu," 3a.

51 Chang Sun Kang-i notes that the consistent emphasis on female authorship in the *Shijing* [*Book of Poetry*] was mostly made in the process of giving the poems of the women poets of Ming–Qing period a canonical place, in "Gender and Canonicity: Ming-Qing Women Poets in the Eyes of the Male Literati," *Hsiang Lectures on Chinese Poetry* 1 (2001).

52 Jing Yuanshan, "Quan nüzi dushu shuo 勸女子讀書說 [Exhortation to Women's Learning]," in Zhu, *Zhongguo jindai sixiangjia wenku*, 233–234.

past to look for learned female paragons. Kang admired Ban Zhao 班昭 in the Eastern Han (25–220) for her prominence as a female historian in completing her brother's unfinished official history of the Han dynasty. Kang praised the daughter of the classical scholar Fu Sheng 伏勝 in the Western Han (BCE 206–9 AD), Ms. Fu 伏女, for her ability to transmit the classics. These women, in Kang's eyes, were truly learned. However, like Jing Yuanshan, Kang lamented that this line of literate women had been woefully broken and discontinued in more recent times.[53]

As Joan Judge has suggested, the rejection of women's literary legacy in the recent past while valorizing literate women in the distant past can be read as a reflection of the reformist intellectuals' attempt to redefine the Chinese literate tradition in general and female literacy capital in particular. Literate women in the recent past, epitomized by the *cainü*, functioned as a potent trope to represent what was denounced as "old" and "backward" in Chinese culture. Writing these women out of history therefore served as a convenient strategy for the reformists to construct a new gendered tradition, one that was fundamentally different from the feminized cultural heritage that led to the purported weakness and emasculation of the Chinese nation.[54] Furthermore, in parallel with the reformists' erasure of the feminine literacy legacy from the more recent history was their passionate elevation of Western ideas of women's education. To different degrees, these reformist writers looked to the West (or Japan) to find models for women's education in China. In this sense, the proximal roots for indigenous local practices were not in China's recent past but, rather, in the contemporary West and China's distant past. The two opposing tracks that operated in the discourse on women's education—the conservative track of finding roots in the distant past and the iconoclastic track of rejecting the validity of recent precedents—therefore revealed the dilemma that the reformist writers faced in envisioning a new female literacy in the modern era.[55]

53 Kang, "Nüxue libi shuo."

54 Judge, "Reforming the Feminine," 164–165. Hu Ying also points out that the late Qing intellectuals' equation of China's cultural tradition in general and the lyrical tradition in particular with the feminine was inextricably linked with the aspiration to construct a new masculine identity for China, in "Naming the First 'New Woman'," 186. Shengqing Wu examines how the Chinese lyrical tradition was dominated by male authors and a masculine ideology across the course of Chinese history, in *Modern Archaics*.

55 This paradoxical combination of archaism and iconoclasm as reflected in the discursive move of rejecting the recent past in favor of a valorization of remote antiquity was also evident in other reformist intellectuals' writings and thought. For the discussion of Yan Fu in this regard, see Theodore Huters, *Bringing the World Home: Appropriating the West in Late Qing and Early Republican China* (Honolulu: University of Hawai'i Press, 2005), 73. Wu Shengqing discerns a similar discursive move in the late Qing poet Chen

Recent critiques of the Western model of modernity have pointed out that the imperatives of modernity tended to subjugate different locales to a homogeneous temporality of progress, which subordinated other historical realities outside Europe and Western modernity.[56] Seen in this light, the Chinese reformists' sweeping criticism of the Chinese cultural tradition in general and the *cainü* in particular could be understood as part of a larger effort to eradicate differences across the boundaries of culture and nation in order to incorporate China's national reinvigoration agendas into a universal modernization project. Notwithstanding the obvious fact that some reformist writers were co-opted into this "smoothing out" process, disruptive voices also appeared, as evinced by Xue Shaohui's reluctance to cut herself off completely from the *cainü* tradition. Rejecting the call to reduce women's learning to that which served the nation and modernization, Xue appropriated the *cainü* legacy to adapt to new social and political circumstances and to reaffirm China's cultural difference in a conscious resistance to modernity's leveling of space and experience.

3 Asserting Intellectual Authority in the Public Space

The female contributors to *Nü xuebao* were conscious of the historical significance of their writing in the new public space. As Pan Xuan 潘璇 declared, "[The journal *Nü xuebao*] has completely destroyed the big signposts and the old fences that marked the division of inner and outer worlds. Isn't it unprecedented that we now can publicly discuss women's education and assume the role of women editors?"[57] Directly attacking the Confucian doctrine, which insisted women's words not be heard outside women's quarters (*nei yan buchu men wai* 內言不出門外), Pan openly called for women's authorial voices and new roles in the public domain.

Sanli 陳三立's negotiation between present particulars and universal values, in *Modern Archaics*, 121–127.

56 For an examination of this revisionist scholarship on Western modernity, see Tang Xiaobing, *Global Space and the Nationalist Discourse of Modernity: The Historical Thinking of Liang Qichao* (Stanford: Stanford University Press, 1996), 7; see also Wu, *Modern Archaics*, 294.

57 直把戒外言內言的這塊大招牌，這堵舊圍牆，竟衝破打通了！堂堂皇皇的講論女學、女主筆，豈不是中國古來所未有的呢？ Pan Xuan 潘璇, "Lun *Nü xuebao* nanchu he Zhongwai nüzi xiangzhu de lifa 論女學報難處和中外女子相助的理法 [On the Difficulties of Founding the *Nü xuebao* and the Way of Mutual Help between Chinese and Western Women]," *Nü xuebao* 3 (1898): 2b.

This attempt to claim a new public identity was first demonstrated in the female writers' deliberate avoidance of the term *guixiu* 閨秀 when referring to themselves or addressing one another. The term, which literally means "flowers in the inner chambers," was often used to designate well-educated, cultured women from gentry or scholarly families in imperial China. As indicated by *gui*, which means "a small gate of the inner courtyard, palace or city,"[58] *guixiu* readily evokes the proper spatial location of women and their roles in the home, although scholars have pointed out that, mostly through the act of writing, some cultivated gentry women also imagined identities for themselves beyond the normative roles defined by kinship and the social system.[59] In the writing circle of *Nü xuebao*, women eschewed this category of identification, adopting appellations such as *nüshi*, *xianyuan* 賢媛 (worthy women), *xianshu mingyuan* 賢淑名媛 (worthy, virtuous women from reputable families), or other variants with the word *xian* as the defining element.[60] Nanxiu Qian associates these reformist women's repeated use of *xianyuan* with what she calls the *xianyuan* tradition. Qian traces the origins of this tradition to the Wei-Jin era (220–420) and notes that the concept of *xianyuan*, unlike its counterparts such as *guixiu* or *cainü* in the late Qing context, connotes intellectual independence and high worth and can be understood as the perfect combination of talent and virtue.[61] By contrast, male reformists tended to use *guixiu* to refer to female writers and titles of collections of these women's writings on the campaign for women's education, such as *Guixiu cizao* 閨秀辭藻 (*Words by Cultivated Women in the Inner Chambers*) and *Guixiu shichao* 閨秀詩鈔 (*Poetry by Cultivated Women from the Inner Apartments*).[62] In this regard, the female

58 Li, *Women's Poetry of Late Imperial China*, 5.

59 Fong, *Herself an Author*; Yang, *Heroines of the Qing*.

60 See, e.g., the women's essays and reports in Jing Yuanshan's "Nüxue jiyi chubian." For a similar observation of this frequent use of *xian*-associated terms, see also Qian, *Politics, Poetics, and Gender*, 124 and 296n7.

61 Qian, *Politics, Poetics, and Gender*, 14–15. However, according to Ko, in the early Qing period, *xianyuan* became a label for the valorization of female talent and used to designate women poets in some county gazetteers, in *Teachers of the Inner Chambers*, 124.

62 See, for instance, Jing Yuanshan, "Nü xuetang Zhangyuan dahui zhu guixiu cizao buyi 女學堂張園大會諸閨秀辭藻補遺 [Supplement to the Words by the Cultivated Women from the Girls' School at the Meeting Held at the Zhang Garden]," in Zhu, *Zhongguo jindai sixiangjia wenku*, 83–84; Jing Yuanshan, ed., "Zai xu Nü xuetang guixiu shichao 再續女學堂閨秀詩鈔 [A Continued Record of Poetry by the Cultivated Women from the Girls' School]," "Nü xuetang jie youren shu bing guixiu shi 女學堂接友人書並閨秀詩 [A Friend's Letter and Poems by Cultivated Ladies Received at the Girls' School]," and "Guixiu shichao lu Ding Suqing shi 閨秀詩鈔錄丁素清詩 [Poems by the Cultivated Lady Ding Suqing]," in *Xinwen bao*, June 7, 1898; January 29, 1898; June 4, 1898. Jing Yuanshan also often referred to these women reformers as *guixiu* when he recorded the

writers' choice of other types of self-identification was a conscious effort to defy men's designation, which suggests an assertion of agency in the gender politics of naming and their aspiration to express a new sense of belonging derived from their ability to write in a new historical context.

The women contributors' effort to transcend the "inner" and "outer" binary not only was illustrated by their rejection of *guixiu*, with its negative connotation of confining women to the domestic sphere, but also reflected their efforts to reach out to a broader female readership beyond their own writing circle. The reformist women, as shown above, had already begun to "go public" through their open gatherings for the promotion of women's education and their poetic correspondence with one another. Because of the availability of the new print media, the traditional literary practice of corresponding with one another in verse was no longer limited to a few learned reformist women but extended to a larger community. As Xia Xiaohong has perceptively pointed out, the practice of exchanging ideas via letters among traditional Chinese literati expanded enormously in the late Qing, thanks to the new newspapers and journals. Even those who were thousands of miles apart from one another could remain in touch by exchanging poems and lyrics published in the newspapers. As a result, the cultivated gentry women in Shanghai were not the only ones to join in the reformist women's poetic correspondence.[63] For example, a woman named Xiu Zhen 秀珍 from Yunjian 雲間 (Songjiang county in Jiangsu Province in the late Qing, present-day Songjiang district in Shanghai) composed a poem in response to poetry by the female faculty members at the Girls' School. Xiu Zhen's text reveals that she was so amazed by these women's "fine verses" that she put down her needlework and read these poems over and over well into the night. In the last line, Xiu Zhen expressed her earnest hope that the admirable cause of developing women's education would spread to her hometown as well.[64]

This vignette was not unique. *Nü xuebao* also published poems and letters written by its female readers. As a result, the female contributors formed a loose literary network with potential female readers across geographical and social barriers, building solidarity with women they had never met or would

activities and events concerning the promotion of women's education in the 1898 reform period.

63 Xia Xiaohong 夏曉虹, *Wan-Qing nüxing yu jindai Zhongguo* 晚清女性與近代中國 [*Late Qing Women and Modern China*] (Beijing: Peking University Press, 2004), 9.

64 Xiu Zhen 秀珍, "Yin du Nü xuetang zhu nüshi shuaicheng sijue 因讀女學堂諸女士詩率成四絕 [Verses Composed after Reading the Poems by the Ladies at the Chinese Girls' School]," in the Supplement to *Xinwen bao* (July 4, 1898).

never meet. Scholars have noted that similar kinds of literary communities formed through exchanges by women of epistles or poems had existed in the late imperial period.[65] But unlike the late imperial female poets and writers, the female contributors to *Nü xuebao* and their female correspondents were less likely to derive their sense of community from the shared goal of advancing their literary talent. Rather, they aimed to promote public causes of national importance, such as women's education. They seemed to pay little attention to the literary value of the poetic responses per se and focused on the act of exchange itself as an effective way to create fellowship and sisterhood through developing common national causes.

Of course, not all female readers of *Nü xuebao* possessed the literary ability to respond with letters or poems, but the wider female readership that the journal could reach increased the "authority" of women's authorship because they no longer needed to have a personal connection or emotional bond with their readers. In contrast to the literary women in the late imperial period who expressed their innermost personal thoughts or feelings and shared them with individual friends, the women writing for *Nü xuebao* declared their ability and courage to speak to strangers and express opinions to people beyond their own immediate circles. Writing in the journal therefore empowered them to claim public authorial authority, rather than sustain the tradition of private emotional expression. As the "Benguan gaobai 本館告白 (Announcement from This Journal)" in the first issue clearly stated, the ideal pieces that the journal expected from female contributors were *lun* or *shuo* essays.[66] By the late nineteenth century, *lun* and *shuo* were pertinent genres for speaking to the public and often associated with political discussions. Whereas women's literary writing had long been perceived as a safe haven from men's cold, intellectual world and distant from politics, women's *lun* or *shuo* writing in *Nü xuebao* was precisely in service to a new politics and open to a national readership.

This dramatic shift from "private" to "public" was demonstrated not only in the female contributors' experiment with new modes of writing but in the new form of publishing enabled by *Nü xuebao*. Scholarship on women's writing culture in the late imperial era has noted that the flourishing of publishing enterprises—family publishing in particular—opened up an unparalleled avenue for the publication of women's works. It challenged the Confucian moral doctrine that "women's words should not be heard in the

65 As for how literary women in the late imperial period created an "epistolary world" to develop and disseminate their female talent, see Ellen Widmer, "The Epistolary World of Female Talent in Seventeenth-Century China," *Late Imperial China* 10 (December 1989).

66 "Benguan gaobai 本館告白 [Announcement from this Journal]," *Nü xuebao* 1 (1898).

outside world" and made the wall between the inner (domestic) and outer (public) spheres more permeable.[67] However, the late imperial women's works had relatively limited impact on the general public and cultural landscape, largely because their works were regarded as symbols of their family's cultural attainments and thus often used to cement social ties, rather than being sold in the market. *Nü xuebao*, in contrast, provided a new model of publishing distinct from the late imperial literary women's publishing venues. Unlike the late imperial literary women, who were often hailed as the pride of their family or clan, the women writing in *Nü xuebao* emerged as reform-minded intellectuals who wrote about social and political concerns for the sake of the nation. Moreover, whereas earlier women's works appealed to readers who wanted to explore the writers' private realm from their own private vantage point, an act of reading that invited a sensual, erotic overtone of "sneaking a peek" into the women's inner chambers, the female writers of *Nü xuebao* drove the readers to start from the private realm and explore a new female-authored public realm for the first time. The material context for women's writing, which had been intimately linked with family honors and clan prestige in the late imperial era, now shifted to national prosperity and politicized female literacy. In helping to carve out a new gendered public discursive space, women's writing in *Nü xuebao* was instrumental in constructing a new womanhood.

4 Ambivalence: a Debate of Linguistic Registers

In their attempt to reach a wide national readership, the female editors of *Nü xuebao* encountered a dilemma: whether to adopt a plain, straightforward vernacular style in contrast to the classical style (*wenyan* 文言) to address the masses with limited education, especially women. Although the classical writing style had long been deemed the primary form of writing adopted by the elite and ruling classes and associated with cultural continuity and unifying the empire, by the turn of the twentieth century, vernacular writing had become a new style and gained increasing popularity in newspapers and

67 Ko, *Teachers of the Inner Chambers*, 29–67. Male family members played a crucial role in the publishing of women's works, offering not only financial sponsorship but also moral and emotional support. See Clara Wing-chung Ho, "Encouragement from the Opposite Gender, Male Scholars and Women's Publications in Ch'ing China, A Bibliographic Study," in *Chinese Women in the Imperial Past: New Perspectives*, ed. Harriet T. Zurndorfer (Leiden: E.J. Brill, 1998).

journals.[68] This new vernacular journalistic style was celebrated for its effectiveness in disseminating new forms of practical knowledge and communication. A number of leading reformist intellectuals, such as Liang Qichao and Kang Youwei, had argued for the transformative power of vernacular writing in turning the uneducated masses into nation-minded people.[69] Under these circumstances, the female contributors to *Nü xuebao* who were conversant in the classical learning and proficient in writing in classical Chinese also realized that in many ways a vernacular style could be more effective in spreading their ideas about women's education and in communicating with their less-educated female readers. The female contributors to *Nü xuebao* originally proposed calling the journal *Guanhua nü xuebao* 官話女學報 (*Mandarin Journal of Women's Learning*), a title highlighting the privileged value of the vernacular in the journal's editorial agenda. However, after the female editors engaged in a serious discussion about the appropriate linguistic register for the journal, this title was not approved.

Xue Shaohui, the editor-in-chief, initiated the debate. Before the journal was published, Xue wrote a letter to the Women's Study Society to solicit opinions with regard to her proposal to call it *Guanhua nü xuebao*. Xue explained, because very few Chinese women knew how to read or write, using *guanhua* (Mandarin), a prominent form of vernacular writing, was therefore a reluctant and yet necessary option.[70] But at the same time, Xue was deeply concerned

68 In the Confucian tradition, *wen* was a significant concept with cultural and political significances. In the broadest metaphysical and cosmological sense, *wen*, referring to "patterns," was a splendid display of Heaven and Earth; in a narrower sense, it simply designated "writing." *Wen* thus had both the function of conveying cultural meaning [*dao* 道] by connecting the past and the present and the power of unifying the country with a great linguistic diversity. In this sense, *wenyan* was deemed able to fulfill this double function of vertical and horizontal unification. For discussions on the concept of *wen* in Chinese literary tradition, see Wu, *Modern Archaics*, 25–33; Elisabeth Kaske, "Mandarin, Vernacular and National Language—China's emerging concept of a National Language in the Early Twentieth Century," in Michael Lackner and Natascha Vittinghoff, *Mapping Meanings*, 266–267; on vernacular writing as a new journalistic style at the turn of the twentieth century, see Zhang, "Feminism in the Vernacular."

69 For example, in 1897, Liang Qichao proposed to use local patois [*liyu* 俚語] to disseminate different kinds of knowledge, cultivate national consciousness, and eradicate evil social customs, in "Bianfa tongyi: lun youxue 變法通議·論幼學 [A General Discussion of Reform—On Education for Children]," in *Yinbing shi heji: wenji* 飲冰室合集文集 [*Collected Writings from the Ice-Drinker's Studio*] (Shanghai: Zhonghua shuju, 1936).

70 By the early nineteenth century, *guanhua* had emerged as regional dialect that was well developed in most parts of China in both spoken and written forms. As a spoken language, *guanhua* even received a certain degree of imperial government support as the *lingua franca* of the state. As a written language, *guanhua* was used in the majority of the

about "the lack of elegance and refinement" inherent in "vulgar" vernacular writing. The members of the Women's Study Society shared Xue's concern and proposed a solution in their response to her letter. They suggested that well-versed writers, such as Xue, use "colorful brushes" (*caihao* 彩毫)—a reference to elaborate and ornate expression—to awaken uneducated women in families of scholar-officials first. They noted that they and these women were of the "same kind" (*tonglei* 同類), and it would be more appropriate to exhort the "upper classes" (*shangdeng ren* 上等人) with "well-crafted and embellished writing" (*wenbi zhi gaomiao* 文筆之高妙).[71] Here the emphasis on literary ornamentation and embellishment made it clear that the preferred written medium was elegant classical writing, as vernacular writing was commonly regarded as lacking stylistic or rhetorical artifice.[72] In proposing to speak to the "upper classes" with a more prestigious classical writing style, the society's members seemed to have drifted away from the journal's goal of addressing the masses of Chinese women. The classical writing functioned not only as a symbol of their literary and cultural prestige but also a mark of their elite class status.

The contested values of "elegant" and "popular" involved in the dichotomy of classical versus vernacular propelled the editorial board to compromise and employ "30 percent of classical writing and 70 percent of vernacular writing" (*ya san su qi* 雅三俗七).[73] But this suggested ratio was not exactly followed, and most essayists still wrote in classical Chinese. Xue Shaohui adopted the classical style in her essays. Qiu Yufang, a seasoned practitioner of vernacular writing and who had penned many vernacular essays in *Wuxi baihua bao*, also opted for the classical style when writing in *Nü xuebao*. This discrepancy in practice made it problematic to achieve the stated objective of "adopting Mandarin to elaborate or explain everything related to women's education" (用官話演說一切女學).[74] *Yan* 演 or *yanshuo* 演說 (to elaborate, to explain, or to render) usually referred to using the vernacular language to bring elite

vernacular literature. On *guanhua* as both a spoken language and written medium, see Kaske, "Mandarin, Vernacular and National Language," 268.

71 The original letter was lost. Xue's comments reappeared in the letter responded by the members of the Women's Study Society. See Shen Ying 沈瑛 et al., "Zhongguo Nü xuehui zhi houguan Xue nüshi shaohui shu 中國女學會致侯官薛女史紹徽書 [To Woman Historian Xue Shaohui of Houguan from the Women's Study Society]," *Zhixin bao* 59 (July, 1898).

72 For a discussion on the association of the classical language with literary ornamentation and the vernacular with linguistic transparency, see Wu, *Modern Archaics*, 26–31.

73 "Benguan gaobai."

74 "Benguan gaobai."

ideas to the uneducated masses. In this sense, the extent to which the ideas of the elite women writers of *Nü xuebao* reached popular audiences remains questionable.

In the face of this general trend to adopt the classical language, however, one nonconformist was not only a vocal advocate of the use of the vernacular but also successfully developed a vernacular style. Pan Xuan was a female contributor whose name appeared on the cover of every issue of *Nü xuebao*. Little is known of Pan's life, except that she was from Shanghai, but her impassioned advocacy of vernacular Chinese may have inspired Qiu Tingliang to write "Lun baihua wei weixin zhi ben 論白話為維新之本 (On the Use of Vernacular as the Basis for Reform)," which became known as the manifesto for the late Qing language reform movement.[75] For Pan, the employment of vernacular writing not only spurred female literacy—or, as she put it, "when one woman reads the journal aloud, dozens of women can understand"—but, more importantly, worked to cultivate a national consciousness.[76]

In "Lun yong guanhua 論用官話 (On the Use of Mandarin)," Pan discussed at length the political imperative of replacing the outmoded, esoteric classical language with the more accessible vernacular, which she valorized as the language most appropriate for schools and newspapers. Unlike fellow female contributors who strove to preserve the prestige of the classical language, Pan sought to dismantle it. She endorsed the use of the vernacular in light of the replacement of Latin by the European vernacular, such as English, French, and German, to justify the legitimacy of the vernacular by putting it into a global context. Moving beyond the dichotomy of vulgar versus elegant, Pan redefined the value of vernacular writing in purely pragmatic terms and considered linguistic transparency its defining feature.[77] She wrote,

> The ancient (classical) writing was of little use other than being used in studying antiques. With the use of the more readable and accessible

75 Xia Xiaohong speculates that Pan Xuan's ideas on the vernacular may have become one of the sources of inspiration for Qiu Tingliang's article because Qiu's niece Qiu Yufang was also one of the female contributors to *Nü xuebao*, and it is likely that Qiu Tingliang read Pan's article before he published his own. See Xia Xiaohong, *Wan-Qing baihua wen yu qimeng duwu* 晚清白話文與啟蒙讀物 [*Late Qing Vernacular Writings and Reading Materials for Enlightenment*] (Hong Kong: Sanlian shudian, 2015), 59–60.

76 Pan Xuan 潘璇, "Shanghai *Nü xuebao* yuanqi (di'er jie): Lun ben bao wei nüxue qi jian 上海女學報緣起（第二節）：論本報為女學起見 [Forward to *Nü xuebao*, Part Two: For the Sake of Women's Education]," *Nü xuebao* 2 (1898): 2a.

77 For a critique of linguistic transparency in the vernacular, see Wu, *Modern Archaics*, 31.

> vernacular (*baihua*) writing, one could save enormous time and energy and be dedicated to the study of useful, practical knowledge.[78]

Another prominent advantage of the vernacular, or *baihua*, Pan argued, was that it represented the unification of both writing and speech, which means vernacular writing was a natural extension of vernacular speech. Pan thus equated written *baihua* with *guanhua*, a koine of the Ming and Qing period that was employed by officials, traveling monks, and merchants for oral communication and that was transregional. She contended:

> Today when we found newspapers and journals, we should consider using *guanhua* first and then local patois. Why is that? Because even if a local patois can be understood in one village or township, it may not be understood in one county or prefecture; even if it can be understood in one county or prefecture, it may not be understood in one province or across the entire country.[79]

The main purpose of using *guanhua*, Pan continued, was to make China a modern nation. In advocating vernacular writing as the common linguistic ground for the formation of Chinese nation-state in general and for journalism in particular, Pan Xuan used the koine of the empire in the service of a new, nationalist mission.

The debate over the choice of linguistic register between classical and vernacular writing in *Nü xuebao* indicates female contributors' complex and ambivalent attitudes toward constructing a modern identity. On the one hand, they were well aware of the political exigency of addressing and enlightening the masses of women, who had been recognized as a subordinated gendered collectivity in the new historical context of national strengthening, as evidenced by the late Qing reformist intellectuals' conception of Chinese women as an intellectually inferior group. The proposal to adopt an accessible vernacular style further suggests that these female contributors recognized the imperative to ally themselves in gender terms with the emergent subordinated

78 古話除了考古外，沒有別用，不如用白話的易讀易曉，可以省却那些無限的功夫，好去揣摩這些有用的實學。Pan Xuan, "Shanghai *Nü xuebao* yuanqi (diyi jie): Lun yong *guanhua* 上海女學報緣起（第一節）：論用官話 [Forward to *Nü xuebao*, Part One: On the Use of Mandarin]," *Nü xuebao* 1 (1898): 3a.

79 如今立報，應當先用官話，次用土話。為什麼呢？因為土話只能行在一鄉一村的，不能通到一縣一州，行在一縣一州的，不能通到一省一國。 Pan, "Shanghai *Nü xuebao* yuanqi (diyi jie)," 3a.

category called "women." However, that the majority of the female journalists failed to realize this proposal also reveals their profound anxiety over vernacular writing's association with being low class and having low tastes. Hailing from elite families, in which they received a superior classical education, these women regarded classical writing as not only their most familiar writing medium but also a mark of their prestigious social and cultural standing. Their choice of classical writing over vernacular writing was thus an indication of their identification in class terms with elite male reformers, rather than the masses of women.

5 Conclusion

Nü xuebao, the first Chinese women's journal, opened up an unprecedented mixed-gender public space for both male and female reformers to the first debate on the woman question in the 1898 reform period. Whereas the male reformist intellectuals envisioned a civic female literacy that was predicted on the disavowal of the elitist, feminized Chinese literate tradition, women presented their own discursive responses. As this chapter shows, although some women joined men in discrediting the *cainü* legacy, subversive voices also emerged, as shown by Xue Shaohui's clear rejection of subsuming China's cultural uniqueness in general and women's literary heritage in particular to utilitarian programs under the universal nationalist discourse. The majority of female contributors expressed their disagreement with men's repudiation of the *cainü* tradition through their successful appropriation of the female talent-boosting practices, such as the use of writing to assert intellectual authority, the employment of specific designations for self-identification purposes, and the exchange of letters and poems. These female writers showed that the practices that had been effective in cultivating female talent could be refashioned for new circumstances, rather than being discarded as obsolete or useless. In the new journalistic public realm, they used writing as an empowering means to assume public authority in the new context of the nation and to transpose the family and clan glories that had been attached to the value of women's writing to nationalist demands.

The contestation over the language register reveals the predicament that female contributors encountered in the process of constructing a gendered modern identity. Amid the sweeping castigations of *cainü* culture and the demanding nationalist calls for a new female literacy, "women" as a collectivity began to emerge as both potential agents capable of transforming society and "ignorant" objects who needed to be enlightened by the elites. In proposing vernacular writing to address the less-educated audience of female readers, the female editors began to recognize the imperative of making an alliance with the socially and politically subordinated category "women." Yet, as members of the highly privileged and educated elite, they also felt compelled to employ the more formal classical writing so as to demonstrate their cultural and social superiority. Ironic as it may seem, even the most radical critics of traditional high culture, such as Kang Tongwei and Qiu Yufang, were at the same time staunch supporters of the language on which this culture was dependent. This profound disjuncture suggests that the gendered modern identity envisioned by the female writers was largely class based and, hence, exclusive of the masses of Chinese women. As we see in the next chapter, the ambivalence in these reformist female writers' identification on the basis of elite status, rather than an identification with Chinese womanhood in general, would soon disappear in the journalistic writings by feminist women in the years that immediately followed 1898.

CHAPTER 2

Nationalism and Beyond: *Nüjie* and the Construction of a New Gendered Collective Identity

In 1903, Jin Tianhe 金天翮 (1874–1947), a prominent writer and feminist advocate, published the first Chinese feminist manifesto entitled *Nüjie zhong* 女界鐘 (*The Women's Bell*).[1] As the titular imagery "bell" suggests, Jin's primary goal of writing such a treatise was to awaken and enlighten Chinese women—a gendered collectivity that he termed *nüjie* 女界. While providing a systematic championing of women's rights to education, marriage freedom, new morality, and suffrage, Jin lamented that Chinese *nüjie* were woefully oppressed and enslaved. He envisioned a woman warrior leading "a women's revolutionary army" (*nüjie zhi geming jun* 女界之革命軍) that would awaken women cloistered in the inner chambers from their nightmares.[2]

Although the reformist intellectuals in the 1898 period had already begun to interpellate women as potential subject-agents in a new national politics, as shown in chapter 1, Jin was the among the first to deploy a gender-specific term to explicitly identify the collectivity of women as an oppressed group in the context of national salvation.[3] For the next several years, *nüjie* resonated through public speeches, the popular press, and fiction as a wide variety of actors used this new word as a tool for realizing their own nationalist agendas through mobilizing women. In these years, *nüjie* became a new signifier

1 For the most recent scholarship on *Nüjie zhong*'s role in the history of Chinese feminism, see Liu, Karl, and Ko, *The Birth of Chinese Feminism*. Li Youning 李又寧 also provides a detailed scholarly commentary of *Nüjie zhong* and a reprint of the 1903 edition, in "*Nüjie zhong* yu Zhonghua nüxing de xiandai hua 女界鐘與中華女性的現代化 [*The Women's Bell* and Chinese Women's Modernization]," in *Nüjie zhong* 女界鐘 [*The Women's Bell*], ed. Li Youning (New York: Outer Sky Press, 2003). Louise Edwards was among the first scholars outside China to study this feminist treatise. See her study "Chin Sung-ts'en's '*A Tocsin for Women*': The Dexterous Merger of Radicalism and Conservatism in Feminism of the Early Twentieth Century," *Jindai Zhongguo funü shi yanjiu* 近代中國婦女史研究 2 (1992).

2 Jin Tianhe 金天翮, "Xulun 緒論 [Preface]," in *Nüjie zhong* (New York: Outer Sky Press, 2003).

3 The earliest adoption of the term *nüjie* that can be dated was in the feminist journalist Chen Xiefen's 陳擷芬 (1883–1923) *Nüxue bao* 女學報 [*Journal of Women's Studies*], a feminist journal that Chen first published in Shanghai in 1902 and then in Tokyo in 1903. But it was not until the publication of Jin's treatise that this term gained currency in the writings of nationalism and feminism.

 DOI:10.1163/9789004438545_004

for collective womanhood that was inevitably subjugated to the demands of nationalism, providing a new language for male feminist writers such as Jin to articulate the relationship between gender and the nation. However, as women also began to actively engage in debates and writings about nationalism and feminism, they reoriented the way in which *nüjie* operated in the context about nationalism and changed its connotations in subversive ways that male writers had not anticipated.

This chapter explores how women feminist writers refashioned *nüjie* as a powerful analytical category to examine a wide range of questions concerning the woman question within and beyond the context of nationalism in the first decade of the twentieth century. A number of scholars have lent attention to historical gendered terms for the collectivity of women in pre-twentieth century China, such as *funü* 婦女, *furen* 婦人, and *nüzi* 女子.[4] Little, however, is known of *nüjie*,[5] a neologism for the collectivity of women that emerged from the context of national salvation and directly associated women with the nation from the outset. As previous scholarship has pointed out, the turn of the twentieth century was a vibrant era of cultural, intellectual, and linguistic exchanges. At this historical juncture, classical Chinese terms began to adopt new vocabularies to produce neologistic constructions facilitated by the transaction of loanwords from Japanese or European languages. *Nüjie* was just such an example. Although this term was composed of two Chinese characters: *nü* and *jie*, it was actually a modern neologism as *jie* was a derivative of *shijie* 世界, a "return graphic loan."[6] Despite its millennia-long existence in the Chinese

4 Mou Zhengyun 牟正蘊, "Jiegou *funü*: jiuci xinlun 解構 "婦女"： 舊詞新論 [Deconstructing *Funü:* New Interpretations of An Old Term]," *Jindai Zhongguo funü shi yanjiu* 6 (1998); see also Tani Barlow's examination of the history of *funü* as a collectivity for kinswomen within the Confucian familial structures in her discussion of "Theorizing Women," in *The Question of Women in Chinese Feminism* (Durham: Duke University Press, 2004), 37–48; and "Theorizing Woman: *Funü, Guojia, Jiating* (Chinese Women, State, and Family)," in *Body, Subject and Power in China*, ed. Angela Zita and Tani E. Barlow (Chicago: The University of Chicago Press, 1994), 263–265.

5 A recent scholarly discussion about *nüjie* investigates how the promotion of sisterhood and the construction of an imagined women's community were associated with the concept in the last two decades of the Qing dynasty. See Yun Zhu, *Imagining Sisterhood in Modern Chinese Texts, 1890–1937* (Lanham, MD: Lexington Books, 2017), 1–34. But in the discussion the author simply renders *nüjie* as "women's sphere," a literal translation that elided the semantic fluidity and multiplicity of the term as a conceptual mechanism, as I treat it in this chapter.

6 Building on Gao Mingkai 高名凱 and Liu Zhengtan's 劉正埮 study of loanwords in modern Chinese, Lydia Liu explains that " 'Return graphic loans' were those classical Chinese terms or expressions used by the Japanese to translate Western terms that were then imported back into Chinese with a radical change in meaning, such as *geming* 革命 (revolution; *kakumei*), *wenhua* 文化 (culture; *bunka*), *jingji* 經濟 (economy; *keizai*); and *kexue* 科學 (science;

classical and Buddhist texts, *shijie* has acquired its modern meaning of "world" from the Japanese *kanji* 漢字 (Chinese character) compound *sekai* 世界 in the late nineteenth century.[7] In this sense, *nüjie* also signified a temporal and spatial boundary specific for women and could be rendered as "women's world."

Such semantic mobility made *nüjie* a unique concept amenable to various interpretations. While it frequently referred to women as an oppressed group, it was also adopted to suggest simultaneously a dark and dismal world in which women had been drenched in ignorance and subordination for thousands of years and a utopian land where women's emancipation and enlightenment were to be realized.[8] In most instances, however, the notion of *nüjie* exceeded and resisted facile rendition into "women's world," "women," or "womanhood." Rather, it was a conceptual totality that signified not only a new connection drawn between women and the Chinese nation but also the relationship between women's past and the present, the gendered social relations between men and women, or more broadly, the relationship between women and the modernizing world. *Nüjie* thus became a powerful category of analysis for women to articulate feminist issues within the confines of nationalism and, ultimately, to transcend these confines. In order to better elucidate the analytical

---

kakagu)." See Lydia Liu, *Translingual Practice: Literature, National Culture, and Translated Modernity—China, 1900–1937* (Stanford: Stanford University Press, 1995), 32–33; see also Gao Mingkai and Liu Zhengtan, *Xindai hanyu wailai ci yanjiu* 現代漢語外來詞研究 [*A Study of the Loanwords in Modern Chinese*] (Bejing: Wenzi gaige chubanshe, 1958). Missionary Evan Morgan identified *jie* as a new word created in Japan and also used to connote the meaning of "world." He argued that Japan probably obtained the idea from European expressions, such as "The Official World," "The World of Letters," and "Political World." See Evan Morgan, *Chinese New Terms and Expressions with English Translations: Introduction and Notes* (Shanghai: Kelly & Walsh, 1913), 192.

7 *Shijie* originally appeared in the Buddhist canon and was later used to connote *tianxia* 天下 (all under the heaven)—a key Confucian concept implying that China was a self-contained cosmos. The equating of 世界 and "world" through the mediation of Japanese significantly replaced the concept *tianxia*. *Shijie* began to denote a new conceptualizing of temporal and spatial boundaries in modern China. See Liu, *Translingual Practice*, 342. On the conceptual shift from *tianxia* to *shijie*, see Joseph R. Levenson, *Confucian China and Its Modern Fate: A Trilogy* (Berkeley: University of California Press, 1972), 98–104; Jin Guantao 金觀濤 and Liu Qingfeng 劉青峰, "Cong *tianxia, wanguo* dao *shijie*—wan Qing minzu zhuyi xingcheng de zhongjian huanjie 從「天下」、「萬國」到「世界」——晚清民族主義形成的中間環節 [From *tianxia, wanguo,* to *shijie*: Intermediary Links in the Formation of Nationalism in the Late Qing]," *Ershi yi shiji* 二十一世紀 94 (2006).

8 *Hei'an* 黑闇 was a prevalent expression characterizing *nüjie* at the time. For example, Qiu Jin 秋瑾 (1875–1907) often used the expression "*nüjie zhi hei'an* 女界之黑闇 [the darkness of *nüjie*]" to refer to the condition of women's oppression. Qiu Jin, "*Jingweishi* xu 精衛石序 [Preface to *Stones of the Jingwei Bird*]," in *Qiu Jin ji* 秋瑾集 [*Collected Works by Qiu Jin*], ed. Shanghai guji chubanshe 上海古籍出版社 (Shanghai: Shanghai guji chubanshe, 1991).

valences of *nüjie* as a category, the term is left untranslated in some situations, whereas in others it is contextually rendered as "women," "womanhood," and "women's world" so as to maintain its semantic flexibility.

As women began to take up feminist writing on *nüjie*, an important question that arises is the extent to which the nationalist-inflected meanings of this term and men's feminist writings about *nüjie* informed women's articulation of their own feminist ideas. Recent scholarship has pointed out that, although male authors began to engage in feminist writing of various types beginning in the nineteenth century, their pursuits, nonetheless, spoke of their concern over national strengthening and Chinese modernization, rather than of women's interests per se.[9] Not until the early twentieth century did a small group of women emerge as vocal advocates and active writers about feminist issues.[10] This does not mean that women's feminist writing was devoid of nationalist concerns or that women's voices were more authentic than men's in the writing of women's issues. Interest in China's national survival was inextricably intertwined with women's feminist writings, as it constituted a crucial part of the larger context that had informed the rise of women's feminist writing in the first place. What marked women's feminist writing is that women maneuvered strategically to appropriate the nationalist discourse as they argued for their own feminist agendas. This was especially true of women's writing about *nüjie*, as the notion initially was defined by male feminist writers for nationalist purposes from the outset. When women first encountered *nüjie* in their feminist writing, they had to subscribe to this male-defined concept, but they soon appropriated it as an analytical category to construct their own visions of modern Chinese womanhood in the context of nationalism and beyond. Thus, the process in which women created their own analyses and definitions of *nüjie* was filled with gendered dynamics and complexity.

The feminist women's press that flourished at this time offers an ideal locus for us to examine writings on *nüjie*. The first of these women's journals was *Nüzi shijie*, the longest-running late Qing feminist publication launched and managed by a group of prominent male intellectuals in Shanghai in 1904. The journal appeared until 1907, with a total of eighteen issues. Both men and women contributed to it. Another influential feminist journal was *Zhongguo xin nüjie zazhi* 中國新女界雜誌 (*Magazine of New Women's World of China*),

9 For a recent argument that Jin's feminist agenda still largely resided within the larger project of China's national strengthening, see Liu, Karl, and Ko, *The Birth of Chinese Feminism*, 1–7. For a thoughtful discussion on men's feminist writing, see Dooling, *Women's Literary Feminism*, 12–13.

10 Dooling, *Women's Literary Feminism*, 36–64; Judge, "Talent, Virtue, and the Nation."

which was established in 1907 by a Chinese woman studying in Tokyo named Yan Bin 燕斌 (full name Luo Yanbin 羅燕斌; b. 1869). Another prominent journal also published in Tokyo was *Tianyi* 天義 (*Natural Justice*), an anarchist-leaning feminist journal that was founded and edited by the noted anarchist-feminist He-Yin Zhen 何殷震 (ca. 1884–1920?) and her husband, Liu Shipei 劉師培 (1884–1919), in 1907–1908.

These feminist journals constituted a unique mixed-gender public space revolving around articulations of *nüjie* by both men and women. As in the mixed-gender public space in *Nü xuebao*, in the feminist public space, women rarely argued directly against men's conceptions of *nüjie*. In some instances, on the pages of *Zhongguo xin nüjie zazhi* and *Tianyi*, men seemed to have completely retreated from writing about *nüjie*. But this does not mean that *nüjie*, a national subordinated gendered collectivity that was first and foremost conceptualized by men, also receded. Rather, it served as a powerful starting point for female feminist contributors to develop their own approaches to *nüjie*. It is in this feminist mixed-gender public space constituted across specific journals that we see the tensions and dynamics of the gendered articulations of *nüjie*.

Preoccupation with the national interests was another prominent characteristic of the feminist women's journals. In varying degrees, the majority of these journals framed their feminist goals in terms of national concerns. One example was the promotion of *guomin zhi mu* 國民之母 (mothers of citizens), a concept that directly related the promulgation of women's education and rights with the nationalist call for citizenship.[11] For this reason, existing scholarship has tended to see the nationalist-leaning writings in these women's journals as evidence of the limits and constraints of the feminist discourse of this period and, in general, of the subordination of Chinese feminism to nationalism.[12] A closer look at the writings by women, however, suggests a more complex relationship between nationalist ideology and feminist writing. It is true that some female writers privileged the nation and emphasized that women should be emancipated for the national good, yet there were also a number of women who strove to foreground women's interests. For these

11 Joan Judge, "Citizens or Mothers of Citizens? Gender and the Meaning of Modern Chinese Citizenship," in *Changing Meanings of Citizenship in Modern China*, ed. Elizabeth Perry and Merle Goldman (Cambridge: Harvard University Asia Centre, 2002).

12 Beahan, "Feminism and Nationalism"; Peter Zarrow, "He Zhen and Anarcho-Feminism in China," *The Journal of Asian Studies* 47 (1988), 796. Tani Barlow also argues that the flourishing of women's journals at the turn of the twentieth century "contributed to what rapidly emerged as 'myths of the nation'," in Barlow, "Theorizing Woman," 263.

authors, writing about the nation was a means that gave them legitimacy to articulate their ideas on women's issues. Women writers' deployment of the term *nüjie* best illustrated this dynamic. Like their male counterparts, women writers first adopted *nüjie* to criticize conditions for women and to conceptualize Chinese women as an oppressed collectivity in terms of the national interest. Later, however, these female writers produced more powerful analyses of *nüjie*, which not only facilitated the separation of the causal links between women and the nation but also constructed a new emancipatory discourse on women.

In this chapter, we examine these three influential women's feminist journals, each of which demonstrated how articulations of *nüjie* were indissolubly linked with advocating the production of "mothers of citizens," "female citizens," and "absolute equality between men and women"—formulations that were indicative of the changing relationships between gender and the nation in the context of nationalism and feminism. Together, they present a comprehensive view of how contesting ideals of modern Chinese womanhood were constructed through the gendered analyses of *nüjie*. Most significantly, this examination reveals the trajectories in which female writers managed to employ *nüjie* to reconfigure Chinese women as a specific oppressed group as well as potentially subversive national subjects whose transformations were closely linked with, but not confined to, the agenda of national strengthening. Through the empowering category of *nüjie*, female writers constructed feminist critiques within—and against—the nationalist discourse and ultimately envisioned a new collective identity for Chinese women. These writings on *nüjie* attested to the innovative ways in which early twentieth-century feminist Chinese women engaged in and expanded the scope of the debate on the woman question in the context of Chinese nationalism and feminism.

This chapter is also intended to fill a lacuna in the current scholarship on the genealogy of Chinese terms for "women." In her theorizing on "women" across Chinese history, Tani Barlow asserts that until the emergence of the term of *nüxing* 女性 in the 1920s, "there is no term present before the twentieth century that might indicate women as group outside the family."[13] By contrast, this chapter shows that *nüjie* was just such a term, emerging at the turn of the twentieth century to designate "women" as a gendered collectivity outside the family—a new concept to verbalize Chinese women's inextricable relationship to the Chinese nation and the modernizing world.

---

13 Barlow, *The Question of Women*, 40.

1 The Cure for the Nation: Mobilizing *Nüjie*

Intensive writings on *nüjie* first abounded in *Nüzi shijie*. The journal was celebrated as the longest standing and most widely circulated women's journal in the late Qing period.[14] It was launched by the liberal educator and active journalist Ding Chuwo 丁初我 (1871–1930) in 1904. The main contributors to it were men, including Jin Tianhe; Jiang Weiqiao 蔣維喬 (1873–1958), an experienced editor at the Commercial Press and an active educator; Liu Yazi 柳亞子 (1887–1958), a young revolutionary and prolific feminist writer; and other progressive male intellectuals who championed women's education, rights, suffrage, and gender equality.

The male authorship was so overwhelming that only two columns were reserved for female authors: "Yinhua ji 因花集 (Uniting Flowers)" and "Nüxue wencong 女學文叢 (Literary Collection for Women's Studies)." The first was part of the larger section "Wenyuan 文苑 (Literary Garden)," which included literary writing by both men and women; in the second, articles by women were at times interspersed with articles by men.[15] Male contributors dominated the core sections, such as "Sheshuo 社說 (Editorials)" and "Jiangtan 講壇 (Speech Forums)." However, a small number of women also wrote for these sections. It is largely in these two discursive domains that ideas and imaginaries of *nüjie* were produced by both men and women writers. In the preface to the inaugural issue, Jin Tianhe envisioned the emergence of "female national people" through the trope of "flowers of civilization" (*wenming zhi hua* 文明之花):

> Neither European winds nor American rains can make it [the flower of civilization] fall or wither. The tides of the Pacific will soak into the soil upon which it grows and nurture it into blossom. The lotuses of the Jade Well will look at it with heartfelt admiration. The plum blossoms of the Luofu Mountains will turn pale while facing it. The sakura of Mount Fuji (in Japan) will die of shame when seeing it.[16]

14 The specific circulation figures were unclear, but the journal had distribution offices across China. For more about this journal, see Xia, *Wan-Qing nüxing yu jindai Zhongguo*, 67–113.

15 Hu Siao-chen notes that a female-specific column in effect confines women's works and implies a different, usually inherently second-class standard for women's literary accomplishments, in "The Construction of Gender and Genre in the 1910s New Media: Evidence from *The Ladies' Journal*," in Qian, Fong, and Smith, *Different Worlds of Discourse*.

16 歐風吹之不落，美雨襲之不零。太平洋之潮流，漫淫灌溉而適以涵濡滋潤助其發達也。玉井之蓮，望之心折。羅浮之梅，對之色變。富士山之櫻，見之而將羞死也。 Jin Tianhe, "*Nüzi shijie* fakanci 女子世界發刊詞 [Inaugural Statement for *Women's World*]," *Nüzi shijie* 1 (1904).

From this position Jin asserted his view that "the world of China's twentieth century will be the world of Chinese women."[17] In a similarly hyperbolic fashion, Ding Chuwo also praised the twentieth century world as "a world of soldiers" (*junren shijie* 軍人世界), "a world of knight-errants" (*youxia shijie* 遊俠世界), and "a world of literature and fine arts" (*wenxue meishu shijie* 文學美術世界).[18] As much as he loved these worlds, Ding declared, he particularly loved "the twentieth-century women's world which is as beautiful as flowers and brocade."[19]

However, both Jin and Ding's enthusiastic advocacy of an imaginary women's world was paralleled with their poignant criticism of the women's world in reality. According to Ding, Chinese men were slaves in a lost country, yet Chinese women were in double enslavement as they were slaves of the enslaved men.[20] Ding bemoaned that women's world of his time was a dark and ignorant one.[21] In stark contrast to his utopian vision of a women's world in which women assumed new roles as national people and "mothers of civilization," Jin consciously realized that China was a lost country where women's education and rights were not developed.[22] Thus, for Jin and Ding, the futuristic women's world filled with "flowers of civilization" that they imagined was nothing more than an effective antidote for redressing China's subjugation and weakness.[23] At the end of his preface, Jin asked, "The women's world emerged in the early

---

17 Jin, "*Nüzi shijie* fakanci," 10.

18 Ding Chuwo, "*Nüzi shijie* songci 女子世界頌詞 [Ode to *Women's World*]," *Nüzi shiji* 1 (1904).

19 Ding, "*Nüzi shijie* songci," 13.

20 Representational tropes such as "slavery," "lost country," and "slaves of the slaves" were prevalent in the late Qing texts. See, Rebecca E. Karl, " 'Slavery', Citizenship and Gender in Late Qing China's Global Context," in Karl and Zarrow, *Rethinking the 1898 Reform Period*, 212–244.

21 Ding, "*Nüzi shijie* songci," 13.

22 Jin, "*Nüzi shijie* fakanci," 10.

23 According to Amy Dooling, the utopian impulse also existed in feminist literary fantasies. For example, Wang Miaoru's 王妙如 (1877–1903) *Nüyuhua* 女獄花 [*Flowers in the Female Prison*] and Qiu Jin's *Jingweishi* 精衛石 [*Stones of the Jingwei Bird*] both offered utopian visions of egalitarian societies in which women's subordination existed only in the past, while at the same time also presenting a dystopian view of women's sufferings and subjugated conditions in Chinese society. In contrast to Wang and Qiu's elaborate description of futuristic societies in which utopian heroines advanced the cause of women's emancipation and rescued the Chinese state, Jin and Ding's utopian vision of a women's world was vague and simply served as a rhetorical device in their call for national salvation and critique of the woeful state of *nüjie*. See Dooling, *Women's Literary Feminism*, 49–64.

years of the twentieth century, and [if it is used as] a remedy for our nation, can all the ills of China be cured?"[24]

The desire for a romanticized "women's world" led many contributors to fuel vehement attacks on *nüjie*—that is, Chinese women and their subordinated feminine conditions. In an article published in the second issue of the journal, Ding Chuwo listed several "evils" that had haunted *nüjie* for thousands of years. He first raised the criticism that Chinese women suffered from the "evil of emotions" (*qingmo* 情魔) as they simply wallowed in shallow romantic sentiment yet were unable to develop feelings for family, society, or the nation. In the following sections, Ding denounced other vices besetting Chinese women, such as the "evil of illness" (*bingmo* 病魔) that caused women's physical weakness and incapacity preventing them from producing strong and healthy citizens, the "evil of superstition" (*shenguimo* 神鬼魔) that resulted in women's benighted intellectual level, and the "evil of money" (*jinqianmo* 金錢魔), which drove women to extravagant consumption of material goods.[25] Behind Ding's critique was his call for the restoration of women's rights that were believed to have existed in ancient China. The author contended that only after these evils for *nüjie* were eliminated could women's rights be reclaimed from the depths of Chinese history. This step would in turn prevent China from perishing.

An author writing under the pseudonym of Tianzuisheng 天醉生 deployed the slogan of *nüjie geming* 女界革命 (women's revolution) to mobilize women to restore their rights. Convinced that that women's rights had long existed in Chinese history, the article traced their origin back to the eras of "Three Sovereigns and Five Emperors" (*sanhuang wudi* 三皇五帝) in China's distant past. However, as the so-called sages and saints increasingly produced those nonsensical theories and doctrines, such as "men are superior to women" (*nanzun nübei* 男尊女卑) and "three obediences and four virtues" (*sancong side* 三從四德), the author asserted, women were invariably demeaned and deprived of their natural rights.[26] Although the article's aim was to promote women's rights, the author devoted great attention to expounding on *nüjie*'s state of subjugation and women's contemporary plights. Like Ding Chuwo, he warned women of the impending crisis of becoming "third-class slaves"

24 女子世界出現於二十世紀最初之年， 醫吾中國，庶有瘳焉？ Jin, "*Nüzi shijie* fakanci," 12.

25 Ding Chuwo, "Shuo nümo 說女魔 [On the Evils of Women]," *Nüzi shijie* 2 (1904).

26 Tianzuisheng, "Jing gao yiban nüzi 敬告一般女子 [Respectfully Exhort the General Women]," *Nüzi shijie* 1(1904): 10.

(*sandeng nuli* 三等奴隸) or even "fourth-class slaves" (*siding nuli* 四等奴隸) in the face of domestic oppression and foreign domination.[27]

These male critics frequently adopted the trope of "slavery" to express their vision of *nüjie*'s predicaments, but a female writer explicitly blamed men for having caused women's subjection. In her article titled "Nüjie geming 女界革命 (Women's Revolution)," Tang Xuezhen 湯雪珍 directed much of her criticism toward men's enslavement of women, rather than simply lamenting women's subordination. She argued that Chinese women were by no means born to be slaves, nor was servility in their nature. Rather, it was men's suppression that trapped women in the "female prison" (*nüyu* 女獄) and rendered them the inferior ones in the evolutionary process.[28] Tang also remarked that men were not only willing to serve as the slaves of the Manchus and foreigners but also coerced women into being slaves. Attributing women's enslavement to men's incompetence, she posed sharp questions for Chinese men: "Why does a dignified Chinese man not enslave other countries but, instead, chooses to be a slave? Why does he not enslave the heinous alien races rather than choosing instead to enslave our own race's precious fellow womankind?"[29]

What distinguished Tang's critique was that she saw "women as slaves" as a result of Chinese men's enslavement of women, accrued over the course of history, rather than a consequence of Chinese women's own failure to overcome their subjugation. Moreover, Tang contended that it was men's servitude, rather than women's alleged subservience, that caused China's national enslavement. At the end of her article, Tang evoked the imagery of "women's revolutionary army" in Jin Tianhe's *Nüjie zhong* to mobilize women to improve their own rights and learning, overthrow men's authority, and be the main agents of women's emancipation.[30]

For most contributors, criticizing *nüjie* was an integral part of their endorsement of women's rights, education, and women's role as "mothers of citizens." In other words, through expounding on women's lamentable conditions, the promulgation of women's rights and their contributions to the nation became

27 Tianzuisheng, "Jing gao yiban nüzi," 12.

28 Tang Xuezhen, "Nüjie geming 女界革命 [Women's Revolution]," *Nüzi shijie* 4 (1904): 14. The imageries and tropes of captivity were closely associated with descriptions of the disempowered and undignified status of *nüjie* at the time. For instance, Amy Dooling points out that in *Nüyuhua* and *Jingweishi* women were often explicitly likened to slaves, draft animals, and prisoners. See Dooling, *Women's Literary Feminism*, 49–56.

29 這麼一個堂堂皇皇的中國男子，為甚麼不去奴隸萬國，而却做了萬國的奴隸？為甚麼不去奴隸異族的狗種猢猻，而却來奴隸我同族同胞的寶貴女子？ Tang, "Nüjie geming," 16.

30 Tang, "Nüjie geming," 17.

imperative and exigent. Writing under his pen name Ya Lu 亞盧 (Asia's Rousseau), Liu Yazi, in his article "Ai nüjie 哀女界 (Lamenting on Women/Women's world)," demonstrated that his critique of Chinese *nüjie* in effect appeared side by side with his aspirations to promote women's rights and education. Like most feminist writers in the journal, Liu Yazi reiterated the imagery and rhetoric of women's oppression and enslavement before he set out to discuss the necessity of developing women's rights. In addition, the author marveled at the development of women's rights in Euro-American countries and Japan while lamenting the status quo of Chinese women of his time.[31]

It is worth pointing out that when Liu Yazi published his article, the journal was in the midst of a heated debate over whether to prioritize women's rights or women's education. Some writers argued that the extension of women's rights should be predicated on the full development of women's education.[32] For example, Jiang Weiqiao argued that women's rights presupposed abilities that were a conditional product of a certain level of education. Women's rights could be granted only in accordance with the individual's demonstrated ability to exercise them effectively. Like attaining freedom, achieving women's rights was determined by women's level of intellect and their ethical quality. Taking the practice of free marriage as an example, he wrote, a young girl who lacked knowledge and experience was more susceptible to deception by the debauched, allowing the practice to easily degenerate into immorality and licentiousness. Therefore, he concluded, "only a person who is literate and moral can speak about freedom; only a woman who is well educated and moral can speak about women's rights."[33]

Liu Yazi rebuked those who held such views and identified Jiang and other like-minded writers who saw women's education as a prerequisite to women's rights as "moderates" (*wenhepai* 溫和派). Liu pointed out that these writers were simply "using crafty measures to violate *nüjie*" (以狡獪手段侵犯女界).[34] The author argued that if one's education were the yardstick for one's rights, Chinese men were no more qualified than women to have rights

31 Ya Lu 亞盧 [Liu Yazi], "Ai nüjie 哀女界 [Lamenting on Women/Women's World]," *Nüzi shijie* 9 (1904).

32 For details on this debate, see Xia, *Wan-Qing nüxing yu jindai Zhongguo*, 83–92. For an extended discussion on women's rights at this period, see Mizuyo Sudo, "Concepts of Women's Rights in Modern China," in *Translating Feminisms in China*, ed. Dorothy Ko and Wang Zheng (Oxford: Blackwell, 2007).

33 惟有自治之學識之道德之人，而後可以言自由；惟有自治之學識之道德之女子，而後可以言女權。 Zhuzhuang 竹莊 [Jiang Weiqiao 蔣維喬], "Nüquan shuo 女權說 [On Women's Rights]," *Nüzi shijie* 5 (1904).

34 Ya Lu, "Ai nüjie," 5.

because only a few Chinese men were educated. Moreover, Liu asserted, it was not women's fault that they lacked education. Rather, it was because women had long been treated as slaves and playthings. Although Liu pointed out women's sorry state of being enslaved, unlike Tang Xuezhen who explicitly dismissed men's enslavement of women, he did not mention who were the culprit that caused the suppression and slavery of *nüjie*. Noting that Chinese women were simultaneously perceived as "enemies of civilization" (*wenming zhi di* 文明之敵) and "mothers of civilization" (*wenming zhi mu* 文明之母), he proposed the establishment of a "women's world" where women enjoyed rights and education. And only when such a women's world was founded, he wrote, would lamentations over *nüjie* disappear.[35]

Accompanying the advocacy of women's rights was espousal of the ideal of "mothers of citizens," a role that Chinese women were encouraged to assume to eradicate their deep-rooted bad habits and traits abhorred by the writers in the journal and to ultimately overcome the oppressed existence of *nüjie*. In contrast to the notion of *nüjie*, which underscored women's unremitting subjugation in the context of nationalism, the ideal of "mothers of citizens" redrew the link between women and the nation in a positive way. For example, in his article "Lun zhuzao guomin mu 論鑄造國民母 (On Forging Mothers of Citizens)," Liu foregrounded the essential role women of women in the making of a national citizenry:

> If there are no mothers of citizens, how can citizens be produced? If a nation does not have citizens that are produced by mothers of citizens, then a nation cannot be called a nation. Thus, if we wish to forge citizens, we must start with forging mothers of citizens.[36]

Liu emphasized women's roles as first and foremost "mothers" who contributed to the nurturing of Chinese citizens. As Joan Judge has pointed out, emphasis on motherhood not only suggested that women's connection with the citizenry was biological, racial, and pre-political but also demonstrated the tension between the traditional Confucian values on the family and the modern concept of the nation.[37] As "mothers of citizens," women were politicized and mobilized for the national cause while maintaining the Chinese family

35 Ya Lu, "Ai nüjie," 5–9.

36 無國民母，則國民安生？國無國民母所生之國民，則國將不國。故欲鑄造國民，必先鑄造國民母始。 Ya Te 亞特 [Liu Yazi], "Lun zhuzao guomin mu 論鑄造國民母 [On Forging Mothers of Citizens]," *Nüzi shijie* 7 (1904): 1.

37 Judge, "Citizens or Mothers of Citizens?" 32.

system. For Liu Yazi, the endorsement of forging "mothers of citizens" was synonymous with the creation of a "women's world" and the fundamental reform of *nüjie*. Through mobilizing *nüjie* who lacked a militant spirit, economic independence, and the sense of patriotism, Liu was convinced that "the day when the women's world is developed is the day mothers of citizens are developed."[38]

The new ideal of "mothers of citizens" provided Chinese women with new possibilities for participating in national affairs and with access to new arenas, allowing feminist writers to redefine the question of women's conditions under the rubric of *nüjie*. Both male and female writers perceived the molding of women into "mothers of citizens" as the most effective way to transform Chinese women from the collectivity of the oppressed into potential national subjects. However, the linkage of "motherhood" and citizenship still suggested that women were construed as actors to create high-quality citizens for the sake of the nation, rather than being full citizens themselves. Furthermore, the notable number of publications by men revealed that women writers remained marginalized in the articulations of the status of women in relation to the nation.

2 A *Nüjie* of Their Own

As women's education was increasingly recognized as a key component of national strengthening and the refashioning of *nüjie*, Chinese women were encouraged to pursue studies both at women's schools in China and abroad.[39] It was at this critical period that a few elite women traveled to Japan to pursue a formal education and became vocal advocates of women's rights and emancipation. These female students abroad, through their activities and writing, encouraged Chinese women to speak on their own terms. Organizations and study societies founded by female students flourished in Japan at this

38 女子世界發達之一日，即為我國民母發達之一日。 Ya Te, "Lun zhuzao guomin mu," 5.

39 Until the late nineteenth century, it was mainly Western missionaries operating schools for girls and women. Not until the 1890s did Chinese-run women's schools begin to emerge. On developments in women's education at this time, see Liao Xiuzhen 廖秀珍, "Qingmo nüxue zai xuezhi shang de yanjin ji nuzi xiaoxue jiaoyu de fazhan, 1897–1911 清末女學在學制上的演進及女子小學教育的發展 (1897–1911) [The Evolution of the Schooling System for Women in the Late Qing (1897–1911)]," in *Zhongguo funu shi lunwen ji* 中國婦女史論文集 [*Collections of Essays on Chinese Women's History*], ed. Li Youning and Zhang yufa (Taipei: Taiwan shangwu yinshuguan, 1988), 2: 203–255.

time.[40] One of the most influential women's organizations was the Society of Chinese Female Students in Japan (Zhongguo liu Ri nüxuesheng hui 中國留日女學生會). Founded in Tokyo by a student named Li Yuan 李元 in September 1906, along with the female students and activists Yan Bin and Tang Qunying 唐群英 (1871–1937) as the secretaries of the organization, the society recruited some seventy female students to become members. Though aiming to provide mutual assistance and form solidarity among Chinese female students in Tokyo, the society embraced a broader goal of mobilizing Chinese women in general. In its manifesto, the society explicitly addressed "we Chinese women" (我們中國女界) as the target audience and encouraged women to rid themselves of their subjugation. Lamenting that, for thousands of years, Chinese women had lived like slaves and had been as disunited as grains of sand, the female organizers of the society expressed the exigency of promoting education and establishing women's associations.[41]

The booming women's groups not only opened up new spaces for female solidarity but also enabled women to demand equal political participation with men. In founding women's organizations and the feminist press, female writers and activists tied women's education to the achievement of full citizenship. For them, education would empower Chinese women to assert their rights and fulfill their duties to the nation, as the overriding formulation *nü guomin* 女國民 (female citizen) suggested.[42] These female advocates of "female citizens" differed from their male counterparts in underplaying or even relinquishing a woman's primary role as a biological or social producer of citizens. In contrast to male writers' conceptions of women as mediators between the economies of family and the nation in *Nüzi shijie*, they called upon

40 Judge, *The Precious Raft of History*, 198–203; idem, "Between *Nei* and *Wai*: Women Students in Japan in the Early Twentieth Century," in *Gender in Motion: Divisions of Labor and Cultural Change in Late Imperial and Modern China*, ed. Bryna Goodman and Wendy Larson (Boulder: Rowman and Littlefield, 2005). Xia Xiaohong, "Wan-Qing de nüzi tuanti 晚清的女子團體 [Women's Organizations in the Late Qing]," *Hangzhou shifan xueyuan xuebao* 杭州師範學院學報 1 (1996).

41 "Zhongguo liu Ri nüxuesheng hui chengli tonggao 中國留日女學生會成立通告 [Announcement of Founding the Society of Chinese Female Students in Japan]," in *Zhongguo funü yundong tongshi* 中國婦女運動通史 [*A General History of the Chinese Women's Movement*], ed. Tan Sheying 談社英 (Nanjing: Funü gongming she, 1936).

42 According to Guo Yanli 郭延禮, the term *nü guomin* first appeared in the regulations of the Humanitarian Association [Gong'ai hui 共愛會], a women's organization founded by female Chinese students in Tokyo in 1903. See Guo Yanli, "Ershi shiji chu nüxing zhenglun zuojia qunti de dansheng 20世紀初女性政論作家群體的誕生 [The Birth of Female Political Polemical Writers in Early Twentieth-Century China]," *Zhongguo xiandai wenxue yanjiu congkan* 中國現代文學研究叢刊 3 (2009), 94.

Chinese women to become individual social and political actors through their economic and political independence. In their numerous polemical articles and speeches, *nüjie* served as an empowering concept for them to connect women's past and present, China and the West, and to transcend their status quo of myriad oppressions for the national good in general and for the sake of women in particular.

Among the women's journals dedicated to the promotion of the ideal of "female citizens" through the trope of *nüjie*, Yan Bin's *Zhongguo xin nüjie zazhi* was of particular significance.[43] Published in Tokyo in 1907, it was regarded as one of the most successful women's journals of the day and had a large circulation.[44] Before launching the journal, Yan Bin was an active member of the Society of Chinese Female Students in Japan and, at the same time, wrote for women's journals such as the famous *Zhongguo nübao* 中國女報 (*Journal for Chinese Women*), run by Qiu Jin 秋瑾 (1875–1907).[45] Yan Bin wrote a wide array of essays in *Zhongguo xin nüjie zazhi* under her pen name Lian Shi 煉石 (smelting stone), an allusion to the Chinese mythological goddess Nüwa's 女媧 heroic feat of repairing the roof of Heaven. Six issues were published before it was forced to shut down by the Japanese government because of its blatant advocacy of assassination in the last issue. Proclaiming its allegiance to the idea of "female citizens," Yan Bin outlined five tenets for the journal and explicated them in vernacular Chinese in the column called "Yanshuo 演說 (Public Speech)":[46]

> To make the latest studies on *nüjie* clear; to import new civilization of *nüjie* from all nations; to promote morality, to advocate education; to

43 Tan Sheying considers it as of equal significance to Chen Xiefen's *Nüxue bao*, Qiu Jin's *Zhongguo nübao* and Tang Qunying's *Shenzhou nübao* 神州女報 [*Shenzhou Women's News*]. See Tan, *Zhongguo funü yundong tongshi*, 15.

44 According to a Singapore journal, *Zhongguo xin nüjie*'s circulation was estimated to be 10,000. See Li Youning, "*Zhongguo xin nüjie zazhi* de chuangkan ji neihan: *Zhongguo xin nüjie zazhi* chongkan xu 中國新女界雜誌的創刊及內涵：中國新女界雜誌重刊序 [The Publication and Significance of *Magazine of New Women's World of China*: Preface to the Reprint of *Magazine of New Women's World of China*]," in Li and Zhang, ed., *Zhongguo funü shi lunwen ji* (Taipei: Taiwan shangwu yinshuguan, 1981), 1: 179–241.

45 For more biographical information about Yan Bin, see Ho, *Biographical Dictionary of Chinese Women*, 258–60.

46 The first four principles were elaborated into independent articles from the second issue to the fourth issue. Yet the fifth issue did not expound on the fifth principle. See Lian Shi 煉石 (Yan Bin's another penname), "Ben bao wuda zhuyi yanshuo 本報五大主義演說 [Five Tenets of This Journal]," *Zhongguo xin nüjie zazhi* 2 (March 5, 1907); 3 (April 5, 1907); 4 (May 5, 1907).

> eradicate the benighted and the superstitious, to create a new society; to unite connections, to make the obscure and the neglected manifest.[47]

By referring to women and their conditions in other countries, Yan Bin expanded the meaning of Chinese *nüjie*. This global consciousness enlarged the sense of time and space previously designated to *nüjie* by the feminist writers in *Nüzi shijie* and signaled the women feminist writers' emerging awareness of re/positioning Chinese women and their status in a global context.[48]

Yan Bin's commitment to constructing a new *nüjie* was first and foremost reflected in her definition of *nüjie* as a collectivity of Chinese women whose oppression was rooted in Chinese history and gendered. In the preface to the journal's inaugural issue, she wrote that Chinese *nüjie* had long been fettered by old conventions and that the practices of inequality between men and women were deeply rooted in Chinese society:

> We Chinese *nüjie* have adhered to ancient precepts for thousands of years, and these ingrained habits cannot be cast off overnight. In today's world competition and communication are becoming fierce, customs of inequality between men and women, and evils of inhibiting intelligence and injuring bodies are still entrenched in our society, and [they] are too deep-rooted to be eradicated easily. Those who are shortsighted say that these ills are not harmful to the progress of the nation. But do they know that while China's population is indeed large, if the majority of its two hundred million women are already like this, then even though China has the [physical] form of female citizenry, it does not have the spirit of female citizens—having such citizens is equivalent to having no citizens whatsoever.[49]

---

47 發明關於女界最新學說；輸入各國女界新文明；提倡道德、鼓吹教育；破舊沈迷，開新社會；結合感情，表彰幽遺。 Lian Shi, "Ben bao wuda zhuyi yanshuo," *Zhongguo xin nüjie zazhi* 2 (1907): 13.

48 This global consciousness of the conditions of women from around the world was also shared by Yan Bin's contemporary, the anarcho-feminist He-Yin Zhen. See Liu, Karl, and Ko, *The Birth of Chinese Feminism*, 28–35.

49 我們中國女界數千年來墨守古訓，積重難返。處今日世界交通競爭劇烈之時，而男女不平等之習慣，痼塞智慧、殘賊肢體之惡魔，依然盤踞於社會上，根深蒂固，未易盡除。淺見者謂此無妨於國運之進步也。豈知中國人口雖眾，此二萬萬中最多數之女子，既已如此，則是中國雖有多數女國民之形質，而無多數女國民之精神，則有民等於無民。 Lian Shi, "Fakanci 發刊詞 [Preface]," *Zhongguo xin nüjie zazhi* 1 (February 5, 1907).

Yan Bin pointed out that gender inequality was a primary source of Chinese women's subjugation and emphasized the significance of cultivating the spirit of female citizens in addition to strengthening women's physical bodies. In contrast to the male feminist writers, who viewed *nüjie* as a separate gender-specific concept, Yan Bin contended that it was always in close relation to *nanjie* 男界—the collectivity of Chinese men, who comprised half of China's population. She also noted that the inequality between men and women was in effect historically produced, rather than inherent or permanent. For example, in another article she explicitly challenged the terms used to signify men and women. She wrote, "The two characters of *nan* 男 and *nü* 女 are not titles ordained by Heaven; rather, they are names created by humans."[50] Calling for a radical break with all the notions of womanhood in the past, she asserted that, from the time that Cang Jie 倉頡 invented Chinese characters four or five thousand years earlier, the four characters *nüzi guomin* 女子國民 had never been used together.[51]

Female writers considered women's education the determining factor in overcoming women's subjugation and becoming qualified as "female citizens." In an article on the relationship between women and the nation, Yan Bin observed the necessity of education for women at different stages of their lives and argued that the intimate relationship between women and the nation would eventually rest on the development of women's education.[52] It is noteworthy that women's education was a common commitment for the advocates of "mothers of citizens" and "female citizens." As expressed in *Nüzi shijie*, women's education remained one of the key concerns in *Zhongguo xin nüjie zazhi*. Although Yan Bin and other female contributors also stressed the necessity of promoting women's education for the sake of family prosperity, national strengthening, and racial survival, they did not view it in terms of preparing

50 況男女兩字者，非天生的徽號，乃人定之名詞也。 Lian Shi, "Nüquan pingyi 女權平議 [On Women's Rights]," *Zhongguo xin nüjie zazhi* 1 (1907): 4. Yan Bin's conception of the differentiation between man and woman as an artificial and historical rather than a natural product might have influenced He-Yin Zhen's notion of *nannü* as "a historical elaboration and a normative distinction internal to patriarchal discourse itself." For an illuminating discussion about He-Yin Zhen's concept of *nannü* and the possible influence of Yan Bin's writings on He-Yin Zhen, see Liu, Karl, and Ko, *The Birth of Chinese Feminism*, 13–18, 45–46.

51 Lian Shi, "Ben bao duiyu nüzi guomin juan zhi yanshuo 本報對于女子国民捐之演說 [A Public Speech on a Female Citizen's Fund]," *Zhongguo xin nüjie zazhi* 1 (1907): 43.

52 Lian Shi, "Lun nüjie yu guojia zhi guanxi 論女界與國家之關係 [On the Relationship between Women and the Nation]," *Zhongguo xin nüjie zazhi* 2 (1907).

women to be "mothers of the citizens."[53] Rather, they viewed women's education as a prerequisite for Chinese women to assume their roles as "female citizens." While proponents of "mothers of citizens" conceived women as biological and moral sources of the cultivation of China's future citizens, the female writers' glorification of "female citizens" accentuated the immediate role that women played in national politics and their direct demand for citizenship. In other words, the centrality of women's education was not in its perceived efficacy in enabling women to better instruct their sons and daughters to be qualified citizens for the nation but, rather, in its potential to empower women to become citizens in their own right.

As the journal was dedicated to enlightening the "200 million Chinese women" (二萬萬中國女界), female contributors self-consciously deployed a vernacular journalistic style which was called *baihua* (lit. "white, clear, plain or straightforward speech"). Although the term *baihua* had long existed in Chinese society alongside *wenyan* and was closely associated with popular literature and thus largely served entertainment and didactic purposes,[54] its meaning and function underwent significant transformation at the turn of the twentieth century. *Baihua* was reintroduced, owing much to the influence of the Japanese *genbun itchi* 言文一致 (unification of spoken and written languages) movement, as an innovative newspaper style to address the less-educated masses.[55] Widely adopted in the booming vernacular journals and newspapers at the time, *baihua* became a powerful medium for the promotion of nationalist agendas.[56] Feminist journals frequently ran regular sections in *baihua* such as "Yanshuo 演說 (Public Speech)," "Yanjiang 演講 (Public Speaking)," or "Yantan 演壇 (Forum for Public Speaking)," and at times even published editorials in *baihua*. For the female feminist writers, *baihua* was not only a useful tool in their advocacy of feminist issues but also an integral part of the message of their feminism. In contrast to the

53 Qing Ru 清如, "Lun nüxue 論女學 [On Women's Education]," *Zhongguo xin nüjie zazhi* 2 (1907).

54 For centuries, *wenyan* and *baihua* have been regarded as having distinctive codes, clearly defined roles, and different targeted audiences. For discussions on the "diglossic" linguistic conditions of *wenyan* and *baihua* in pre-modern China, see Elizabeth Kaske, *The Politics of Language in Chinese Education, 1895–1919* (Leiden and Boston: Brill, 2007), 1–56.; Gang Zhou, *Placing the Modern Chinese Vernacular in Transnational Literature* (New York: Palgrave Macmillan, 2011).

55 For a discussion of *baihua* as a newspaper style in this period, see Kaske, "Mandarin, Vernacular and National Language," 272–275.

56 On the close relationship between *baihua* writing and Chinese nationalism, see Kaske, *The Politics of Language*, 161–232.

nationalist vernacular journalists of the time who spoke prescriptively for the lower classes and barely looked to the "unenlightened" people in their search for authenticity and identity,[57] the feminist journalists used writing in *baihua* to identify themselves as part of the socially and politically subordinated *nüjie*.

Most of the female writers in *Zhongguo xin nüjie zazhi* were perfectly capable of writing in the classical literary style, but, unlike the female contributors to *Nü xuebao*, they had a strong aspiration to experiment with writing in *baihua*, with the aim of reaching their female compatriots who were less literate or relegated to the margins of public life. The essays in vernacular, under the category of "Public Speech," evidenced female writers' efforts to mobilize the masses of Chinese women to realize the ideal of "female citizens." In one of them, Yan Bin declared, "our journal admires most the four characters *nüzi guomin*, and even though we have five tenets, the gist of these tenets is these four characters."[58] Another of these essays, by Mulan Tongxiang 木蘭同鄉, asked her female readers: "How is it that men are considered citizens, but women are not? How is it that men can enjoy rights while women do not enjoy an iota of rights?"[59] Several of these essays underscored the necessity of gender equality and equal education rights that had been available only to men. Insisting that women's talent and virtue had equal significance, one short essay refuted the long-held and widespread doctrine that "women without talent are virtuous" (女子無才便是德).[60] Some articles called upon women to participate in the national cause by undertaking concrete deeds. For example, Yan Bin exhorted her female compatriots to

57 Kaske argues that although Chinese nationalists saw the vernacular as a medium of their nationalism, they failed to make it part of the message of nationalism as they largely viewed the uneducated masses as the target of their efforts to disseminate nationalist ideas, in *The Politics of Language*, 224; on the relationship between *baihua* and feminism, see Zhang, "Feminism in the Vernacular."

58 本社最崇拜的就是 "女子國民" 這四個大字，本社創辦雜誌的宗旨，雖有五條，其實也只是這四個大字。 Lian Shi, "ben bao duiyu nüzi guomin juan zhi yanshuo," 42.

59 難道只認男子為國民，女子就不是國民麼？只要男子享權利，女子就毫無權利麼？ Mulan Tongxiang 木蘭同鄉, "Gonghe xinnian 恭賀新年 [Best Wishes for a New Year]," *Zhongguo xin nüjie zazhi* 2 (1907): 30.

60 "Nüzi wucai bianshi de bo 女子無才便是德駁 [A Rebuttal to 'Women without Talent are Virtuous']," *Zhongguo xin nüjie zazhi* 3 (1907). According to Paul J. Bailey, the phrase "women without talent are virtuous" was not an age-old Confucian doctrine, as many early twentieth-century Chinese reformers had claimed. He identified that it was an adage coined in the seventeenth century, in Paul J. Bailey, *Women and Gender in Twentieth-Century China* (Basingstoke, UK: Palgrave Macmillan, 2012), 8–9.

make contributions through the foundation of a Female Citizen's Fund (Nüzi guomin juan女子國民捐).[61]

As indicated by the journal's principal tenets, the information about *nüjie* from other countries was a crucial inspiration for female writers to envision a new *nüjie*. Unlike the contributors to *Nüzi shijie* who used the images of Western women to magnify the painful conditions of Chinese women, female writers in *Zhongguo xin nüjie* perceived Euro-American women as exemplary models that Chinese women could emulate or even surpass.[62] The journal was replete with articles and translations featuring stories of Western women. The column on "Yishu 譯述 (Translations and Elaborations)," renamed as "Shizhuan 史傳 (Historical biography)" in the third issue and "Zhuanji 傳記 (Biography)" in the fourth issue, in every issue included articles with stories of Western heroines. Seven prominent Western women—all European or American—were featured in lengthy articles.[63]

Although these Euro-American women differed from one another in terms of occupation and nationality, they were all glorified as exemplars or heroines because of their commitment to national causes or their daring entrance on the broader public stage. For example, in the story about Joan of Arc (Ruoan

61 Lian Shi, "Ben bao duiyu nüzi guomin juan zhi yanshuo," *Zhongguo xin nüjie zazhi*, nos. 1–3 (1907). See also Hui Jian nüshi 慧劍女士, "Quan nüjie jiefei gou tielu gupiao xiaoqi 勸女界節費購鐵路股票小啓 [Announcement of Calling on Women to Conserve on their Expenses to Buy Railroad Stocks]," *Zhongguo xin nüjie zazhi* 4 (1907).

62 On Chinese views of Western women in the early twentieth century, see also Carol C. Chin, "Translating the New Woman: Chinese Feminists View the West, 1905–1915," *Gender & History* 18 (2006); Bailey, "Chinese Women Go Global."

63 These women include Florence Nightingale [Naitingge'er 奈挺格爾, 1820–1910], Margaret Fuller Ossoli [Aisuoli 阿索里, 1810–1850], Mary Lyon [Lihen 梨痕, 1797–1849], Joan of Arc [Ruoan 若安, 1412–30], Mary Livermore [Lifuma 黎佛瑪, 1820–1905], George Eliot [Qiyuqi Ailiatuo 奇欲奇愛里阿脫, 1819–80], and Lucretia Mott [Mode 墨德, 1793–1880]. Xia Xiaohong notes this journal has only two biographies of non-Western women. Xia also points out that these biographies are widely appropriated from the Japanese accounts of Western women in the Meiji period. See Xia Xiaohong, "Wan Qing nübao zhong de Xifang nüjie—mingzhi 'furen lizhi' duwu de Zhongguo zhi lü 晚清女報中的西方女傑——明治"婦人立志"讀物的中國之旅 [Western Heroines in Late-Qing Women's Journals: The Voyage to China of Meiji-Era Writings on Women's 'Self-Help']," *Wen shi zhe*文史哲 4 (2012); the stories of some of Western exemplars, such as Florence Nightingale, Mary Lyon, and Joan of Arc were also widely translated and recounted in other late Qing journals or textbooks. See Joan Judge, "Expanding the Feminine/National Imaginary: Social and Martial Heroines in Late Qing Women's Journals," *Jindai Zhongguo funü shi yanjiu* 15 (2007); idem, "Blended Wish Images: Chinese and Western Exemplary Women at the Turn of the Twentieth Century," *Nan Nü: Men, Women, and Gender in Early and Imperial China* 6, no. 1 (2004).

Dake 若安達克), the author Mei Zhu 梅鑄 expressed her utmost admiration for the sacrifice of the Maid of Orléans to the national interest of France. Mei Zhu claimed that Joan's heroism and fame exceeded those of Hua Mulan 花木蘭, the most renowned Chinese woman warrior who disguised herself as a man, standing in for her father over twelve years. While Mulan was merely famous for her filial devotion to her father and her story was only well known in China, Mei Zhu argued that, in contrast, Joan extended her devotion to the state and earned honor worldwide.[64]

Similarly, the American abolitionist and philanthropist Lucretia Mott (Mode 墨德) was celebrated for her transcendence of conventional gender norms when venturing out in public. The author of her biography devoted considerable space to elaborating on Mott's career trajectory as an anti-slavery activist with extensive experience in public service. According to the author, Mott was also a pacifist and outspoken advocate for women's suffrage movement and prohibition in the United States. The author thus portrayed Mott's social and political engagement as motivated by a resolution to reform society and the country. She was among the national heroines whose accomplishments received international recognition.[65]

The capacity to transcend geographical boundaries was another key marker of women's global prominence. The biography of the journalist Margaret Fuller Ossoli (Aisuoli 阿索里) underlined her wide range of travel experience and foreign exposure. The article mentioned Ossoli's extensive travel, including to Britain, France, and Italy.[66] Almost all these biographies celebrated the ideals of devotion to their country and venturing into public spaces.

64 Mei Zhu 梅鑄, "Faguo jiuwang nüjie Ruoan zhuan 法國救亡女傑若安傳 [Biography of Joan of Arc, a French Heroine Who Saved the Nation]," *Zhongguo xin nüjie zazhi* 3 (1907): 61–62. For an analysis of Mei Zhu's exaltation of Joan of Arc as a great patriot, see also Judge, "Expanding the Feminine/National imaginary," 21–23. One could argue that Mulan's story was not yet presented as a tale of filial sacrifice for "national" service until the early twentieth century. Louise Edwards demonstrates it was only in the early twentieth century that the conflicts between family interests and those of the state began to diminish in Mulan's narrative. For the transformations of Mulan's story, see Louise Edwards, "Transformations of The Woman Warrior Hua Mulan: From Defender of The Family to Servant of the State," *Nan Nü: Men, Women, and Gender in China* 12, no. 2 (2010).

65 Lian Shi, "Boaizhuyi shixingjia Mode nüshi zhuan 博愛主義實行家墨德女士傳 [Biography of the Philanthropist Lucretia Mott]," *Zhongguo xin nüjie zazhi* 5 (June 5, 1907).

66 Ling Xi 靈希, "Meiguo da xinwenjia Asuoli nüshi zhuan 美國大新聞家阿索里女士傳 [Biography of the Great American Journalist Ms. Margaret Fuller Ossoli]," *Zhongguo xin nüjie zazhi* 1 (1907).

The stories of these Western heroines are at times embellished with familiar Chinese tropes, such as filial sacrifice and knight-errantry.[67] Mei Zhu's biography described Joan of Arc as a devoted daughter who was initially conflicted between serving her father and devoting herself to her country. At first, Joan was depicted as an unenlightened peasant who had no intention of going beyond her role as a dutiful daughter. Although consumed with intense hatred for the English soldiers who looted and pillaged her hometown, Joan, Mei Zhu wrote, realized that "after all she was a woman ... except for shedding tears and gashing her teeth in anger, there was little she could do."[68] The narrative then shifted to Joan's enlightenment after receiving visions from three saints that made her determined to defend France and recover it from the English domination. Joan's father strongly opposed her decision to fight for her country because he was unwilling to subject Joan to the danger of battle. Nonetheless, Joan eventually chose to declare her devotion to the country over her family: without asking for her father's permission, she left home and joined the army. The author Mei Zhu defended Joan's seemingly rebellious act by asserting that had Joan obeyed her parents and remained at home, her country would have perished. If the country perished, she would have been unable to protect her family, which in turn would be an unfilial act.[69]

As Louise Edwards has aptly pointed out in her discussion of Hua Mulan's story, at the start of the twentieth century, the virtue of filial piety was militarized and "subsumed into the statist discourse and was best performed through the demonstration of militarized sacrifice to the state."[70] This is also true in Mei Zhu's version of Joan's story: Joan's demonstration of filial piety was possible only through her sacrifice to the state. The addition of Joan's filial devotion and her privileging of national duties over family obligations showed the female writers' desire to contribute to the Chinese nation, and their call for empowered and enlightened female heroes in China.

67 For more discussion of the prevailing practice of assimilating Western female exemplars into "traditional" or Confucian virtues in the late Qing, see Nanxiu Qian, "Borrowing Foreign Mirrors and Candles to Illuminate Chinese Civilization: Xue Shaohui's Moral Vision in the *Biographies of Foreign Women*," *Nan Nü: Men, Women, and Gender in Early and Imperial China* 6, no. 1 (2004); Judge, "Blended Wish Images."

68 自己終究是女子……除了流淚切齒之外，亦是一些主意沒有的。 Mei, "Faguo jiuwang nüjie," 61.

69 Mei, "Faguo jiuwang nüjie," 63–64.

70 Louise Edwards, *Women Warriors and Wartime Spies of China* (Cambridge: Cambridge University Press, 2016), 19.

In contrast to the struggles between filial devotion and national sacrifice highlighted in Joan's story, other prominent women's stories merged the two from the outset. The American journalist and orator Mary Livermore (Lifuma 黎佛瑪) was also hailed as an extraordinarily devoted daughter who treated her parents with reverence and her younger siblings with kindness.[71] In a similar fashion, a biography of the British novelist George Eliot (Qiyuqi Ailiatuo 奇欲奇愛里阿脫) presented her as a filial daughter who carefully tended to her sick father for years.[72] Some women, such as Mary Lyon and Florence Nightingale, were portrayed as having maternal sentiments and "righteousness and knight-errantry" (*yixia* 義俠) driven by an extended love for humankind.[73] This integration of traditional Chinese motherly virtues and universal (Westernized) qualities attested to the journal's vision of an ideal "female citizen" who was characterized by "gentle kindness and extended love for humanity" (*cihui boai* 慈惠博愛).[74]

These representations of Western women in the journal illustrated the female writers' efforts to create a new category of Chinese womanhood in two prominent ways. First, these Western women served as models in the female writers' imaginary of a new *nüjie*. Highlighting Western women's role in a national context suggests that the formation of a new Chinese *nüjie* was also predicated on women's devotion to the Chinese nation. Second, the reworked narratives of Western women demonstrated the female writers' attempts to justify Chinese women within a national and universal world order. By creating ample narrative space to adorn these stories with traditional Chinese motifs, the authors aligned Chinese women with their Western counterparts and legitimatized their access to broader public spheres in a global context. In this sense, the construction of a new *nüjie* reconfigured the female subjects under the Confucian order as citizens who were an integral part of a new national order and whose active participation in national affairs was key to the creation of a new national collective identity for Chinese women.

---

71 Zhuo Hua 灼華, "Da yanshuojia Lifuma nüshi zhuan 大演說家黎佛瑪女史傳 [Biography of Ms. Mary Livermore, A Great Orator]," *Zhongguo xin nüjie zazhi* 4 (1907).

72 "Yingguo xiaoshuojia Ailiatuo nüshi zhuan 英國小說家愛里阿脫女士傳 [Biography of the English Novelist Ms. George Eliot]," *Zhongguo xin nüjie zazhi* 4 (1907).

73 Joan Judge notes that possessing metaphorical maternal qualities was a marked feature in the representations of Western heroines in the late Qing, in "Blended Wish Images."

74 Joan Judge points out that the emphasis on the maternal sentiments highlighted their roles as metaphorical and social mothers which is in effect a re-inscription of Chinese female models as biological mothers, in "Expanding the Feminine/National Imaginary," 13.

3 Beyond Nationalism: Demanding a Revolution in *Nüjie*

Unlike the female writers in *Zhongguo xin nüjie zazhi*, who invoked *nüjie* as an effective trope to declare Chinese women's autonomy in obtaining full citizenship and to construct new womanhood within the framework of nationalism, anarcho-feminist writers employed *nüjie* as an analytical category to express their concerns about women beyond the context of nationalism. Peter Zarrow points out that, as anarcho-feminism emerged in around 1907, it began to liberate Chinese feminism from the demands of nationalism, as anarchist publications on women "spoke less of women's rights as an independent variable and more of how the liberation of an oppressed element in society depended on the liberation of all."[75] Although the cause of women was still inextricably linked to the larger project of liberating society as a whole, Zarrow explains, it was no longer subsumed to national duties. In these anarcho-feminist writings, women were still largely construed as an "oppressed element" of society, as recurrent uses of the term *nüjie* manifested, but women's liberation was considered contingent on a fundamental social revolution, rather than merely serving the national interest.

Among the anarchist-feminist writers, He-Yin Zhen emerged as the most vocal and representative one to articulate through the category of *nüjie* women's central role in realizing a thorough social revolution. Born to a moderate family in Jiangsu Province, He-Yin received considerable education in traditional Chinese literature and philosophy. She was married to Liu Shipei, a noted philologist and anarchist, in 1903, and in 1907 they left for Tokyo, where they co-founded the influential anarcho-feminist journal *Tianyi*.[76] She combined the surnames of both her father (He) and mother (Yin) as her family name for her feminist writing.[77] The journal was published by the Society for the Restoration of Women's Rights (Nüzi fuquan hui 女子復權會), an association that He-Yin organized to advocate anarchism. The association's bylaws called for the suppression of men's privilege, resistance to hierarchy, a prohibition on respecting and trusting any government, and ending women's submission to

75 Zarrow, "He Zhen," 797. For a recent thoughtful analysis of anarcho-feminism in early twentieth-century China and the works by the most renowned anarcho-feminist, He-Yin Zhen, see Liu, Karl, and Ko, *The Birth of Chinese Feminism*.

76 The journal was called *Tianyi bao* 天義報 in the first two issues. From the third issue onward, it was renamed *Tianyi* 天義 with the romanization *Tian Yee*.

77 Liu, Karl, and Ko, *The Birth of Chinese Feminism*, 2–3.

men.[78] These topics were reflected and developed in He-Yin's contributions to *Tianyi*.

Along with other founding members and main contributors to the journal, He-Yin stipulated that the journal's objective was "to abolish the old society and practice human equality."[79] To achieve this goal, she proposed, "in addition to promoting a revolution in *nüjie*, we also promote racial, political and economic revolutions."[80] The opening statement of the journal further explicated that the rationale underpinning its objective was to realize "true equality" (*zhengong* 真公) in the world. The old societies needed to be abolished because they were all hierarchical and thus the sources of increasingly unequal systems and practices. According to the statement: "among the classes in the world, the class [division] between men and women was even more rigid."[81] For example, the practices of valuing men over women had long existed in the countries of the East, and even though Western countries proclaimed gender equality, women there were still restrained from enjoying equal political rights with men. The statement thus declared, "if we wish to abolish classes in society, we ought to start by abolishing the class [distinction] between men and women."[82]

A revolution in *nüjie* was thus considered the most fundamental and effective means to eradicate gender hierarchy and bring about true social equality. Unlike earlier feminist depictions of *nüjie* as unenlightened and submissive, the anarcho-feminist writers conceived of *nüjie* as a united group of women who actively, and at times violently, sought ways to revolt against oppression by men. For instance, the opening statement revealed that if men were to lord over or exploit women, then "*nüjie* should rise together and kill them" (女界共起而誅之).[83] He-Yin also exhorted: "If *nüjie*

78 He-Yin Zhen, "Nüzi fuquanhui jianzhang 女子復權會簡章 [Bylaws of Society for the Restoration of Women's Rights]," *Tianyi bao* 天義報 1 (1907).

79 以破壞固有之社會，實行人類平等為宗旨。 He-Yin Zhen, "*Tianyi bao* jianzhang 天義報簡章 [Bylaws of *Natural Justice*]," *Tianyi bao* 1 (1907): 7.

80 於提倡女界革命外，兼提倡種族、政治、經濟諸革命。 He-Yin, "*Tianyi bao* jianzhang," 8.

81 世界固有之階級，以男女階級為嚴。 He-Yin Zhen, "*Tianyi bao* qi 天義報啓 [Announcement of *Natural Justice*]," *Fu bao* 復報 10 (1907) (reprinted in Wan Shiguo 萬仕國, ed., *Liu Shenshu yishu buyi* 劉申叔遺書補遺 [Supplement to the Posthumous Works by Liu Shipei][Yangzhou: Guangling Press, 2008], 661).

82 故欲破社會固有之階級，必自破男女階級始。 He-Yin, "*Tianyi bao* qi," 661.

83 He-Yin, "*Tianyi bao* qi," 662.

wish to realize gender equality, they cannot simply employ strategies of resistance. Rather, they must use brute force to compel men to be equal with women."[84]

In "Nüzi xuanbushu 女子宣布書 (The Women's Manifesto)," He-Yin offered a detailed critique of the inequalities between men and women covering a variety of aspects, calling for *nüjie* to fight for absolute gender equality. She wrote, "Men are the archenemy of women, and as long as women fail to be men's equals, anger and sorrow will never be abated."[85] She suggested that *nüjie* take measures to strive for equality with men, such as demanding men to practice monogamy, renouncing concubinage, merging both parents' surnames as their family name, and asking for equal participation in politics with men. Nevertheless, He-Yin continued, the demand for equality did not arise because women aspired to seize "power and profit" (*quanli* 權利) but, rather, because men and women were naturally endowed with equal rights. She further contended that terms such as *nanxing* 男性 (men) and *nüxing* 女性 (women) referred more to the results of different social customs and education and less to differences in nature.[86] If sons and daughters were to be treated equally, raised and educated in the same manner, she argued, then men and women could perform the same duties, the terms "men" and "women" could be abolished, and the goal of gender equality could be achieved.

He-Yin was convinced that economic equality was the prerequisite and basis of *nüjie*'s attainment of gender equality. In "Jingji geming yu nüzi geming 經濟革命與女子革命 (Economic Revolution and Women's Revolution)," He-Yin contended that Chinese women's economic subjugation had been produced over the course of history and was the primary source of *nüjie*'s overall subordinated social status. Using marriage practices as an example, she pointed out that Chinese men had long treated women as private possessions. The reason that women could be privately possessed was that men held power over money and thus had control over women's fate. Only after money was abolished, He-Yin asserted, could women refuse to submit to men financially and obtain economic equality with men. She argued,

---

84 女界欲求平等，非徒用抵制之策也。必以暴力使彼不得不與己平。 He-Yin Zhen, "Nüzi xuanbushu 女子宣布書 [The Women's Manifesto]," *Tianyi bao* 1; reprinted in Wan, *Liu Shenshu*, 656.

85 男子者，女子之大敵也。女子一日不與男子平等，則此恨終不磨。 He-Yin, "Nüzi xuanbushu," 655; translation in Liu, Karl, and Ko, *The Birth of Chinese Feminism*, 182.

86 For an insightful analysis of He-Yin Zhen's employment of these two neologisms, see Liu, Karl, and Ko, *The Birth of Chinese Feminism*, 16.

> *Nüjie*'s revolution must go hand in hand with an economic revolution. If an economic revolution cannot be accomplished, then the common phrase heard today calling for "a revolution between men and women" cannot be said to have touched the essence of the problem.[87]

He-Yin's critique of *nüjie*'s subjugation obviously was directed not only against Chinese men's oppression of women in general but specifically at the unequal gender relations that originated in the overall system of unequal property. The revolution of *nüjie*, therefore, had to place its primary emphasis on eliminating the private property system protected by the Chinese state.

For this reason, He-Yin regarded the existence of the state as the prime culprit reproducing wealth and power in society and hence the source of all social hierarchies. By fueling attacks on the state, the critical analysis of *nüjie* by He-Yin was distinguished from that of the majority of feminist writers, who subordinated women's liberation to the general logic of the Chinese state. For He-Yin, the liberation of *nüjie* was predicated on radically reconfigured social and gender relations in which men and women no longer submitted to any form of inequity. In this sense, her anarchist stance was crucial to her feminist critique of *nüjie*.[88] Moreover, unlike most contemporaneous nationalist feminists, who glorified the level of gender equality achieved in Euro-American countries, He-Yin expressed suspicion of this idea. For example, she criticized the system of unequal property in the West and condemned marriages built on such a system as nothing but "mutual prostitution between men and women" (男女互相賣淫者也).[89]

---

87 故女界革命，必與經濟革命相表裡。若經濟革命不克奏功，而欲昌言男女革命，可謂不揣其本矣。 He-Yin Zhen, "Jingji geming yu nüzi geming 經濟革命與女子革命 [Economic Revolution and Women's Revolution]," *Tianyi* 13–14 (1907); reprinted in Wan, *Liu Shenshu*, 909; translation in Liu, Karl, and Ko, *The Birth of Chinese Feminism*, 103.

88 The relationship between He-Yin Zhen's anarchist stance and her feminist theory has remained a matter of contention in contemporary scholarship. For example, Xia Xiaohong argues that He-Yin Zhen's conception of gender equality was heavily colored by her anarchist theory. Xia considers He's advocacy of women's revolution to be mere lip service without practical grounds. See Xia Xiaohong, "*Tianyi bao* and He Zhen's Views on 'Women's Revolution,'" in Qian, Fong, and Smith, *Different Worlds of Discourse*, 293–314. This English version, translated by Hu Ying, is part of Xia's original article in Chinese; see "He Zhen de wu zhengfu zhuyi 'nüjie geming' lun 何震的無政府主義 "女界革命" 論 [He Zhen's Anarchist Thought on 'Women's Revolution']," *Zhonghua wenshi lun cong* 中華文史論叢 83 (2006); Liu, Karl, and Ko, however, have proposed a different view of He-Yin Zhen, and deemed anarchism as inseparable from and intertwined with her feminist thoughts (*The Birth of Chinese Feminism*, 1–26).

89 He-Yin, "Jingji geming," 906.

He-Yin also criticized men's advocacy of women's rights as conducive to the attainment of citizenship for the elite and propertied class. She called for Chinese women to win the cause of women's rights by themselves. In her essay "Nüzi jiefang wenti 女子解放問題 (On the Question of Women's Liberation)," she dismissed the cries for women's emancipation that were imposed upon women and initiated by men, who, she believed, were not truly concerned about women's interests. He-Yin outlined three reasons that men supported women's liberation. First, Chinese men attempted to learn from the so-called civilized countries, such as the United States, Japan, and countries in Europe, where men granted women a certain degree of freedom. He-Yin saw these Chinese men's actual purpose as not so much promoting liberation for women's benefit as acquiring power, authority, and distinction for themselves. He-Yin criticized their efforts as nothing but "men's pursuit of self-distinction in the name of women's liberation" (男子因求名而解放女子).[90] The second reason was that, when men encouraged women to earn a livelihood and be economically independent, they did not do so in order to advance women's interests but, rather, to lighten men's own burdens. He-Yin called these actions "men's pursuit of self-interest in the name of women's liberation" (男子因求利而解放女子).[91] She also attacked men who advocated the significance of household management for women, claiming that these men were not genuinely concerned about enriching women's domestic skills. Rather, they were evading their own family responsibilities in order to enjoy themselves. She described this practice disparagingly as "men's pursuit of self-comfort in the name of women's liberation" (男子因求自逸而解放女子).[92]

He-Yin thus exhorted her fellow Chinese women (*nüjie*) to achieve autonomy and liberate themselves, instead of relying on men as their liberators. In addition to opposing the male project of liberating women, He-Yin also severely criticized some women's misconceptions and misuses of liberation. She pointed out that, although these women appeared to be actively removing all ethical and legal constraints in the name of freedom and equality, they were actually misconstruing the meaning of liberation as simply self-indulgence. According to He-Yin, these misinterpretations would only be harmful for the

---

90 He-Yin Zhen, "Nüzi jiefang wenti [On the Question of Women's Revolution]," *Tianyi* 7 (1907), in Wan, *Liu Shenshu*, 779–780; translation in Liu, Karl, and Ko, *The Birth of Chinese Feminism*, 60.

91 He-Yin, "Nüzi jiefang," 780; translation in Liu, Karl, and Ko, *The Birth of Chinese Feminism*, 61.

92 He-Yin, "Nüzi jiefang," 780; translation in Liu, Karl, and Ko, *The Birth of Chinese Feminism*, 62.

cause of women's liberation and the realization of absolute sexual equality. She further emphasized that her understanding of gender equality implied equality among all human beings, which was not only about ending men's oppression of women but also about ending men's oppression by other men and women's oppression by other women. She wrote:

> As for the idea of equal division of power between men and women, most people seem to believe that since there are power holders among men, there should be among women as well. But did such powerful sovereigns as Queen Victoria of the British Empire or Empresses Lü Zhi and Empress Wu Zetian in the dynastic history of China ever bring the slightest benefit to the majority of women?[93]

He-Yin's call for absolute equality imparted new connotations to the concept of *nüjie*. In her analysis, *nüjie* was reconfigured as a collectivity of Chinese women who not only took the initiative to overthrow men's oppression and win women's rights through their own effort but also struggled to dismantle hierarchies among women. With this new interpretation of *nüjie* in mind, He-Yin wrote extensively on problems concerning the interests of the masses of Chinese women, such as women's labor and livelihood.[94]

He-Yin Zhen's anarcho-feminist writings in *Tianyi* developed the notion of *nüjie* in three significant ways. First, He-Yin understood *nüjie* as the collectivity of Chinese women, whose subjugation was historical and institutionalized. In stark contrast to the prevalent nationalist feminists who saw women's subjection as the source of national backwardness, He-Yin identified women's inferior status as historically reproduced through a wide array of accumulated unequal economic, social, political, and cultural practices. For her, the totality of oppressed Chinese women would no longer bear responsibility for national strengthening or the degeneration of civilization but, rather, were victims of the latter. Second, in her original and creative analysis of *nüjie*'s revolution, she conceived of *nüjie* as a useful category of analysis beyond the confines of

93 若倡男女分權之說，謂男界既有握權之男，即女界應有握權之女，則英帝維多利亞，中國之呂雉、武則天、均為女主,曾有絲毫利益及於女子者乎？以是少數女子握權，決不足以救多數女子。 He-Yin, "Nüzi jiefang," 782; translation in Liu, Karl, and Ko, *The Birth of Chinese Feminism*, 66.

94 Peter Zarrow has discussed in detail on He-Yin Zhen's writings on women's labor, in "He Zhen," 800–803. The introduction to *The Birth of Chinese Feminism* suggests that *shengji*生計 (livelihood) is a "more enabling rubric than 'class' " in analyzing He-Yin Zhen's feminist critique of political economy. See Liu, Karl, and Ko, *The Birth of Chinese Feminism*, 10.

nationalism. Rather than mobilizing women's liberation for the sake of national interests, she construed women as subversive agents demanding recognition of their own interests and rights, producing a radical break with previous writings that drew a causal link between *nüjie* and the Chinese nation. Third, He-Yin's theorization of *nüjie* was the first to pay attention to the significant roles that less privileged Chinese women (lower-class women, in particular) played in society. Her rigorous critique of the potential generation of a group of powerful and wealthy women, as revealed by her criticism of the empresses in Chinese history, suggested that, for her, *nüjie* consisted primarily of Chinese women who, while numerous, were located at the bottom of society economically and sociopolitically.

4 Conclusion

Nüjie was a unique neologistic construction that reconfigured "women" as a new gendered collectivity in relation to the Chinese nation and the modernizing world in the early years of the twentieth century. Although this term was initially coined to refer to Chinese women as an oppressed group and as an object of critique in the pressing calls for national strengthening, it was later developed as a useful analytical category to examine a wide range of questions concerning women, such as women's education, female citizenship, women's emancipation, and gender equality, and to signify women's autonomy and agency within and beyond the context of nationalism.

Through a close analysis of various feminist articulations of *nüjie* in the three important women's journals, this chapter reveals the gendered dynamic and complexity in the evolution of the term. In the journal *Nüzi shijie*, both male and female feminist writers deployed *nüjie* to integrate women as mediated national subjects through the ideal of "mothers of citizens," paying little attention to women's individual rights and personal interests vis-à-vis the nation. Women's education, for example, was not promoted for the sake of women's own betterment and development; rather, it was construed as an indispensable instrument assisting the cultivation of national citizens. In *Zhongguo xin nüjie zazhi*, female feminist writers emerged as vocal and active proponents of "female citizens" under the enabling rubric of *nüjie*. They envisioned a new Chinese womanhood in accordance with national interests as immediate subjects as well as possessing heightened awareness of women from other countries in the face of the modernizing world. In *Tianyi*, He-Yin Zhen's innovative feminist critiques of the existence of national, economic, social, and gender inequalities provided a prime example of how *nüjie* continued to operate as a powerful category of analysis in anarcho-feminist writings. *Nüjie* was identified as a collectivity of subversive agents who opposed nationalist calls, demanded women's liberation without male intervention, and called for absolute gender equality.

The gendered articulations of *nüjie* destabilized or even ruptured the causal link between women and the nation drawn by late Qing nationalist intellectuals. Although at times female feminist writers were co-opted into the nationalist discourse in their conceptions of *nüjie*, they managed to produce alternative ideas of "women" in the context in which Chinese feminism was presumably subjugated to nationalism. Their creative analyses of *nüjie* reflected the fact that the women's roles prescribed and designated by the male nationalist intellectuals were being contested, challenged, or resisted. These female writers' critiques through the category of *nüjie* revealed their female agency in redefining women's social, political, and cultural identities within and beyond the overriding modernization project of national strengthening and their authority in constructing competing feminist critiques with men.

By the 1910s, the term *nüjie* had gained wide currency and frequently appeared in almost all feminist women's journals as well as various other modern publications.[95] However, as the government under Yuan Shikai thwarted the first wave of activism in support of women's suffrage beginning in 1913, women feminist activists became increasingly disenchanted with participation in national politics and advocation of women's emancipation. Moreover, even the female suffragists were less interested in struggling for equal suffrage rights for all Chinese women than merely demanding equality with men in suffrage rights. As Louise Edwards notes, "in many of the women activists' minds, illiterate and propertyless women should also be excluded."[96] Such elitism began to make *nüjie*—the once-powerful and effective watchword in women's feminist journals signifying a solidarity for the collectivity of Chinese women—gradually lose its potential for mobilizing the masses of women for political and feminist involvements in early Republican China.

The Yuan Shikai government's sweeping suppression of women's suffrage movements also exacerbated the decline in women's feminist journals after 1913, and the term *nüjie* began to lose its feminist vigor and political tension and came to stand in simply for "women." For example, the first commercial

95 Barbara Mittler points out the frequent uses of *nüjie* after 1907 in the commercial newspapers such as *Shenbao*. She notes that the term *nüjie* often appeared in advertisements concerned with women's health and hygiene, in *A Newspaper for China?* 263.

96 Louise Edwards, *Gender, Politics, and Democracy: Women's Suffrage in China* (Stanford: Stanford University Press, 2008), 69.

women's journal *Funü shibao* promoted *nüjie* as desired consumers in China's expanding urban spaces and usually associated it with consumerism and images of modern women.[97] The semantic history of *nüjie* is beyond the scope of this investigation, yet without a doubt *nüjie* was a powerful notion and useful analytical category with considerable influence on the Chinese feminist discourses in the first decade of the twentieth century.

97 For a discussion of *nüjie* and the emerging modern women images in commercial women's magazines in early Republican China, see Zhang Yun, "The Emerging Modern Woman: Representations of the 'Girl Student' in Early Twentieth-Century Urban China," *Harvard Asia Quarterly* 16, no. 3 (2014).

CHAPTER 3

The Manchu Woman Commits Suicide: Ethnicity and the Composition of the New Chinese Woman

Nüjie did not remain a term that signified merely the subjugated feminine conditions of Chinese women in the context of nationalism. It also became a powerful category of analysis through which female feminist writers could articulate female subjectivity and construct a gendered collective identity for Chinese women within and beyond the confines of nationalism. But even though these writers intended *nüjie* to be a referent for all Chinese women, regardless of class, they would not have chosen to look to Manchu women, or any other non-Han ethnic women in China, in their search for authenticity and identity. In a polemic penned in 1904 by a prominent feminist journalist, Chen Xiefen 陳擷芬 (1883–1923), *nüjie* was conceived as a specific collectivity of Chinese women that "were slaves of those enslaved by foreign races (異族奴隸之奴隸, i.e., both the Manchus and Westerners)."[1] Although Chen did not specify whether Manchu women were included as part of the oppressive Manchu race, given Chen's radical antipathy to them, a position she shared with most of her fellow feminist writers, it is clear that these writers' conception of China's *nüjie* was a gendered, racial category exclusive to Han women.

This chapter investigates the role of non-Han ethnicity in the imagining of modern Chinese womanhood by focusing on the portrayal and resonance of a Manchu woman's suicide in 1905 in the popular press, official accounts, and the women's press. This woman was Huixing 惠興, a widowed mother who poisoned herself by swallowing opium because of her failed attempts to collect funds to maintain a girls' school that she had established for Manchu women.

1 Chen Xiefen, "Nüjie zhi ke wei 女界之可危 [Crisis in Women's World]," *Zhongguo ribao* 中國日報 (March 11 and 12, 1904)(reprinted in Li and Zhang, *Jindai Zhongguo nüquan yundong shiliao*, 1: 416–418). As a correlate of *tongzhong* 同種 [same race], a term that was frequently adopted in Han revolutionary discourse to suggest the racial and national "otherness" of the Manchus, *yizu* 異族 was often employed to indicate both Westerners and the Manchus. Frank Dikötter argued that both *zhong* 種 [breed, species] and *zu* 族 [lineage, race] could be rendered by the notion "race." See Frank Dikötter, *The Discourse of Race in Modern China* (Hong Kong: Hong Kong University Press, 1992), 70–71. For an analysis of the *tongzhong* discourse and its racial implications in the context of nationalism, see Rebecca E. Karl, "Creating Asia: China in the World at the Beginning of the Twentieth Century," *American Historical Review* 103, no. 4 (1998); and idem, " 'Slavery,' Citizenship and Gender," 225–226.

© KONINKLIJKE BRILL NV, LEIDEN, 2020 | DOI:10.1163/9789004438545_005

The incident took place in a critical political environment in the final years of the Qing, when anti-Manchu sentiment was intensifying and the strained relationship between the Manchu and Han communities became increasingly hostile. Although Huixing's suicide soon received some media attention in major national newspapers based in Shanghai, her Manchu background was underplayed, if not completely omitted, in reports on the incident. The limited news coverage of Huixing's death in the Shanghai press focused mainly on honoring her act as an extreme example of self-sacrifice for a national cause—the promotion of women's education. In contrast to the reticence of the southern Chinese newspapers to report her suicide, northern Chinese newspapers were far more responsive and passionate. Huixing's story was featured in the northern press and was extensively described and appropriated in a wide variety of forms: essays, public speeches, eulogies, biographies, and plays. Huixing's Manchu ethnicity was highlighted in the northern press because a group of Manchu reformist intellectuals participated in the retelling and remaking of her story. As Xia Xiaohong points out, that the Manchu reformers were keen on promoting Huixing's suicide and highlighting her Manchu ethnicity was reflective of the Manchu-Han tensions at the time.[2] Indeed, Manchu promoters' avid valorization of Huixing's heroic sacrifice and extraordinary behavior as a Manchu heroine could be read as an effort to assert their ethnic identity in response to the threat of Han nationalism.[3] But most significantly, as discussed in this chapter, the process through which Huixing's story was constantly refashioned and repackaged also attested to the Manchu reformers' aspirations to construct a recognizable national female exemplar who could compete with the visions of modern Chinese womanhood widely circulated in the writings by Han feminist intellectuals.

---

2 For an insightful discussion on Huixing's suicide and its association with the Manchu-Han discontent of the time, see Xia, *Wan-Qing nüxing*, 223–256.

3 For scholarly works on the development of the Manchu racial and ethnic identity in late imperial China, see Pamela Kyle Crossley, *A Translucent Mirror: History and Identity in Qing Imperial Ideology* (Berkeley: University of California Press, 1999); Mark Elliott, *The Manchu Way: The Eight Banners and Ethnic Identity in Late Imperial China* (Stanford: Stanford University Press, 2001); Edward J. M. Rhoads, *Manchus and Han: Ethnic Relations and Political Power in Late Qing and Early Republican China, 1861–1928* (Seattle: University of Washington Press, 2000). For an overview of the development of the Manchu identity after the fall of the Qing dynasty, see Patrick Fuliang Shan, "Elastic Self-Consciousness and the Reshaping of Manchu Identity," in *Ethnic China: Identity, Assimilation, and Resistance*, ed. Xiaobing Li and Patrick Fuliang Shan (Lanham, MD and Oxford: Lexington Books, 2015). For a recent study on the Manchu racial identity envisioned by a Manchu writer, Dehai (a.k.a. Donjina), from the Qing frontier in the early twentieth century, see David C. Porter, "Manchu Racial Identity on the Qing Frontier: Donjina and Early Twentieth Century Ili," *Modern China* 44, no. 1 (2018).

This chapter focuses on how Manchu reformers took an ethnic-based approach to the woman question to articulate their visions of the nation, gender, and ethnicity through their representations of Huixing and her suicide. Whereas the Han feminist writers in Chapter 2 drew upon the heroic characteristics of Western women in their creation of ideal modern womanhood, the Manchu reformers turned to Confucian virtues and tropes to legitimate and amplify Huixing's exemplarity as a modern Chinese woman. In this process of reconstruction, Huixing emerged as a figure created from merging a recognizable Manchu woman with a familiar Han woman. This also led to the question of gendered differences in the understanding of Manchu ethnicity: whereas male Manchu reformers sought to remodel Huixing as an ethnic Manchu ideal in order to assert their Manchu identity, the female Manchu writers tended to identify themselves in gender terms more than in ethnic terms. They perceived Manchu women as woefully oppressed by men, as were their Han sisters, and frequently waged fierce attacks on the evil social customs that harmed all women, including those who were Manchu and Han, Eastern and Western. This gendered divergence suggests that female Manchu writers had a significantly different conception of modern womanhood and approach to the woman question from their male counterparts.

Huixing's death, as she herself had correctly anticipated, not only inspired massive public sympathy but also prompted impassioned calls to action among her fellow reform-minded Manchu intellectuals and activists. In addition to numerous memorials held for her, a girls' school was opened in her name and a women's journal, titled *Huixing nüxue bao* 惠興女學報 (*Journal of Huixing Girls' School*), was also launched as both the mouthpiece of the Huixing Girls' School and a platform for promoting her cause. This journal featured a regular section called "Huixing nüshi jishi 惠興女士紀事 (The Chronicle of Huixing)" to publish articles on Huixing's life and deeds: some were reflective essays by Manchu reformist writers or reports collected from different newspapers on the significance of her death; others were fictional retellings of her life story.[4] This intermingling of the factual and the fictional significantly changed the social and cultural meanings attributed to Huixing's suicide, working to produce an alternative ideal of new Chinese womanhood.

Reports of Huixing's suicide and debates on the questions of gender, nation, and ethnicity also appeared in *Beijing nübao* 北京女報 (*Beijing Women's News*), a pro-Manchu feminist daily that was founded in 1905 by a male social

4 This special column existed from the journal's inaugural issue in May 1908 until the twentieth issue in November 1909. Most of the materials about Huixing's life and suicide that this chapter draws from are from publications in this section.

activist named Zhang Zhanyun 張展雲 and his mother.[5] *Beijing nübao* also served as a site, where in some instances, male and female contributors directly encountered with one another in making sense of questions of gender and ethnic differences related to Huixing's case.

This chapter begins with an overview of Huixing's case as represented in media reports, emphasizing her suicide as a window onto the production of new tropes of martyrdom and female suicide and as an instantiation of the ideal of the self-sacrificing modern woman who was committed to national or public causes. Then I examine how Manchu reformers built on Huixing's role as a figure of sacrifice for national causes and accentuated her Manchu ethnicity to construct ideal modern "Chinese" (specified as Manchu) womanhood that they deemed legitimate and exemplary. The remainder of the chapter analyzes a group of Manchu women's writing in two pro-Manchu women's journals to probe the gendered differences in understanding Manchu ethnicity and the authors' desire to imagine the Manchu women as qualified modern women.

1 A Sacrificial Martyr for a National Cause

At the end of December 1905, *Shenbao* 申報, one of the most influential and widely distributed Shanghai-based daily newspapers, first reported on Huixing's suicide. The news article, titled "Huixing nüshi wei xue xisheng 惠興女士為學犧牲 (Ms. Huixing Sacrificed for Education)," opened with a brief biographical account of Huixing and ended with Huixing's own suicide note. Born to a military official family from the Hangzhou banner garrison in Zhejiang province, Huixing was widowed at the age of nineteen. She maintained steadfast loyalty to her deceased husband. After reading the *Quanxue pian* 勸學篇 (*An Exhortation to Learning*) by Zhang Zhidong 張之洞 (1837–1909), a prominent reformist official who was then the governor-general of Hunan and Hubei, Huixing was deeply inspired and determined to commit herself to the cause of promoting women's education. In August 1904, Huixing gathered a cohort of locally prestigious townspeople to discuss her proposal to open a school for girls. In the middle of the gathering, in an attempt to emphasize the gravity of the occasion, she abruptly exposed her arm to the audience and sliced off a piece of flesh. She declared, "Today marks the founding day of

5 The journal was published in vernacular Chinese until 1909. For more information about the journal, see Jiang Weitang 姜緯堂 and Liu Ningyuan 劉寧元, ed., *Beijing funü baokan kao* 北京婦女報刊考, 1905–1949 [*A Study of Women's Journals and Newspapers in Beijing, 1905–1949*] (Beijing: Guangming ribao chubanshe, 1990), 35–72.

the girls' school, and my blood will commemorate this event." She then solemnly vowed that she would "perish with it" (*yi shen xun zhi* 以身殉之) if the school ever faced closure. The school finally opened but suffered from a severe lack of sustained and sufficient funding. About a year later, the school was almost forced to close because of financial crisis and Huixing fell into despair. After preparing letters petitioning the local government for more funds, she committed suicide by ingesting opium. At the time of her death, she was just thirty-five years old.[6]

Although this article appeared in the form of a brief biography and did not include the editorial comments added by later news reports, it encompassed almost all the crucial elements that recurred in later accounts of Huixing: women's education, flesh cutting, female suicide, and self-sacrificing martyrdom. An article from *Dongfang zazhi* 東方雜誌 (*Eastern Miscellany*) also recorded the incident and devoted particular attention to Huixing's act of flesh cutting. After the initial shock, the audience was moved by this extreme, self-destructive act—an act that was performed publicly and inspired sympathy for Huixing's cause as well as respect for her sacrifice. In hailing Huixing's heroic act, the reporter stressed that Huixing possessed the laudable virtues of *yi* 義 (righteousness) and *xia* 俠 (knight-errantry)—two traits often invoked in the Chinese historical and literary tradition.[7] The *xia* usually referred to an individual who was known for rejecting conventional norms and was prone to altruistic self-sacrifice for grand causes.[8] As Hu Ying has pointed out, the *xia*'s selfless sacrifice held great potential for depicting heroic women's fighting for a national cause in the late Qing context of national crisis.[9] At the turn of

---

6 "Huixing nüshi wei xue xisheng 惠興女士為學犧牲 [Ms. Huixing Sacrificed for Education]," *Shenbao* (December 30, 1905). This news report reappeared in full length in the first issue of *Huixing nüxue bao* 惠興女學報. See "Hangzhou Huixing nüshi wei xue xunshen jielüe 杭州惠興女士為學殉身節略 [A Brief Account of Ms. Huixing's Sacrifice for Education in Hangzhou]" and "Hangzhou Zhenwen nüxuexiao xiaozhang Huixing nüshi jueming yi zhong xuesheng shu 杭州貞文女學校惠興女士絕命遺眾學生書 [A Suicide Note to Students of Hangzhou Zhenwen Girls's School from its Principal Ms. Huixing]," *Huixing nüxue bao* 1 (May 1908).

7 "Huixin nüshi xun xue ji 惠馨女士殉學記 [Account of Ms. Huixin's Sacrifice for Education]," *Dongfang zazhi* 東方雜誌 3, no. 5 (1906).

8 The female knight-errant, *nüxia*, who surfaced in Tang literature, is also a prominent figure in the *xia* tradition. Like her male counterpart, the *nüxia* is conventionally linked with unconventional behavior and martial prowess. But the trope of cross-dressing is often associated with the *nüxia*. For a brief survey of the far-reaching genealogy of the female knight-errant in the Chinese literary tradition and a detailed analysis of how female knight-errants embodied examples of heroic transformations during the Ming-Qing dynastic transition, see Li, *Women and National Trauma*, 205–293.

9 Hu, *Tales of Translation*, 112–113.

the twentieth century, knight-errantry appeared in various representations of heroic, nationalist women figures and was reiterated as a specific virtue integral to the ideal of the new Chinese woman. In this portrayal of Huixing, she emerged as a legitimate knight-errant who sacrificed her life for a national cause—women's education. In addition, she was described as "a female hero with frail substance" (*jinguo ruozhi* 巾幗弱質)—an seemingly contradictory expression that simultaneously emphasized her "masculine" valor and her feminine physical frailty. This reattribution of physical weakness to a heroic woman could be read, to use Hu Ying's terms, as "an attempt to fortify the heroine's femininity," which in turn made her unconventional behavior even more heroic.[10]

This combination of heroic sacrifice and feminine virtues prompted impassioned sympathy from the public. A longer and more elaborate biography of Huixing in the northern newspaper *Shuntian shibao* 順天時報 (*Shuntian Times*) thus presented her as both an iconoclastic figure whose action on behalf of national causes was worthy of emulation and a virtuous wife and mother.[11] This biographical account was originally presented as a speech at a memorial held for Huixing. It added more detail about Huixing's life than had appeared in *Shenbao* and *Dongfang zazhi*. She was depicted as a well-educated woman who had entertained great ambitions from a very young age. As a widowed mother, she experienced great ordeals in bringing up her son. Her adherence to traditional womanly behavior was further implied by the school's name Zhenwen 貞文, as the character *zhen*, according to the author of the biography, explicitly denoted "purity and chastity." The biography not only framed her as the exemplar of a traditional virtuous woman but also a nation-minded modern heroine: She had always admired Harriet Beecher Stowe and aspired to achieve lofty goals in her own life as well. She constantly spoke about the urgency of developing women's education and saw it as the highest priority in national strengthening. She proclaimed that a nation must have virtuous mothers before it could have quality offspring. Recognizing the "darkness of the women's world" (*nüjie hei'an* 女界黑闇), she regarded the promotion of

10 Hu Ying, "Gender and Modern Martyrology: Qiu Jin as *Lienü, Lieshi, or Nülieshi*," in *Beyond Exemplar Tales: Women's Biography in Chinese History*, ed. Joan Judge and Hu Ying (Berkeley: University of California Press, 2011), 127.

11 The integration of heroism and traditional Chinese female virtues was also prevalent in the late Qing representations of Western heroic women. On the one hand, they were depicted as the most iconoclastic figures, while on the other hand they were also the most traditional and virtuous women in conventional Confucian terms. For such an example of biographies of Sophia Perovskaia in the late Qing context, see Hu, *Tales of Translation*, 111–120.

women's education as the first and most important task.[12] The invocation of Stowe, one of the best-known Western female figures in the late Qing imagination of modern Chinese womanhood,[13] and of the phrase *nüjie hei'an*, a new locution that late Qing feminists often employed to criticize the subjugated status of Chinese women,[14] further attested to Huixing's global consciousness and feminist aspiration—two qualities that were essential to the ideal of modern womanhood.

The public setting for Huixing's flesh–cutting display was also described in the biography including the gory details. To a certain extent, Huixing's self-inflicted mutilation readily invoked the ritualized filial practice of *gegu* 割股 (lit. "slicing the thigh or limb"), cutting one's flesh to be made into medicine for ailing parents or other elders in the family.[15] In fact, a later official biographical account of her changed this act of cutting her flesh for women's education into just this kind of "filial slicing": she was presented as a filial daughter-in-law who served her own flesh to nurture a sickly parent.[16] But in the biography published in *Shuntian shibao*, her act of flesh slicing was a clear manifestation of her commitment to a national cause and, by extension, the nation. In this regard, Huixing grafted the object of filial sacrifice from parents onto the new nation. Moreover, in contrast to the potential controversy that acts of filial

12 "Buji Hangzhou Zhenwen nüxue xiao xiaozhang Huixing nüjie lishi 補記杭州貞文女學校校長惠興女傑歷史 [The Supplement to the Life Story of the Principal of Hangzhoug Zhenwen Girls' School, Huixing]," *Shuntian shibao* (February 8, 1906) (reprinted in Li and Zhang, *Jindai Zhongguo nüquan yundong shiliao*, 2: 1449–1451).

13 Harriet Beecher Stowe was a renowned American abolitionist and author of the anti-slavery novel *Uncle Tom's Cabin*. In 1902, the intellectual and writer Jiang Zhiyou 蔣智由 (1865–1929) provided a first translation of the biography of Stowe and elevated her as a symbol of cosmopolitanism [*shijie zhiyi* 世界主義]. For a detailed study on the translation and appropriation of Stowe's story in late Qing China, see Xia, *Wan-Qing nüxing*, 172–186.

14 On the trope of *nüjie hei'an*, see Chapter 2.

15 In Chinese culture, *gegu* became a stock expression that included many other parts of the body, such as an arm or a chest, and could refer to any behavior of filial slicing. For a discussion of the *gegu* phenomenon in the Tang dynasty, see Ch'iu Chung-Lin 邱仲麟, "Bu xiao zhi xiao: Sui Tang yilai gegu liaoqin xianxiang de shehuishi chutan 不孝之孝: 隋唐以來割股療親現象的社會史初探 [Filial Piety of the Unfilial: A Socio-Historical Study of the Phenomenon of 'Cutting Flesh to Heal Parents' from the Sui and Tang Dynasties to Modern China]," *Xin shixue* 新史學 6 (1995). By the late imperial period, *gegu* had become an established cultural expression of filial piety. See Jimmy Yu, *Sanctity and Self-Inflicted Violence in Chinese Religions, 1500–1700* (Oxford: Oxford University Press, 2012), 62–84.

16 Zhao Erxun 趙尔巽et al., *Qing shi gao* 清史稿 [*Draft History of the Qing*] (Beijing: Zhonghua shuju, 1977) vol. 46, *juan* 509: 14082.

sacrifice could incite,[17] Huixing's action of cutting her flesh as sacrifice to the nation was nonetheless decidedly respectable and central to her status as a "female hero" (*nü zhong haojie* 女中豪傑).[18]

Just as Huixing's act of flesh cutting was reframed as a nationalistic action, the meaning of her suicide had also to be redefined in the late Qing context of social and political calls for female martyrdom for national causes. Recent scholarly works have pointed out that in the late imperial period, female suicide was an important site for the production of state-sanctioned female virtue and chastity, as demonstrated by the large number of suicidal chaste women documented in compendia of national and local histories.[19] At the same time, female suicides created a vast space for public fascination and consumption, as a variety of actors, including official bureaucrats, male literati, and sometimes even the emperors, harnessed them for different purposes.[20] Despite the multifaceted interpretations, female suicides in the late imperial era were typically understood in relation to the virtue of chastity and had limited resonance beyond the domestic realm or familial relations.[21] In the last decade of

17 For instance, in her study of Ming fiction Maram Epstein notes that the practice of *gegu* was regarded as "counter to orthodox ritual" [*fei zhengli* 非正禮] and as an expedient act only permissible during times of crisis. In the story that Epstein examines, the parent discovered the way by which she was revived and disapproved of the act, rebuking it as "ignorant filiality" [*yuxiao* 愚孝]. Epstein points out that, despite the disapproval, the filial act was nonetheless proved through the immediate efficacy of the unorthodox cure. See Maram Epstein, *Competing Discourses: Orthodoxy, Authenticity, and Engendered Meanings in Late Imperial Chinese Fiction* (Cambridge: Harvard University Asia Center, 2001), 246.

18 "Buji Hangzhou Zhenwen," 1450.

19 See, e.g., Mark Elvin, "Female Virtue and State in China," *Past and Present* 104 (1984); Paul Ropp, "Passionate Women: Female Suicide in Late Imperial China," *Nan Nü: Men, Women and Gender in China* 3, no. 1 (2001); Janet Theiss, *Disgraceful Matters: The Politics of Chastity in Eighteenth-Century China* (Berkeley: University of California Press, 2004); Lu Weijing, *True to Her Word: The Faithful Maiden Cult in Late Imperial* China (Stanford: Stanford University Press, 2008).

20 Katherine Carlitz has examined the wide range of motives in male literati writing about female suicides, ranging from the propagation of female virtue and chastity, erotic fascination with female bodies, literary fame, career advancement, enhancement of male friendship and literary network, to commercial profit. See her "The Social Uses of Female Virtue in Late Ming Editions of the *Lienü zhuan*," *Late Imperial China* 12, no. 2 (1991); and idem, "The Daughter, the Singing-Girl, and the Seduction of Suicide," *Nan Nü: Men, Women and Gender in China* 3, no. 1 (2001). Janet Theiss has demonstrated that female suicides were used to serve statecraft goals and imperial agendas in the Qing dynasty. See her "Managing Martyrdom: Female Suicide and Statecraft in Mid-Qing China," *Nan Nü: Men, Women and Gender in China* 3, no. 1 (2001).

21 Male suicides were usually considered in relation to the virtue of political loyalty during dynastic changes. Paola Zamperini has argued that although female suicides during the

the Qing dynasty, however, the scope for the interpretation of female suicide was broadened as notions of gender boundaries and virtue underwent radical reformulations. If suicide remained an effective way for a woman to publicly demonstrate her virtue, this virtue was no longer necessarily associated with her chastity and loyalty to her husband or betrothed. Instead, suicide could be deployed as self-willed means of sacrifice to a noble cause in the public realm. This shift in the meaning of female suicide is best illustrated by Huixing's suicide. Knowing that her suicide might elicit unintended interpretations, as it did not fit into the familiar types of virtuous and chaste female suicides worthy of public glorification, she attempted to define the meaning of her death in her suicide note (*jueming shu* 絕命書):

> That I am renouncing my life cannot be called committing suicide. Rather, this is called "making a sacrifice," a custom established from ancient times that would make one realize commitment to a cause. It is like praying to the gods when you are ill, and when you recover you ought to burn candles and incense to redeem your vows to the gods. Now the school has been successfully founded, like a sickly person being cured. The vows made earlier must be repaid with sacrifice.[22]

She then stated that she had contemplated killing herself for months. Her concern over the insufficient funds and the already-hired teachers at the school, however, made her postpone her suicide. For her, death was a deliberate, carefully planned act under her control, not one that she passively suffered. In describing her actions, she rejected the term *duanjian* 短見 (lit. "myopic view"), a stock expression that often carried a negative connotation when used to refer to suicide, and attempted to justify it as principled martyrdom by linking it

---

traumatic periods of social and political disorder also had political overtones, such as the suicide of Consort Yu 虞姬, the concubine of Xiang Yu 項羽, they were more often understood as actions following male initiative. See her "Untamed Hearts: Eros and Suicide in Late Imperial Chinese Fiction," *Nan Nü: Men, Women and Gender in China* 3, no. 1 (2001): 98–100; Janet Theiss has noted that suicides of women who defended their chastity in the midst of the dynastic conquest by the Manchus were sanctioned by the Qing rulers as actions demonstrating their loyalty to the dynasty. But I would argue that their suicides were still more associated with chastity than with the loyalist martyrdom by men.

22 我今雖捐生，這不叫短見，這是古時候定下的規矩，名叫 "盡犧牲"，是為所興的事求其成功。譬如為病求神保佑，病好之後，必買香燭還願。如今學堂成了，就如同病好了，這個願是一定要還的。 "Hangzhou Zhenwen nüxuexiao xiaozhang Huixing nüshi jueming yi zhong xuesheng shu," 9.

with ritual sacrifice. Written at the point of her death, this self-inscription not only linked her with self-sacrificing, quasi-religious fervor but also suggested a powerful sense of personal agency.[23]

At the time of Huixing's death, an increasing number of self-sacrificing, political Western women martyrs were introduced to the Chinese. The stories of these heroic Western women were variously translated, appropriated, and at times rewritten to adapt to Chinese soil via different channels, such as books and periodicals. As seen in Chapter 2, translated biographies of Western heroines were a prominent feature of the feminist women's press. Among these widely circulated figures were Madame Roland, an influential French revolutionary who was identified by Liang Qichao as the first heroine in the modern world; Sophia Perovskaia, an iconoclastic Russian anarchist and assassin; and Joan of Arc.[24] All these women were characterized by their commitment and self-sacrifice to public or national causes and thus were heralded by late Qing reformers and revolutionaries as models for emulation by Chinese women. For example, Qiu Jin, a renowned revolutionary feminist who martyred herself in 1907, two years after Huixing's death, mobilized Chinese women to follow the lead of these imported heroic female figures to fight for their own emancipation and freedom.[25]

Concurrent with the valorization of these Western heroines was the abundance of writing that recast traditional Chinese heroic women warriors, historical or imagined, as sacrificial nationalist martyrs. The appropriation of these Chinese heroines was widespread in newspapers, educational materials, and the women's press. For example, turn-of-the-century renditions of the story of Hua Mulan, probably the best-known Chinese woman warrior, constantly represented her as a symbol of nationalist aspirations. The core values of filial piety and resistance to the central state, which underlined the pre-twentieth-century narratives about her, were significantly undermined. Rather, as Louise Edwards has aptly noted, she was refashioned as an example to promote " 'militarized filial piety' as the modern social virtues of patriotism and sacrifice to the nation-state."[26] These Western and Chinese heroic women and their stories

---

23 For discussion of the female agency in women's suicide writings in the Ming-Qing period, see Grace Fong, "Signifying Bodies: The Cultural Significance of Suicide Writings by Women in Ming-Qing China," *Nan Nü: Men, Women and Gender in China* 3, no. 1 (2001).

24 For a detailed study of the translations and transformations of the stories of Madam Roland and Sophia Perovskaia in the late Qing context, See Hu, *Tales of Translation*, 106–196. These figures were often invoked in late Qing literature and their stories frequently appeared in various forms in newspapers and journals.

25 Qiu Jin, "*Jingweishi* xu."

26 Edwards, *Women Warriors*, 17.

injected an ideal of self-sacrifice and self-willed nationalist martyrdom into the conception of the new Chinese woman.

This is the atmosphere in which the press coverage attempted to portray Huixing as the first modern Chinese female martyr. Press commentaries, and a proliferation of eulogies and commemorative poems and lyrics generated on different occasions, consolidated her image as an assertive martyr. Whereas Huixing had to link her suicide with ritual sacrifice so as to fix the meaning of her death and gain public attention and visibility, press coverage and mourners in the public had less difficulty in establishing the national significance of her sacrificial martyrdom. For example, her biography in *Shuntian shibao* hailed her as the "greatest person in the six thousand years of history of women's world" (六千年來女界第一偉人) because of the self-sacrificial spirit in her devotion to women's education.[27] As discussed in earlier chapters, women's education had become an integral part of the project of national strengthening in the late Qing, and a commitment to the promotion of women's education was shared by almost all women with a modern consciousness. Huixing's strong dedication to women's education, through an extreme act of committing suicide, thus made her decidedly a nationalist martyr, distinguishing her from traditional chaste female martyrs. Nevertheless, the fact that Huixing's sacrifice was also publicly glorified in a way that was similar to virtuous female suicides in the late imperial period suggests that at the turn of the twentieth century, female suicide continued to serve as a site for the production of new meanings. In the new context of national salvation, the object of traditional feminine virtues of purity, chastity, and self-sacrificing loyalty could readily be transposed from husbands and families unto the new nation.

2 Making a Manchu Heroine

As seen in the previous section, news reports on Huixing devoted a great deal of attention to the meaning and significance of her suicide and to establishing her as a model nationalist heroine. Public speeches at the memorials held for her also tended to associate her death with the larger agenda of China's national salvation. For example, the speech at one of the public memorials in Beijing directly linked Huixing's sacrifice to the urgency of national renewal. Delivered in vernacular Chinese, the speech stressed that her death could "awaken national spirit" (*huanxing guohun* 喚醒國魂), "encourage the development of

27 "Buji Hangzhou Zhenwen," 1451.

education" (*jili xuejie* 激勵學界), and most importantly, "rejuvenate the country" (*xingqi guojia* 興起國家), foregrounding her as a shining patriotic exemplar for the four hundred million Chinese people. At the end of the speech, the speaker warned the audience against focusing on Manchu-Han differences and admonished them to make concerted efforts to "preserve the country" (*baoguo* 保國) instead.[28] Although this admonition was intended to emphasize that the significance of Huixing's sacrifice went beyond the boundaries of region and ethnicity, at the same time, it inadvertently served as a reminder of Huixing's Manchu identity, which was often underplayed or even eschewed in the representations of her as an ideal nationalist martyr.

The attempt to play down mentions of Huixing's ethnicity was further reflected by the scant media focus on the real causes of her death. Although most reports mentioned that she had died because of the lack of school funds, a brief account in *Jingzhong ribao* 警鐘日報 (*Alarming Bell Daily*), a prominent nationalist newspaper at the time, suggested that her motivations for promoting women's education and her suicide were far more complex than they seemed. The report stated that Huixing was determined to found a girls' school because she had once been denied admission to a girls' school established by Han Chinese. The Han girls' school rejected her because of her non-Han ethnicity. The term *fei wo zulei* 非我族類 (not a member of my race) used in the report not only indicated her racial "otherness" but also evoked explicit overtones of anti-Manchu sentiment among those who denied her admission.[29] However, the revelation that ethnic discrimination was a contributing factor to the series of events that led to her death was not mentioned in other contemporary news reports. Not until three years after her death did a Manchu reformist intellectual raise this scenario, confirming that Huixing killed herself in part to protest the discriminatory admission policy of a Han girls' school.[30]

In major national publications such as *Shenbao* and *Dongfang zazhi*, the general lack of interest in probing the causes of Huixing's death from the perspective of ethnic conflicts should be understood in the late Qing context of increasingly strained Manchu-Han relations. As existing scholarship has

28 "Xu ji Shufan nüxuexiao zhuidaohui yanshuo ci 續記淑範女學校追悼會演說詞 [The Supplement to the Speech at the Memorial Held in the Shufan Girls' School]," *Shuntian shibao* (February 7, 1906) (reprinted in Li and Zhang, *Jindai Zhongguo nüquan yundong shiliao*, 2: 1448–1449).

29 "Qinü yi wei bi xingxue hu 旗女亦為彼興學乎 [Manchu Women also Promoted Education for Themselves?]," *Jingzhong ribao* 警鐘日報 (November 8, 1904).

30 "*Huixing nüxue bao* fakanci 惠興女學報發刊辭 [Opening Statement for *Journal of Huixing Girls' School*]," *Huixing nüxue bao* 1 (April 15, 1908).

emphasized, in the last decade of the Qing dynastic, the young, revolution-minded intellectuals, particularly those who had studied in Japan, created a loud chorus of anti-Manchuism. Following the lead of outspoken anti-Manchu critics, such as Zhang Binglin 章炳麟 (1869–1936), Zou Rong 鄒容 (1885–1905), and Chen Tianhua 陳天華 (1875–1905),[31] Han Chinese students studying abroad, both male and female, fueled anti-Manchu sentiment through their many anti-Manchu writings and their involvement in anti-Qing activity.[32] Prominent women feminists such as Qiu Jin and Chen Xiefen were also known for their anti-Qing proclamations. These revolutionaries founded various organizations and journals to spread their anti-Manchu propaganda. In contrast to these publications, which had an openly anti-Manchu agenda, newspapers, especially those based in Shanghai with a national circulation and influence, tended to be cautious and refrain from aggravating the Manchu-Han tensions.[33] Rather than spilling ink on investigating Huixing's case in a way that might give rise to ethnic controversy, these national newspapers were more interested in celebrating her demonstrated qualities of martyrdom and making her into an ideal modern Chinese heroine as a counterpoint to the widely circulated images of Western women who embodied modern womanhood.[34]

---

31 On the influence of their radical, anti-Manchu works in the late Qing, see Rhoads, *Manchus and Han*, 12–13.

32 For an analysis of how Zou Rong and his fellow radical revolutionaries conceptualized and justified their contemporary Manchus as an "alien race" [*yizhong* 異種] by invoking traumatic historical memories of the Qing conquest in the seventeenth century, see Peter Zarrow, "Historical Trauma: Anti-Manchuism and Memories of Atrocity in Late Qing China," *History and Memory* 16, no. 2 (2004): 78–80.

33 In her examination of *Shenbao*'s reports on the Wuchang rebellion as an example, Barbara Mittler points out that, although *Shenbao* and other Shanghai newspapers "stoke the revolutionary fire," they never became "the voice of violent anti-Manchuism or anti-imperialism." See Mittler, *A Newspaper for China?* 384.

34 In her recent study of the commemoration of Liangbi 良弼 (1877–1912), a Manchu military official who was assassinated during the 1911 Revolution, as a martyr by both Qing loyalists and revolutionaries, Hu Ying points out that a martyr's death had universal characteristics such as "a dramatic demonstration of the hero's determination and valor and the recognition of these qualities by an audience, either an actual witness or a historian-biographer." Fulfilling these requirements thus rendered the hero's martyrdom a good death worthy of universal celebration, regardless of ideological divergences or partisan divisions among the dead. Likewise, the national presses' concerted effort to celebrate the martyrdom of Huixing could also be understood as a universal aspiration to honor a good death, in spite of the martyr's ethnic difference. See Hu Ying, "Enemy, Friend, Martyr: Commemorating Liangbi (1877–1912), Contesting History," *Late Imperial China* 38, no. 1 (2017): 13.

As the news of Huixing's suicide spread, it struck a particularly strong chord with her fellow Manchus, especially the Manchu officials and reform-minded intellectuals. *Beijing nübao*, an influential pro-Manchu women's newspaper, published a series of reports about Huixing. Zhang Zhanyun, the journal's founder and editor in chief, was later actively engaged in raising funds to support Huixing's unfinished cause. Several months after Huixing's death, Ruixing 瑞興, then the general of the Hangzhou banner garrison, submitted a memorial to petition the Ministry of Rites to give her an imperial award of merit that was historically awarded to faithful maidens or chaste widows, called *jingbiao* 旌表, to honor her sacrificial martyrdom.[35] Ruixing saw Huixing as a unique example of Manchu women's efforts to promote women's education and declared that her death had honored the Eight Banners.[36] He further praised Huixing's sacrifice as "rarely seen among Manchu and Han women."[37] Other Manchu writers also highlighted Huixing's non-Han ethnicity by lauding her as a shining exemplar of "our great Qing dynasty," "our Tungusic race," and "our East Asian womankind."[38] Unlike the national newspapers, which often referred to her as a heroine of China with an unspecified ethnicity, these writers explicitly identified her as a model for Manchu women. In addition to resonating with the Manchus, Huixing's death also caught the attention of other banner people. A short biography of her penned by Sanduo 三多 (1871–1941), a late Qing literati and a Mongol banner man, praised her as a Manchu female exemplar above all others in Chinese history, whose achievements were on par with those of Madame Roland:

> Women's education has long been underdeveloped in China. The most refined of those modestly educated women were only capable of assuming the roles of talented women, wise mothers, or virtuous chaste

35 The *jingbiao* practice could be traced back to the Han dynasty when the court rewarded both men and women for their exemplary moral behaviors by issuing imperial plaques and "honorific tablets." But in the Ming and Qing periods, the *Jingbiao* awardees were primarily chaste wives or chaste widows who preserved sexual fidelity for their deceased husbands or fiancés, either by committing suicide or refusing to remarry. See Lu, *True to Her Word*, 32–33, 69–82.

36 The Eight Banners in the Qing dynasty were administrative and military divisions in which all banner households were placed. In addition to the Manchu banners, the Eight Banner system had two other significant ethnic components: the Mongol banners and the Hanjun. See Rhoads, *Manchus and Han*, 67.

37 Ruixing 瑞興, "Baqi xieling gong cheng 八旗協領公呈 [Memorial from a Regiment Colonel]," *Beijing nübao* (July 9, 1906). This memorial was also published in *Huixing nüxue bao* 4 and 5 (1908).

38 Rhoads, *Manchus and Han*, 93.

> martyrs—these were the most they could achieve. There has not yet been a woman like Madame Roland who cast aside her personal feelings and desires and sacrificed herself for the benefits of her fellow compatriots and later generations. Now my fellow townswoman Huixing is the first heroic woman of this kind.[39]

The most ardent supporter of Huixing's life and deeds was Guilin 貴林, a fellow native of the Hangzhou garrison and a Manchu reformist intellectual. He was then a regimental colonel (*xieling* 協領) of the Zhangzhou garrison who had known about Huixing's dedication to women's education.[40] According to one of his accounts, he was right by Huixing's side several hours after she ingested the opium and she asked him to transmit her petition to the local government.[41] After Huixing died, Guilin actively sought support from the local government and initiated a wide range of fund-raising events, together with other Manchu bannermen, to carry out Huixing's wishes. He finally managed to collect enough funds to reopen the school in April 1906 as a government institution. In Huixing's memory, it was renamed the Huixing Girls' School, and Guilin served as its new superintendent. At the same time, Guilin was active in spreading Huixing's story and promoting her commitment to women's education. In May 1908, he launched *Huixing nüxue bao* (Figure 3) as both the

39 蓋中國女教不昌久矣，庸中佼佼，或能為才女、為賢母、為節烈婦，已達極點，未有如羅蘭夫人所謂真正人物，去私情，絕私慾，身獻同胞，而酬報待諸後世者。有之，自吾同里惠興女傑始。 Sanduo 三多, "Ji Huixing nüjie wei xue xunshen shi 記惠興女傑為學殉身事 [An Account of the Female Hero Huixing's Sacrifice for Education]," *Dagong bao* 大公報 (March 14, 1906).

40 Guilin was executed by the revolutionaries during the 1911 Revolution for his resistance to surrender (Rhoads, *Manchus and Han*, 200, 204). Recent scholarship has suggested that Guilin's persistent opposition against the prevailing anti-Manchuism and his implicit criticism of Qiu Jin's anti-Qing revolutionary martyrdom may have attributed to his execution. See Shen Jie 沈潔, "Cong Guilin zhi si kan Xinren zhi ji de zhongzu yu zhengzhi 從貴林之死看辛壬之際的種族與政治 [Ethnicity and Politics during the Xinhai Revolution, from the Perspective of Guilin's Death]," *Shi lin* 史林 4 (2013); Xia Xiaohong, "Qiu Jin yu Guilin 秋瑾與貴林 [Qiu Jin and Guilin]," *Dushu* 讀書 9 (2007).

41 This detail was recorded in both a public speech at Huixing's one-year death anniversary ceremony and another speech at a theater. See Guilin, "Huixing nüshi xunxue zhounian jinianhui yanshuo 惠興女士殉學週年記念會演說 [A Speech at the First Anniversary Memorial for Huixing's Sacrifice for Education]" *Huixing nüxue bao* 3 (July 1908): 10; "Sanyue ershiliu ri Huixing nüxuexiao zongban Guilin zai Guangdelou xiguan zhi yanshuo 三月二十六日惠興女學校總辦貴林在廣德樓戲館之演說 [A Speech Delivered at the Guangde Theater on 26th March by Guilin, the Superintendent of Huixing Girls' School]," *Beijing nübao* (May 11, 1907).

FIGURE 3 Cover of the inaugural issue of *Huixing nüxue bao* (May 14, 1908)
SOURCE: HARVARD-YENCHING LIBRARY

organ of the school and a platform for writings about Huixing that he collected and composed.

The first and second issues of *Huixing nüxue bao* serialized a lengthy article about Huixing by Guilin. The article was originally a speech that he had delivered at a memorial service for Huixing held in the Hangzhou garrison in 1906.[42] In this eulogy-*cum*-hagiography, Guilin first celebrated Huixing as an extraordinary individual who embodied the virtues of filial piety, righteousness, valor, and knight-errantry. Responding to some people's narrow-minded views that regarded Huixing's death as futile and self-promotional, Guilin asserted that Huixing died in the interest of the Manchu people, which he called *wo zu* 我族 (our lineage/race). This use of the first-person plural and *zu*, a term

42 Guilin, "Hangzhou qi cheng wei Huixing nüshi kai zhuidaohui yanshuo 杭州旗城為惠興女士開追悼會演說 [A Speech at the Memorial for Ms. Huixing in the Hangzhou Banner Garrison]," *Huixing nüxue bao* 1 and 2.

that connoted the meaning of "lineage/race" at the turn of the twentieth century, clearly indicated his imagining of a community of Manchus linked by a common origin and a shared racial identity.[43] His adoption of the expression *wo zu* also suggests that he was influenced by the theories of racial difference that gained prominence among the Han Chinese nationalists at the time and had applied them to his own understanding of Manchu-ness and his emphasis on Huixing's Manchu identity.[44] For Guilin, Huixing was decidedly a Manchu nationalist heroine.

With this ethnic consciousness in mind, Guilin further maintained, "our race has long possessed the noble qualities of righteousness and knight-errantry (我族素有高貴義俠之特質), but these qualities have woefully degenerated in the recent years."[45] Huxing's death thus could reawaken these long-inherited virtues of the Manchus and make them known to the world. As noted earlier, Although Chinese literary and historical tradition has long included knight-errantry, it never had a specific ethnic connotation. This designation of the attributes of righteousness and knight-errantry as a Manchu legacy revealed Guilin's attempt to claim the Manchus as the legitimate inheritors and producers of traditional Chinese culture. Moreover, as righteousness and knight-errantry were often invoked qualities in the representations of the ideal new Chinese woman in the late Qing context, Guilin's reconceptualization of these qualities as exclusively Manchu also showed an aspiration to create a modern female Manchu model comparable to the images of ideal Chinese women circulated at the time.

Guilin's intention to fashion Huixing as a Manchu heroine became more evident when he tried to make Huixing's death more prominent in a global context:

> Huixing is not merely a person from the Hangzhou garrison. Rather, she is a great person in world terms. She is not only a great person of our generation but also a great person for many generations to come. Huixing's death brings the three hundred years of "dead" Qing history alive,

43 This resembles Benedict Anderson's description of the use of the first-person plural as a common feature of nationalist novels, which worked to the development of national identity. See Benedict Anderson, *Imagined Communities: Reflections on the Origin and Spread of Nationalism* (New York: Verso, 1983). For a thoughtful discussion on the discourse of "race as lineage," see Dikötter, *The Discourse of Race*, 61–96.

44 Guilin's Manchu contemporaries were also influenced by the racial theories. See, e.g., Porter's discussion of Donjina, in "Manchu Racial Identity on the Qing Frontier."

45 Guilin, "Hangzhou qi cheng wei Huixing nüshi kai zhuidaohui yanshuo," *Huixing nüxue bao* 2: 9.

> the noble qualities of our race manifest to the world, and enlightens the masses of the East Asian *nüjie* who have been drenched in darkness for thousands of years.[46]

Guilin's elevation of Huixing as an exemplar of the East Asian *nüjie* deserves particular attention here. As discussed in Chapter 2 and earlier in this chapter, the term *nüjie*, when used in the context of Chinese nationalism, carried ethnic overtones and was primarily used to designate Han Chinese women. Guilin's linking of Huixing to the broader category of *Dongya nüjie* 東亞女界 (East Asian womanhood) rather than the often invoked *Zhongguo nüjie* 中國女界 (Chinese womanhood) demonstrates a conscious effort to build an alternative Chinese female model—one that not only was marked by her Manchu ethnicity but also enjoyed international recognition.

Guilin also made an effort to reframe Huixing's case as exceptional in his time, reaffirming the uniqueness of her sacrifice. In July 1909, *Huixing nüxue bao* reported a similar suicide by a young married woman named Wang Yuying 王玉英.[47] Wang committed suicide on the day that her husband had died of illness. She left a suicide note asking her parents to sell all her jewelry and belongings, which were worth over ten thousand silver dollars, and contribute the proceeds to schools. To honor Wang's "act of martyring herself for her husband and education" (*xunfu xunxue* 殉夫殉學), local officials petitioned higher authorities to give her a *jingbiao*, requesting that a memorial arch be built in her honor and that her name and story be recorded in local gazetteers. Guilin wrote an editor's commentary for this short report. After briefly praising Wang's decision to donate all her money for educational purposes, Guilin considered her act of following her husband in death problematic. He argued that she had been misled by hidebound scholars with pedantic ideas and that her suicide was an act of ignorant loyalty—he explicitly compared Wang's death unfavorably to Huixing's. He maintained that Huixing had sacrificed herself because of a severe lack of funds, whereas Wang was by no means short of material resources. Therefore, in Guilin's view, it was questionable whether her suicide could be

---

46 惠氏非杭州駐防人，乃世界之大人物也；非一世之人，乃百世之大人物也。惠氏一死，我大清三百年之死歷史為活歷史，我族高尚之特性可以表白於世界，我東亞女界數千年之黑暗可以復明。 Guilin, "Hangzhou qi cheng wei Huixing nüshi kai zhuidaohui yanshuo," *Huixing nüxue bao* 2: 10.

47 "Qing jiang xunfu xunxue zhi nüshi 請奬殉夫殉學之女士 [A Petition to Award the Woman Who Martyred Herself for Her Husband and Education]," *Huixing nüxue bao* 16 (1909).

considered martyrdom for education. He viewed it as a reckless action and cast doubt on the view that Wang had martyred herself for her husband. He then discouraged other women from taking life so lightly. Guilin's appraisal of Wang as a negative foil to Huixing underlined the exemplary nature of the latter's sacrifice, distinguishing her suicide from normative virtuous or chaste suicides.

In another speech to memorize Huixing, Guilin emphasized that the meaning of Huixing's death was its inspirational power. He warned people against indiscriminately emulating Huixing's act of suicide unless they had a genuine and serious purpose. This kind of emulation, in his view, was not a proper course of action and could only make one's death inconsequential, which would not benefit society at all. Huixing's death, on the contrary, had greater weight because it was for the sake of the development of women's education.[48] In short, the justification and veneration of Huixing's death on different occasions clearly showed Guilin's intention to portray Huixing as an exceptional, self-assertive martyr who died in the public interest.

Huixing's death gained increased public recognition, in large part thanks to the fact that Guilin dedicated considerable time and energy to promoting her causes through writing, public speeches, and memorial activities. Broader public fascination with the now-dead heroic female martyr meant that there was demand for retelling Huixing's story in other literary forms as well. For example, Huixing's story was adapted into a Western-style "civilized drama" (*wenming xi* 文明戲) in 1906 and staged under the title *Huixing nüshi zhuan* 惠興女士傳 (*The Story of Huixing*) many times in different places.[49] The play was mostly based on biographical information and stories about Huixing provided by Guilin, but it added many fictional details for dramatic effect. Although Guilin frowned upon these additions, he was nevertheless satisfied

48 Guilin, "Huixing xiansheng xunxue disi zhounian yanshuo 惠興先生殉學第四週年演說 [A Speech for the 4th Anniversary of Huixing's Martyrdom]," *Huixing nüxue bao* 21 (1909).

49 About "civilized drama," see Ouyang Yuqian 歐陽予倩, "Tan wenming xi 談文明戲 [On Civilized Drama]," in *Zhongguo huaju yundong wushinian shiliao ji* 中國話劇運動五十年史料集 [Collection of Historical Sources of Fifty Years of Spoken Drama Movements in China], ed. Tian Han 田漢 et al. (Beijing: Zhongguo xiju chubanshe, 1985): 51–52, 57. For a detailed analysis of the society that performed plays on Huixing, see Xia Xiaohong, "Jiu xitai shang de wenmingxi: Tian Jiyun yu Bejing Funü kuangxuehui 舊戲台上的文明戲：田際雲與北京 "婦女匡學會" [The Civilized Drama on the Old Stage: Tian Jiyuan and the Women's Association of Rectifying Learning in Beijing]," in *Beijing: dushi xiangxiang yu wenhua jiyi* 北京：都市想像與文化記憶 [*Beijing: Urban Imaginations and Cultural Memories*], ed. Chen Pingyuan 陳平原 and Wang Dewei 王德威 (Beijing: Peking University Press, 2005).

with the play's portrayal of Huixing as a reform-minded Manchu woman who was devoted to women's education.[50]

Another modern play featuring Huixing's story was written and performed by Wang Zhongsheng 王鐘聲, the founder of a drama school called the Tongjian School 通鑑學校.[51] An outline of the play and information on performance of it were documented by Guilin in *Huixing nüxue bao*.[52] In this play, Wang made considerable changes in the core of Huixing's story by introducing many topical social concerns at the time. Huixing was represented as a sort of new-style woman who was concerned about social reforms and progress. She criticized social ills such as smoking and other unhygienic habits engaged in by Chinese people. On the day that she founded the girls' school, she gave a long speech criticizing the weaknesses in the Chinese national character. She was convinced that Chinese women's lack of education was the root cause of Chinese inferiority. Founding the girls' school, she asserted, would be the starting point for the cultivation of wise mothers and good wives and facilitating "racial improvement" (*renzhong gailiang* 人種改良).[53] As scholars have pointed out, the concept of the wise mother and good wife was introduced from Japan at the turn of the twentieth century to clarify women's role in relation to the formation of Chinese citizenship, whereas the project of racial improvement was propagated as crucial to China's national survival.[54] Through the invocation of these two nationalist-inflected notions of the time, the play reinforced the image of Huixing as a nationalist heroine who sacrificed for the Chinese

---

50 "*Huixing nüshi zhuan* xinxi 《惠興女士傳》新戲 [A New Play Called *The Story of Ms. Huixing*]," *Huixing nüxue bao* 12–17 (1909).

51 Wang first founded the Chunyang she 春陽社, which was famous for its production of *Uncle Tom's Cabin* in 1907. The society was renamed the Tongjian School in March 1908. About Wang Zhongsheng and his promotion of the new-style drama, see Zhong Xinzhi 鐘欣志, "Yuejie yu manyou: xunmi xiandai guanzhong de 'Zhongsheng xinju' 越界與漫遊：尋覓現代觀眾的"鐘聲新劇" [Boundary Crossing and Wandering: In Search of Modern Audience in Wang Zhongsheng's New Drama]," *Xiju xuekan* 戲劇學刊 14 (2010).

52 "Zhi Tongjian xuexiao xuesheng banyan Huixing nüshi xinxi 誌通鑑學校學生扮演惠興女士新戲 [A New Play of Ms. Huixing Performed by Students at the Tongjian School]," *Huixing nüxue bao* 4 (1908).

53 "Zhi Tongjian xuexiao," 6.

54 About the significance of the ideology of "wise mothers and good wives" in the late Qing context, see Judge, "Talent, Virtue, and the Nation," 771–775; The notion of racial improvement had been introduced into China from the West by the 1910s as a new way of understanding China's rise and decline. See Jing Tsu, *Failure, Nationalism, and Literature: The Making of Modern Chinese Identity, 1895–1937* (Stanford: Stanford University Press, 2005), 100–101.

nation as represented in the national press. No particular attention was paid to her Manchu ethnicity. Guilin did not make any particular comment on these embellishments to Huixing's story, but the great popularity of the play suggests that it had succeeded in realizing Guilin's objective of making Huixing's story known to national audiences.[55]

Unlike the national media, which presented Huixing as a national martyr whose Manchu ethnicity was often elided or concealed, Manchu reformers promoted her as a Manchu nationalist heroine. The emphasis on her Manchu identity, on the one hand, was derived from a political need among the Manchu reformists to use her as a potential unifying force to create solidarity, and, on the other hand, it grew out of the larger context of constructing competing ideals of modern Chinese womanhood. Moreover, the male Manchu writers' concerted effort to fashion a national heroine with Manchu ethnicity disclosed their own profound ethnic insecurity in the face of prevailing anti-Manchu sentiment and activism. Guilin expressed this shared anxiety and his concern about racial survival in one of his essays supporting the Qing government's preparations for the establishment of a constitutional system in 1907.[56] He first bemoaned the fact that Manchus were gradually losing their military prowess to the Han because all the military preparatory schools (*wubei xuexiao* 武備學校) across the country were filled with Han students. This situation, he feared, would inevitably endanger the future of the Manchus. He proclaimed that a constitutional government would particularly benefit the Manchu race and prevent it from perishing. If a constitution were not established, he warned,

> Our race will be consigned to a different place, … those with some special talents will naturally assimilate into the Han communities, … over time the authenticity of our race will be completely lost.[57]

We can gain some insight into these Manchu intellectuals' desire to fix Huixing's image as an identifiable Manchu heroine by comparing what Ching-Kiu

55 Guilin attached a brief note describing that he was entranced by the play and deeply moved by the performance. See "Zhi Tongjian xuexiao," 7.

56 Guilin, "Hangfang Yulihui qingzhu lixian yanshuo 杭防豫立會慶祝立憲演說 [A Celebratory Speech on the Establishment of a Constitutional System, by the Preparatory Society for Constitution in the Hangzhou Banner Garrison]," *Huixing nüxue bao* 8 (December 8, 1908).

57 我族則為另一區域之族，……略有特才者自然而然同化於漢族，……而我族本真則積久失亡殆盡矣。 Guilin, "Hangfang Yulihui," 8.

Stephen Chan writes about the fascination among the May Fourth Chinese intellectuals with disciplining the New Woman image:

> In the turbulent times of the May Fourth cultural movement in modern China, the search for a new subjectivity was carried out quite frequently in terms of capturing, in a new form, the identity crisis of the "new women" [*xin nüxing*]. Yet the control of this form was everywhere disciplined by the intellectual (male-centered) self, whose own dilemma of identity tended to be posited in relation to the alien, repressed, but emerging "other" of the woman in question.[58]

Similarly, Manchu intellectuals such as Guilin projected their own discomfort and anxiety about losing their Manchu identity onto the figure of a female Manchu martyr, who died for a national cause. Huixing's case offered solid and legitimate ground for them to dispel their palpable concerns about the impending erasure of their distinct ethnic identity. Whereas Han writers often looked to Western female exemplars in their search for modern Chinese womanhood, as did the women feminist writers in Chapter 2, the Manchu creators of Huixing's image turned to Confucian virtues and tropes, claiming them as their own in their effort to construct her as an "authentic" female Manchu model.

3 Ethnicity and Gender: Manchu Women's Envisioning of Modern Womanhood

The persistent focus on Huixing's Manchu ethnicity in newspapers found little expression in Huixing's own self-representation. In her suicide note, she exhorted the students to adhere in their future studies to "loyalty, filial piety, integrity, and righteousness" (*zhong xiao jie yi* 忠孝節義)—the four classic Confucian virtues. Although she also advised them to compete with "outsiders" (*wairen* 外人) rather than their fellow people (*tongburen* 同部人), her use of the term *wairen* indicates her consciousness of the larger context of the development of women's education, and *tongburen* did not carry the same overtones of racial struggle as did the term *wo zu* used by Guilin. After all, her school enrolled both Manchu and Han female students.[59] Moreover, as Guilin

58 Ching-kiu Stephen Chan, "The Language of Despair: Ideological Representations of the 'New Women' by May Fourth Writers," *Modern Chinese Literature* 4 (1988): 19.

59 Guilin revealed that the Zhenwen Girls' School was open to both Manchu and Han girls, in "Huixing nüshi zhounian jinianhui yanshuo," 9. Huixing's school was probably among

later revealed, she encountered widespread ridicule and indifference from her fellow Manchus when she turned to them for support in establishing the girls' school.[60] Advancing women's education was indeed a key motivation for her radical decision to take her own life, but she was not primarily driven by ethnic consciousness to contribute to the general welfare of the Manchu people, as her male Manchu promoters suggested. The paucity of writings she left makes it difficult for us gain a fuller picture of Huixing's perceptions of her Manchu ethnicity, but her suicide note clearly suggests that she was not as keen on identifying herself along ethnic lines as were her male Manchu counterparts.

Mark Elliott notes that the Qing court imposed fewer restrictions on Manchu women than Manchu men, and they welcomed acculturation to Han norms more than they resisted it.[61] But this does not mean that the ethnic differences between Manchu and Han women were negligible. An obvious difference between Manchu and Han women was related to the Han practice of footbinding. Dorothy Ko points out that "footbinding became the terrain on which the ethnic and cultural boundaries between the Han Chinese and the 'Other' were being drawn."[62] Huixing's upholding of Confucian doctrine in her admonition and her virtuous conduct as a chaste widow and wise mother, however, suggest that she was not a cultural "other" to her Han sisters—at least the cultural difference was not significant enough to be identified as threatening to the Han Chinese.

In the first decade of the twentieth century, reformist Manchu women also assimilated the nationalist discourse on the causal link between women's education and national strengthening. In his study of Beijing women's activism

---

the first girls' schools whose selection of teachers and students was not based on ethnicity. In his study of Beijing girls' schools established in 1908 and 1909, Weikun Cheng notes that both Han and Manchu women imposed no ethnic boundaries on their schools and their curriculum, except for one vocational women's school for poor Manchu women in 1909, in "Going Public Through Education," 121.

60 Guilin, "Sanyue ershiliu ri Huixing nüxue xiao."

61 Mark Elliott, "Manchu Widows and Ethnicity in Qing China," *Comparative Studies in Society and History* 41, no. 1 (1999): 62–67.

62 Dorothy Ko, "The Body as Attire: The Shifting Meanings of Footbinding in Seventeenth-Century China," *Journal of Women's History* 8, no. 4 (1997): 10; for more on the history of footbinding, see also her *Cinderella's Sisters: A Revisionist History of Footbinding* (Berkeley: University of California Press, 2005). A recent study shows that, unlike the forced imposition of the queue among Han men, Han women's practice of footbinding never faced severe prohibitions after the Qing conquest, except for a ban in 1664 which was soon aborted in 1668. See John R. Shepherd, "The Qing, the Manchus, and Footbinding: Sources and Assumptions under Scrutiny," *Frontiers of History in China* 11, no. 2 (2016).

about women's education in the late Qing, Weikun Cheng notes that Manchu women played a visible role in promoting women's education as an effective means to both improve women's status and advance the nation.[63] Little evidence indicates that these women's agenda on women's education had an ethnic component. As a Manchu woman named Hui Xian stated:

> It has been an illness in China for thousands of years to value boys over girls. ... Women are so incapable and self-denying as to depend on the income made by men. They thus have their men over-loaded. If a woman obtains elementary knowledge or a living skill, she can support herself through an occupation like a man. The country will therefore get rid of poverty.[64]

With its highly similar rhetoric, this statement echoed, if not repeated, the nationalist narratives on women's education by Han female writers. Hui Xian's criticism implied that Chinese women in general, regardless of their ethnicity, were a dependent and subjugated collectivity that needed to be enlightened and liberated through education.

Like Hui Xian, most female Manchu writers contended that Manchu women should devote themselves to establishing solidarity and alliances with Han women, rather than concentrating on the seeming differences revealed through their external appearance. In an article published in *Beijing nübao* in 1905, a female Manchu author writing as Changbai nüzi 長白女子 (Daughter of Changbai), which refers to the mountains along the Korean border where the Manchu people originated, severely criticized her Manchu sisters for thinking that they were better than Han women. She wrote that although Manchu women (*Manzhou nüzi* 滿洲女子) took pride in themselves for not binding their feet, they wanted to have "willow branch feet" (*liutiao jiao* 柳條腳), a practice among bannerwomen of compressing their feet to achieve a narrow, knife-like effect.[65] To the author, the "willow branch feet" were no different from Han women's bound feet. She further stated wryly that Manchu women's excessive application of rouge would embarrass a stage actor. She thus urged her fellow sisters to "stop distinguishing between Manchus and Han" (*bu fen*

63 Cheng, "Going Public Through Education," 107–144.

64 Cited from Cheng, "Going Public Through Education," 113.

65 Also referred to as *daotiao* 刀條 or "loose binding." It is unclear how many Manchu women adopted this practice. Some sources suggest it was widespread in the late Qing. For more information on the practice, see John Robert Shepherd, *Footbinding as Fashion: Ethnicity, Labor, and Status in Traditional China* (Seattle: University of Washington Press, 2018), 145.

Man Han 不分滿漢) and instead to unite to enliven their spirit and awaken the two hundred million fellow women. *Beijing nübao* added a commentary to the article, likely by the journal's male editor in chief Zhang Zhanyun, disagreeing with the author's exhortation not to make ethnic distinctions: "In our view, there are areas where Han women (*Hanren nüzi* 漢人女子) do not measure up to Manchu women." The comment did not expound on the ways in which Manchu women were better than Han women, but it concurred that the development of women's education was pivotal for both Manchu and Han women to achieve "civilization."[66]

In an essay published in *Huixing nüxue bao* in 1908, a female Manchu student named Foying 佛英 at Huixing Girls' School discussed the social customs that were detrimental to women in general, whether Manchu, Han, Western, or Japanese. While condemning the piled-up hairdo, excessive make-up, and the high platform shoes of banner women, she also criticized the three-inch bound feet of Han women, the practice among Western women of wearing a corset, and the heavy and complicated clothes worn by Japanese women. Lamenting that such practices had caused women to be dependent on men, she maintained: "I would say that we women—whether Manchu or Han, from the West or the East—have all lost our personhood" (我們女子，不拘滿漢東西各國的人，學生都說是不合人格的). She was proud of her school for eradicating these social customs that constricted and "harmed us women." Only in this way could women be human. If, in addition, they could learn some skills to support themselves, she concluded, then they would be free, and if they could make rapid progress in learning, without any doubt they could be qualified as civilized people.[67]

In another essay, Foying highly extolled a range of unconventional and heroic female exemplars who broke gender barriers in both ancient China and the West. She first debunked the millennia-long Confucian doctrine and practice that women be confined to the domestic realm and not participate in affairs outside it. She then provided a list of female historical paragons who had not adhered to these old precepts, including Ms. Fu 伏女, a talented scholar known for her transmission of the Confucian classics; Ban Zhao, the eminent female historian in the Eastern Han dynasty; Madame Wei 衛夫人, a noted calligrapher in the Eastern Jin dynasty, and Ti Ying 緹縈, a heroine in

66 "Lun Manzhou nüzi de duoluo 論滿洲女子的墮落 [On the Degeneration of Manchu Women]," *Beijing nübao* (October 18, 1905).

67 Foying 佛英, "Yanshuo nü xuetang zhi guanxi 演說女學堂之關係 [A Speech on the Benefits of Girls' Schools]," *Huixing nüxue bao* 1 (May 1908): 7–8. This article was also published in *Beijing nübao* (May 15, 1908).

the Western Han dynasty who courageously petitioned the emperor to rescue her father from corporeal punishment.[68] Foying continued to valorize Chinese women warriors, such as Hua Mulan and Liang Hongyu 梁紅玉 (1102–1135), for their extremely heroic acts. She also included two Western women, Madame Roland and Mrs. Archibald Little, the wife of the British businessman Archibald John Little and an active campaigner against footbinding in China. While admiring these unconventional and exemplary heroines, however, Foying suggested that contemporary women use moderate and practical means to refashion themselves in a historical period that she called a "transitional era" (*guodu shidai* 過渡時代). She advised her fellow female students to start by ridding themselves of excessive trappings and extravagant adornment and choose plain cotton clothing instead. But she also conceded that the process of dress reform did not need to be radical; rather, a moderate amount of makeup and dressing up was acceptable. In so doing, female students would not appear too progressive to the outside eye, and women's education could be more widely promoted.[69]

For most Manchu women writers, the main distinction between Manchu and Han women was the latter's practice of footbinding, but it was seen not so much as an ethnic or cultural difference as a trope for the general oppression of Chinese women, regardless of their ethnicity. More often, it was invoked to reflect Manchu women's own conditions. As one Manchu woman wrote, "Isn't it abnormal and lamentable that we Manchu women are tightening our own natural feet to [make them look slim] whereas Han women are unbinding their feet?"[70] Another woman described her experience witnessing footbinding by one of her Han relatives, gaining sympathy for them after seeing how much pain the process caused. She was grateful that, as a Manchu woman, she was spared this practice and its excruciating pain. She also criticized Western women's custom of wearing a corset, maintaining that it was even more harmful than footbinding, which at best mutilated a woman's muscles and bones, but wearing a corset could be destructive and harm her internal organs (heart, liver, spleen, lungs, and kidneys) because of their position relative to the waist.

---

68 These historical women often served as local inspiration in the late Qing literary imagination of ideals of modern womanhood. See Zhu, *Imagining Sisterhood*, 8–9; for a discussion of Ti Ying's story in the late Qing context of national salvation, See Judge, *The Precious Raft of History*, 146–148.

69 Foying, "Yanshuo guodu shidai zhi nüzi 演說過渡時代之女子 [A Speech on Women in the Transitional Era]," *Huixing nüxue bao* 2 (June 1908): 6–8.

70 Xinghua 興華, "Pinglun yanshuo 評論演說 [Commentary and Speech]," *Huixing nüxue bao* 5 (September 10).

The writer viewed all these evil practices as indicators of physical and psychological suffering by women that had to be ended.[71]

Manchu women writers frequently contemplated their own feminine condition in comparison to that of Han women, whereas Han women tended to exclude Manchu women in their conception of modern womanhood. As seen in previous chapters, writings by Han Chinese women considered only Western women or prominent historical female paragons in China's distant past worthy of emulation or at a higher level in a symbolic hierarchy. Non-Han ethnic women, if mentioned at all, were often put at a lower level in that hierarchy. For example, in 1907 *Zhongguo xin nüjie zazhi* serialized a lengthy essay on the conditions of non-Han ethnic women (except for Western women) in various parts of the world, including Central and South Asia, Africa, and South America.[72] The author revealed that by including those suppressed, victimized, and "uncivilized" ethnic women, she intended for Chinese women to reflect on their own sorrowful subjugated state.[73] However, Han women's envisioning of modern womanhood and nationhood rarely invoked or featured non-Han Chinese women.[74]

Nevertheless, Manchu women saw themselves as part of the newly recognized subordinated category of "women" and allied themselves with their contemporaneous Han sisters in gender terms. Although their attitudes toward the long-held Confucian doctrines might have differed, as shown by Foying's departure from Huixing's invocation of Confucian virtues, like Han reform-minded women, they believed in the transformative power of women's education in preparing new roles for them in the new context of the nation.

---

71 Xingyong 興永, "Yanshuo nüzi zhi waixiang 演說女子之外相 [Speech on Women's External Appearance]," *Huixing nüxue bao* 15 (July 2, 1909).

72 For a detailed discussion of how non-Western women were represented in a negative light in the Chinese women's periodical press as "backward" and "primitive," see Bailey, "Chinese Women Go Global."

73 Zhuan Kun 轉坤, "Furen daiyu lun 婦人待遇論 [On Women's Conditions]," *Zhongguo xin nüjie zazhi* 1–5 (1907).

74 Non-Han women in China did appear in late Qing literary works and were usually represented as a combination of exoticism and differing degrees of "Chinese-ness." For example, the late Qing popular novel *Niehai hua* 孽海花 [*Flower in a Sea of Retribution*] depicts two Miao women as seen by a Han official. In spite of these two Miao women's recognizable ethnic dress, they are nonetheless portrayed as having bound feet. Moreover, readers are later informed that these two Miao women were also heroic women warriors who had fought on the battlefield against the aggression of Western troops. Clearly, they were not only imbued with Han feminine qualities but also contemporary political aspirations circulating in the late Qing. See Zeng Pu 曾樸, *Niehai hua* [*Flower in a Sea of Retribution*] (Taipei: Wenhua tushu gongsi, 1990).

Similarly, they understood women's oppression as derived from unequal gender relations produced over history, rather than from ethnicity. As one Manchu woman astutely noted, "In this men's society, we women have been treated like playthings and useless creatures for thousands of years."[75] In response to such historical and gendered conditions of women, the author further contended that all men, whether Manchu or Han, should be held responsible for their domination over women.[76]

These writings by Manchu women revealed that gender, rather than ethnicity, played a visible role in their conception of a modern identity. In contrast to their male counterparts, who canonized Huixing as a Manchu nationalist heroine to assert the authenticity of their Manchu identity, female Manchu writers saw their ethnicity as neither a mechanism of distinction nor a marker of difference but, rather, as a point of departure for articulating a universal vision of women's subjugated condition across regional, ethnic, and racial boundaries. By drawing on the same vocabulary of female suffering and suppression as female Han writers, they added Manchu women to the oppressed collectivity of Chinese women—a category that often had overtones of concealing or excluding Manchu women's subjugation. In so doing, they explicitly wrote against such danger of concealment, which pointed to the emergence of a particular female subjectivity from the intersection of the nation, ethnicity, and gender.

4 Conclusion

In August 1907, *Shibao* 時報 (*The Eastern Times*) published a lengthy essay by a certain Mingyi nüshi 明夷女史 on the execution of Qiu Jin on July 15, 1907. In this article, which was later regarded by scholars as one of the earliest works contributing to her canonization as a revolutionary martyr,[77] the pseudonymous author compared Qiu's execution and Huixing's suicide:

> Huixing's death aroused a stir across the entire country, but she only possessed national spirit, whereas Qiu Jin at the same time upheld the

75 男社會上把我們女子當耍貨當廢物已經有幾千年了。 Xingyong, "Yanshuo nüxuesheng zhi zeren 演說女學生之責任 [A Public Speech on Female Students' Responsibilities]," *Huixing nüxue bao* 7 (November 8, 1908): 7.

76 Xingyong, "Yanshuo nüxuesheng zhi zeren," 7–8.

77 See, e.g., Li Xizhu 李細珠, "Qiu Jin nüxing gemingjia xingxiang de lishi jiangou 秋瑾女性革命家形象的歷史建構 [The Historical Construction of Qiu Jin's Image as a Female Revolutionary]," *Shehui kexue yanjiu* 社會科學研究5 (2007).

> principles of nationalism and had the spirit of national people. Hence her purposes were particularly great and grand, how could we let her sink into oblivion easily?[78]

As the author had wished, Qiu Jin's death attracted immense media attention. Almost all the influential national newspapers at the time reported on her execution and life story.[79] She immediately became the subject of poetry, plays, and fiction and was portrayed alternately as an innocent wronged woman and a patriotic, nationalist hero like Madame Roland.[80] Despite the variety of interpretations of motives or meanings ascribed to Qiu Jin's execution, she was hailed as the first and foremost prominent Chinese model of self-sacrificing martyrdom for public and nationalist causes.[81] Given that Qiu Jin herself had actively engaged in publicizing her iconoclastic behavior through her activities

---

78 惠興女士之死也，全國為之震動，然彼僅具國民之思想，而秋女士則舉民族之主義，國民之精神，兼而有之，其宗旨尤為大，豈可聽其湮沒乎？ Mingyi nüshi 明夷女史, "Jinggao nüjie tongbao: wei Zhejing Mingdao nü xuetang nü jiaoyuan Qiu Jin beisha shi 敬告女界同胞——為浙江明道女學堂女教員秋瑾被殺事 [Respectfully Exhort Our Female Compatriots: On the Execution of Qiu Jin, a Female Instructor at the Zhejiang Mingdao Girls' School]," *Shibao* (August 10) (reprinted in Li and Zhang, *Jindai Zhongguo nüquan yundong shiliao*, 1: 454–455).

79 Reformist and revolutionary newspapers, such as *Shibao*, *Shenbao*, and *Shenzhou ribao* 神州日報, both printed extensive reports on her. For a detailed analysis of the late Qing media coverage of her, see Xia Xiaohong, *Wan-Qing shehui yu wenhua* 晚清社會與文化 [*Late Qing Society and Culture*] (Wuhan: Hubei jiaoyu chubanshe, 2000), 209–218.

80 Xia, *Wan-Qing nüxing*, 286–325; For a discussion on the controversy over Qiu Jin's hasty and poorly managed trial procedure and the Qing officials involved in her execution, see Li Xizhu, "Qing mo minjian yulun yu guanfu zuowei zhi hudong guanxi: yi Zhang Zengyang yu Qiu Jin an wei li 清末民間輿論與官府作為之互動關係——以張曾敭與秋瑾案為例 [The Interactions between Local Government and Public Opinion in the Late Qing: The Cases of Zhang Zengyang and Qiu Jin]," *Jindaishi yanjiu* 近代史研究 2 (2004).

81 Qiu Jin's demonstrated penchant for dramatic public sacrifice encountered criticisms from both her contemporaries and later generations. For example, Lu Xun cast doubt on the effectiveness of her martyrdom and saw her spectacular sacrifice as a result of the publicity machine she was herself complicit in making. For an analysis of Lu Xun's comments on Qiu Jin's death, see Eileen J. Cheng, "Gendered Spectacles: Lu Xun on Gazing at Women and Other Pleasures," *Modern Chinese Literature and Culture* 16, no. 1 (2004); In 1937, the prominent playwright Xia Yan 夏衍 wrote a play titled *Ziyou hun* 自由魂 [*The Spirit of Freedom*]. In the play he questioned Qiu Jin's suicidal martyrdom. *Ziyou hun* was later renamed *Qiu Jin zhuan* 秋瑾傳. Scholars have analyzed the vital role that *Qiu Jin zhuan* has played in the reproductions of Qiu Jin's story. See Hu, "Gender and Modern Martyrology," 121–136; Xia Xiaohong, "Qiu Jin wenxue xingxiang de shidai fengmao: cong Xia Yan de huaju dao Xie Jin de dianying 秋瑾文學形象中的時代風貌——從夏衍的話劇到謝晉的電影 [Historical Changes in Qiu Jin's Literary Imagery: From Xia Yan's Play to Xie Jin's Movie]" in *Zhongguo xiandai wenxue congkan* 中國現代文學叢刊 4 (2009).

and writings, it is not surprising that Chinese readers for generations came to view her as a perfect modern nationalist martyr, while less-known figures such as Huixing inevitably "sank into oblivion."

As Mary Rankin has pointed out, later reproductions of Qiu Jin's story have accrued to become mythology that embellished the real facts of her life, obscuring the similarities between her story and those of other women who first demanded independence.[82] The same could also be said of her martyrdom, which became so well known that it overshadowed those of others. Huixing's suicide marked the first emblematic event in which female martyrdom for national causes was valorized as a new virtue that was essential to the ideal of modern womanhood. Martyring herself for the highly visible public and nationalist cause of the time—women's education—Huixing redefined the frameworks of the meaning of female suicide that had largely been associated with familiar interpretations of chastity martyrdom or heroic expressions of virtue in the late imperial period. At the same time, in a context in which self-sacrificial, nationalist women figures were widely circulated and reproduced, Huixing's death appealed to the public imagination of a contemporary female Chinese model who willingly sacrificed herself to turn a spotlight on the nationalist cause. As discussed above, journalistic coverage of her illustrated this process of implanting the self-willed, nationalist female martyrdom into the core of the new Chinese woman image.

The construction of Huixing as a martyr, however, was inextricably linked with the politics of ethnicity and gender. In the late Qing climate of heightened Manchu-Han tensions, Manchu reformers seized on Huixing's sensational sacrifice, accentuating her Manchu ethnicity in order to make her a recognizable Manchu nationalist heroine. On the one hand, this refashioning of Huixing's story reflected the Manchu intellectuals' own fears about losing their Manchu identity in the face of the overpowering Han race. On the other hand, these Manchu reformists' effort to build Huixing into a legitimate and "authentic" nationalist model of China contested the Han exclusiveness in the putatively unified identification of "Chinese women," providing an alternative mode of envisioning modern Chinese womanhood, one that was marked by explicitly racial politics.

In contrast to the Manchu men's insistence on highlighting their Manchu ethnicity, Huixing and her Manchu sisters identified themselves in gender terms more than in ethnic terms. By integrating their distinct gendered

82 Mary Backus Rankin, "The Emergence of Women at the End of the Ch'ing: The Case of Ch'iu Chin," in *Women in Chinese Society*, ed. Margery Wolf and Roxanne Witke (Stanford: Stanford University Press, 1975).

sufferings as Manchu women into the new universal subordinated category of "women," the female Manchu writers sought to construct a modern identity on the basis not of ethnic difference but of gender sameness. In placing Manchu women at the very heart of the new narrative of Chinese women as an oppressed collectivity, they helped redefine the discursive contours of *nüjie* as constructed by nationalist and feminist female Han writers. In the process, they articulated a new female subjectivity.

CHAPTER 4

Fashioning Hygienic Womanhood: Women's Health and Bodies in Commercial Women's Journals

In June 1911, the inaugural issue of *Funü shibao* 婦女時報 (*Women's Eastern Times*), the first commercial women's journal in China, included an article titled "Chanfu zhi xinde ji shiyantan 產婦之心得及實驗談 (On Knowledge and Experience from Women Who Have Just Given Birth)." The article was written by a woman named Qiu Ping 秋蘋. The term *shiyantan* (discussing real-life or personal experience) in the title indicates that Qiu Ping's account was based on the personal experience of childbirth by two of her friends. She began by criticizing traditional Chinese midwifery practices, which caused her friends' tragic death in childbirth. Lamenting that matters of life and death such as childbirth were in the hands of old midwives who had little knowledge about scientific biomedicine, Qiu Ping exhorted her young female compatriots to dedicate themselves to the study of modern midwifery and nursing. Using a profusion of terminologies and views from Western medicine, she recounted the changes of women's bodies in pregnancy and after childbirth. For example, she explained that "sanitization maintains women's nipple hygiene and reduces the risk of breast infection" and that a childbearing woman's uterus expanded from "two inches to the point where the stomach is," as well as describing other aspects of labor.[1]

This candid account of childbirth drew an immediate reaction from the general public. One reader wrote to the journal's editorial office and criticized the article's lack of "refinement and elegance" (*yaxun* 雅馴), qualities usually celebrated in women's literary writing. Bao Tianxiao 包天笑 (1876–1973), the editor-in-chief, waved away such criticism. He contended that the country had no shortage of women who specialized in literature and the fine arts, whereas "practical sciences" (*qieshi zhi kexue* 切實之科學) that concerned life and death and were "women's natural duties" (*nüzi zhi benfen* 女子之本分) were treated with contempt.[2] Promoting modern midwifery and nursing, Bao further declared, was one of the primary objectives of *Funü shibao*.

1 Qiu Ping 秋蘋, "Chanfu zhi xinde ji shiyan tan 產婦之心得及實驗談 [On Knowledge and Experience from Women Who Have Just Given Birth]," *Funü shibao* 1 (1911).

2 "Bianjishi 編輯室 [Editorial Office]," *Funü shibao* 2 (1911).

 | DOI:10.1163/9789004438545_006

During the 1910s, discussions on the importance of using scientific knowledge to manage and cultivate women's health filled the pages of commercial women's journals such as *Funü shibao*. The newly articulated association between women and scientific knowledge also imparted new meaning to the woman question in the early Republican era. Informed by modern Western science, contributors to commercial women's journals began to draw causal links between women's scientific learning and national revitalization and construct a scientized notion of the female body as central not only to the national polity but also to women's individual bodily practices and health in their daily existence. As Qiu Ping commented in her essay, because "women were excluded from the world of politics" (吾女子既見屏於政界), empowerment with practical, scientific knowledge thus signified a new and pragmatic means by which women could serve the new Republic.[3] A good command of scientific knowledge and skills not only would help women engage in new occupations such as modern midwifery and nursing, but, more significantly, was integral to the cultivation of "wise mothers and good wives," an ideal ardently promoted by both *Funü shibao and Funü zazhi* 婦女雜誌 (*Ladies' Journal*). In this new ideal, women were expected to manage the household and educate their children in a scientific and modern way; they were encouraged to become practitioners of domestic hygiene and education and personal hygiene for the sake of both the family and the nation.

While female authors such as Qiu Ping employed scientific knowledge to engage in open debates about women's health and bodies, male contributors, most of whom were medical professionals and students, also discussed the need for obstetrical reform and offered specific kinds of biomedically-based knowledge about women's reproductive health. But they had different emphases and approaches. Men often relied on medical expertise to instruct women in how to properly manage their health and bodies, whereas women offered explicit and detailed descriptions of women's reproductive bodies and emphasized women's bodily experience. Moreover, while men valorized a scientized understanding of the female body mainly for the sake of the prosperity of the national body, women put more emphasis on using the knowledge of biomedicine to create a new epistemology of their own gendered bodies.

In addition to this gendered tension in discussing reproduction, other tensions were also present in the mixed-gender public space of the commercial women's journals—between male editorial agendas and female authorial agency and between different visions of the "wise mothers and good wives"

3 Qiu, "Chanfu zhi xinde," 17.

ideal. This chapter explores these tensions and how they led to gendered articulations of the woman question and conceptions of new womanhood in the early Republican era. The first section examines women's important yet understudied role as agents of knowledge production, rather than objects of consumption, in the early commercial women's journals. It then investigates men's and women's distinct ways of envisioning "wise mothers and good wives" through the lens of *wesheng* 衛生 (the science of hygiene), a notion best encapsulated both men's and women's valorization of scientific knowledge. The last section illustrates the different ways in which men and women appropriated the modern science of hygiene to discuss various aspects related to women's reproductive health and bodies, including menstruation, pregnancy, childbirth, and postpartum care.

1 The Mixed-Gender Public Space of the Commercial Women's Journals: Male Editorial Agency and Female Authorial Subjectivity

Commercial women's journals appeared at a moment when women's role in the political world was becoming increasingly marginalized. In August 1912, a few months after the establishment of the new Republic, the government and the electoral laws explicitly stated that women did not have equal rights to political participation.[4] This public exclusion ignited outrage among female activists and drove them to wage campaigns against this political inequality. A number of women's journals were launched in the context of these fights for equal political rights, either organs for women's suffrage associations or mouthpieces for some leading suffragists' political agendas.[5] One of the commonly stated aims of these journals was "to promote the cause of women's suffrage," focusing on the education of women in political studies, which was considered a prerequisite for women to become enfranchised. But as the Yuan Shikai government initiated a direct campaign against women's suffrage activism in

4 Edwards, *Gender, Politics, and Democracy*, 67–69; see also Wang Jiajian 王家儉, "Minchu de nüzi canzheng yundong 民初的女子參政運動 [Women's Suffrage Movement in Early Republican China]," *Shida Lishi xuebao* 11 師大歷史學報 (June, 1983).

5 For example, *Shenzhou nübao* 神州女報 [*Shenzhou Women's News*, 1912–1913] was the organ of the Chinese Women's Assistance Society [Shenzhou nüjie gonghe xie ji she 神州女界共和協濟社], which was organized by Zhang Mojun 張默君 (1883–1965), an active member of Sun Yat-sen's Revolutionary Alliance [Tongmenghui 同盟會]. Another more radical woman activist Tang Qunying 唐群英 (1971–1937) founded *Nüquan ribao* 女權日報 [*Women's Rights Daily*, 1913] and *Nüzi baihua bao* 女子白話報 [Women's Vernacular News, 1912–1913] to promote her suffragist agenda.

November 1913, these publications were soon forced to shut down.[6] By 1914, both radical and moderate women's suffragists had lost their position in demanding sexual equality in the constitution and the right to prepare women for future political participation by educating them in politics. Compounding these defeats, the political environment in the years that followed became increasingly chaotic as Yuan died in 1916, and women were almost completely excluded from political participation at both the national and provincial level.[7] They thus began to seek roles outside the political arena and envision new womanhood befitting the new Republic.

The commercial women's periodical press thus provided a rich source of information on the new areas of knowledge and social and occupational roles for women. Thanks to the unprecedented development of the modern printing industry and commercialism, in the 1910s, publishing companies in Shanghai blossomed and engaged in vigorous competition.[8] The pressure of competition produced a profusion of periodicals featuring fiction writing, as well as an increasing fascination with women's journals.[9] By the 1910s, two of the most influential women's journals had appeared in Shanghai and fiercely vied for market share. One of them was *Funü shibao*, which was published by Youzheng Book Company (Youzheng shuju 有正書局), owned by *Eastern Times* Office (Shibao guan 時報館). The *Eastern Times* Office was run by Di Baoxian 狄葆賢 (1872–1941), an entrepreneur who was also the founder and manager of *Funü shibao*. Di had successful experience in publishing fiction journals and other popular journals and he made available to *Funü shibao* all the resources of *Shibao*, a reformist daily newspaper that he had founded in 1904, as well as financial backing from the Youzheng Book Company.[10] Di invited Bao

6 Edwards, *Gender, Politics, and Democracy*, 101.

7 During 1917 and 1918, Beijing held elections for national and provincial legislatures, but no records show that women had taken part in any of these electoral events as voters or candidates. See Edwards, *Gender, Politics, and Democracy*, 101; Andrew J. Nathan, *Peking Politics, 1918–1923* (Berkeley: University of California Press, 1976), 93–113.

8 From the 1910s to the 1930s, the Commercial Press, Zhonghua Book Company, and World Book Company were regarded as "the three legs of the tripod" and dominated publishing in Shanghai. In addition to these three publishers, numerous smaller publishing houses also competed with one another. See Christopher A. Reed, *Gutenberg in Shanghai: Chinese Print Capitalism, 1876–1937* (Vancouver: UBC Press, 2004), 212–256.

9 On the flourishing of the popular fiction in urban China in the early twentieth century, see Perry Link, *Mandarin Ducks and Butterflies: Popular Fiction in Early Twentieth-Century Chinese Cities* (Berkeley: University of California Press, 1981), 80–95.

10 For a comprehensive study of *Shibao*, see Joan Judge, *Print and Politics:* Shibao *and the Culture of Reform in Late Qing China* (Stanford: Stanford University Press, 1996).

Tianxiao, who had served as an editor at *Shibao*, to be the chief editor of *Funü shibao*, which put out twenty-one issues from 1911 to 1917.

In 1915, the Commercial Press, Shanghai's leading publisher, launched *Funü zazhi* in response to the publication of *Funü shibao*. Despite its rise and fall over the years, *Funü zazhi* proved to be the longest-standing and most successful women's journal in the Republican era, lasting until 1931. *Funü zazhi* was one of most extensively studied women's journals of the Republican era, and scholars often divided its history into four periods: the initial stage (1915–1919), during which it advocated idealized domesticity, motherhood, and marriage, through the notion of "wise mothers and good wives"; a liberal period (1920–1925), marked by questioning traditional morality; a return to the original conservatism (1926–1930); and a tentative revival of the liberal period (1930–1931).[11] *Funü zazhi* not only became the strongest competitor to *Funü shibao* but also forced other competitors to close down after a short period. For example, the strongest rival of the Commercial Press was Zhonghua Book Company, which created *Zhonghua funüjie* 中華婦女界 (*Chung Hwa Women's Magazine*) in 1915. In the face of the competition from *Funü zazhi*, however, it folded within two years.[12]

Although these commercial women's journals constituted only a small part of Shanghai's rapidly booming publishing industry, competition among publishers was extremely intense.[13] These women's journals not only emerged over

11 Nivard, "Women and the Women's Press," 38; Chiang, "Womanhood, Motherhood and Biology," 521.

12 This women's magazine was in the Zhonghua Book Company's "Eight Major Magazines" series, which covered various subjects and catered to different target readers, such as *Zhonghua xiaoshuojie* 中華小說界 [*The World of Chinese Fiction*], *Zhonghua xueshengjie* 中華學生界 [*The World of Chinese Students*], *Zhonghua shiyejie* 中華實業界 [*The World of Chinese Industry and Commerce*], *Zhonghua jiaoyujie* 中華教育界 [*The World of Chinese Education*], *Zhonghua tongzijie* 中華童子界 [*The World of Chinese Children*], *Da Zhonghua* 大中華 [*Grand China*], and *Zhonghua ertong huabao* 中華兒童畫報 [*Chinese Children's Pictorial*].

Another short-lived women's journal was *Nüzi shijie* 女子世界 [*Women's World*], which was launched by a small publisher in 1914. The editor of *Nüzi shijie* was Chen Diexian 陳蝶仙 (1879–1940), an influential newspaper publisher who also wrote romance novels and was an industrial entrepreneur. For an analysis of Chen Diexian's career as a cultural entrepreneur, see Eugenia Lean, "The Butterfly Mark: Chen Diexian, His Brand, and Cultural Entrepreneurism in Republican China," in *The Business of Culture: Cultural Entrepreneurs in China and Southeast Asia, 1900–65*, ed. Christopher Rea and Nicolai Volland (Vancouver: UBC Press, 2015); idem, "Recipes for Men: Manufacturing Make-up and the Politics of Production in 1910s China," *Osiris* 30, no. 1 (January 2015).

13 In the first thirty years of the twentieth century, publishing in Shanghai expanded sixfold. For example, in the late 1930s, the Commercial Press published as many titles every year

short period but also had similar content and sometimes featured the same authors. For example, Xu Yongqing 徐詠青 (1880–1953), a commercial artist who created half the covers for *Funü shibao*, also drew the first twelve covers for *Funü zazhi*.[14] Wang Jieliang 汪傑樑, one of the most prolific contributors to *Funü shibao*, also wrote several articles for *Zhonghua funüjie*.[15] An article on breast health by a woman named Shen Weizhen 沈維楨 was published in both *Funü zazhi* in January 1915 and *Funü shibao* in February 1915.[16] Liu Sheng 劉塍, a female educator, contributed an "Opening Statement" to the premiere issue of *Funü zazhi* in January 1915 and a similar one for the publication of *Zhonghua funüjie* in the same month. In both statements, Liu Sheng stressed the imperative of cultivating "wise mothers and good wives" in a new national setting and addressed the adversity she had endured throughout her life.[17]

As with the late Qing women's journals examined in previous chapters, early Republican commercial women's journals also constituted a unique mixed-gender public space. But this public space was characterized by a dynamic tension between male editorial agency and female authorial subjectivity. Some scholarship argues that because both *Funü shibao* and *Funü zazhi* had distinctive commercial concerns, the reformist themes these journals attempted to advocate became nothing more than lip service, and the attraction of these women's journals in fact "lay not in progressivism but in the curiosity and interest of 'new style' women."[18] In her recent seminal study of *Funü shibao*, Joan Judge noted that the journal was governed by a prominent tension between

---

as all American publishing houses, with more than a hundred magazines of fiction in the 1910s. For more details on these numbers, see Perry Link, "Traditional-style Popular Urban Fiction in the Teens and Twenties," in *Modern Chinese Literature in the May Fourth Era*, ed. Merle Goldman (Cambridge: Harvard University Press, 1977), 329; Christopher Howe, ed., *Shanghai, Revolution and Development in an Asian Metropolis* (Cambridge: Cambridge University Press, 1981), xv.

14 For analyses of Xu Yongqing's covers in *Funü shibao* and *Funü zazhi*, see Judge, *Republican Lens*, 81–88; Julia F. Andrews, "Persuading with Pictures: Cover Art and *The Ladies' Journal*," in Judge, Mittler, and Hockx, *Women and the Periodical Press*, 21–56. Some of Xu's cover images are discussed in detail in Chapter 5.

15 On Wang's articles in *Funü shibao*, see Judge, *Republican Lens*, 72–77. Wang also wrote articles in *Zhonghua funüjie*, nos. 1, 3, and 4.

16 Shen Weizhen 沈維楨, "Lun xiaobanbi yu nüzi tiyu 論小半臂與女子體育 [On Brest Binding and Women's Physical Education]," *Funü zazhi* 1 (January 1915); "Lun xiaobanbi zhi hai yu nüzi tiyu 論小半臂之害與女子體育 [On the Harm of Breast Binding and Women's Physical Education]," *Funü shibao* 16 (February 1915):.

17 Liu Sheng 劉塍, "Fakanci er 發刊詞二 [Inaugural Statement Two]," *Funü zazhi* 1 (1915); idem, "*Zhonghua funüjie* zhuci 中華婦女界祝辭 [Congratulatory Speech for *Chung Hwa Women's Magazine*]," *Zhonghua funüjie* 1 (1915).

18 Link, *Mandarin Ducks and Butterflies*, 250.

its reformist aspirations and commercial objectives.[19] The journal had a clear reformist agenda, as evidenced in the "Inaugural Statement" (Fakanci 發刊詞) by Bao Tianxiao.

The statement begins with a description of China's deplorable conditions in a global context. "In face of the European winds and American rains that invaded our sacred land," Bao wrote, "our women (*wu nüjie* 吾女界) are also deeply concerned about the increasing decline in national power and social morals and want to provide assistance." Although women's education had bright prospects, it was merely a ray of light in the "heavy haze and darkness" (*chenmai hei'an* 沉霾黑暗). Bao thus declared that the publication's first goal was to encourage "refined, bright, and reasonable ladies" (亦雅不乏明敏通達之閨彥) as well as nation-minded women to contribute their words and knowledge to awaken the nation's citizens from their slumber.

The second goal was to remove all barriers to the development of women's education. Bao stated that they included not only social and economic barriers but also millennia-old restrictive customs and morals that were deep-seated and could not be abandoned overnight. Those who were anxious to eradicate these barriers advocated radical reforms, even the abandonment of morality as if it were a pair of worn-out shoes. Taking this extreme tack hurt the development of women's education because it gave old conservatives fuel for their attacks. Bao suggested, concerned reformers, such as the editorial staff at *Funü shibao*, would regret taking such extreme positions. Instead, he declared, "This women's magazine aims to obliterate these barriers and build a broad road on which women can walk with ease and elegance!"[20]

At first glance, the invocation of feminist-inflected phrases such as "heavy haze and darkness" and its emphasis on the importance of women's education and women's writing made this foreword sound like any progressive manifesto that promulgated women as actors and agents of reforms in the late Qing feminist press.[21] But it did not continue in that vein because it soon obliquely criticized reformers who preferred a radical approach to overthrowing old morals. In his closing, Bao portrayed the bright, patriotic female writers with stereotypical images of traditional feminine beauty:

> Our land expects the collaboration of those with *dexterous weaving hands*, and our country will rely on the union of *fragrant shoulders*. National

---

19 Judge, *Republican Lens*, 6–8.

20 "Fakanci 發刊詞 [Inaugural Statement]," *Funü shibao* 1 (1911): 1.

21 On the frequent use of the expression of "darkness" in the late Qing feminist writing, see Chapter 2.

> affairs should be equally shouldered [by men and women], and national advisers can be sought in *golden boudoirs*. Do not be unworthy of the unyielding moral integrity and preserve the fervor of life in the *jade-like body*. Would all our female compatriots bloom as flowers among the national citizens on this divine and splendid land? [emphasis added][22]

The dense use of opulent classical language and vocabulary could be attributed in part to the fact that Bao was representative of the Mandarin Duck and Butterfly School (*Yuanyang hudie pai* 鴛鴦蝴蝶派) of fiction writing.[23] One prominent characteristic of this school was that its writers produced highly popular fiction by adhering to traditional written styles. But more significant, this passage reflects the journal's commercial objective. These feminized and objectified images, as shown by stock expressions such as "dexterous weaving hand," "fragrant shoulders," "golden boudoirs," and "jade-like body," could easily become commodifiable products that appealed and were sold to readers and consumers of the journal, including both men and women.[24] The juxtaposition of women as both potential subjects of national reform and objects of consumption not only discloses a profound tension between the journal's reformist agenda and its commercial orientation but also implies that male editors were the creators or delineators of textual and visual representations of women.

However, as Judge has also noted, "periodicals ultimately do much more than their editors say they will do, their publishers intend them to do."[25] Similarly, the female contributors to the commercial women's press did more than their male editors had expected them to do—revising, expanding, and even challenging the editorial agendas largely set by men. In spite of the male-prescribed editorial strategies and the dangers of commodification, they employed their

22 江山倩織手同扶，家國憑香肩共擔。平分天下事，求國士於金閨。莫負歲寒心，葆長生於玉體。凡吾同胞姊妹，其亦於此神皋繡壤， 一放此燦爛國民之花矣乎？ "Fakanci," 1.

23 Bao Tianxiao refused to identify himself as a "Mandarin Duck and Butterfly" fiction writer. See Judge, *Republican Lens*, 29.

24 Women's roles as both consumers and objects of consumption were best illustrated in the cover page of the first issue of *Funü shibao*. On the cover, two young women hold an issue of the journal and look at the cover of the issue where their own images appear. On the one hand, this self-reflexive act of gazing signifies the possibility of self-possession in the sense that they are gazing at themselves rather than being gazed at, and, on the other hand, it also implies their own complicit role in consuming their own images. This cover is treated more fully in Chapter 5.

25 Judge, *Republican Lens*, 12.

own tactics to write about their own ideas and experience. They wrote about the necessity of cultivating "wise mothers and good wives" as the male editors had laid down, but their focus was more about how this ideal would provide an alternative way for them to serve the nation, rather than using it a retreat to domesticity. They composed expository essays on themes that male editors advocated, such as adopting practical knowledge to manage the household and a biomedical approach to improving women's health, but their writings did not merely rely on the scientific or medical expertise, as most male contributors did. Rather, they infused their understanding of these topics with their daily personal experience. Female writers concurred with their male counterparts that women's reproductive health was closely linked to the well-being of the Chinese national body and that the protection and cultivation of the female reproductive body was both a medical and nationalist imperative. But they also managed to use the knowledge of scientific biomedicine, as exemplified by the notion of women's hygiene, to create a new epistemology for the female body: female hygiene not only signified the ability and power to prevent disease but, more important, it empowered individual women to understand and publicly talk about their own gendered bodies. Female writers' open discussion of the many intimate aspects of women's bodies with both medical knowledge and lived experience defied male writers' stereotypical representation of women as ignorant of and pathologically reticent about their own bodies.

2 The Ideal of "Wise Mothers and Good Wives"

The commercial women's journals remained attuned with topics on the women's movement. For example, when the women's suffrage movement was at its peak in 1912, *Funü shibao* solicited articles on the discussion of women's political rights.[26] But this kind of fascination about women's political participation did not last long, as the tide of the movement was waning. Even discussions of women's political participation were less about the importance of women's political rights than about whether they conflicted with women's natural duties, related to domesticity. An article titled "Duiyu nüzi canzheng zhi yanjiu 對於女子參政之研究 (On Women's Participation in Politics)" held that

26 *Funü shibao* organized a series of essay competitions (*xuanshang wen* 懸賞文) and the prescribed title of the competition in the sixth issue was "Shuo nüzi canzheng zhi liyou 說女子參政之理由 [Reasons for Women's Political Participation]." The editorial office also called for submissions on suffrage and women's movements. "Bianjishi 編輯室 [Editorial Office]," *Funü shibao* 6 (1912).

women's political involvement did not necessarily mean that women had to abandon their domestic responsibilities because the latter were "natural duties for women just as politics is for men" (家務為女子天職, 政事為男子天職).[27]

In the first several years of the new Republic, promoting idealized domesticity became a pervasive topic in most of the commercial women's journals.[28] The new emphasis on women's natural domestic duties was closely tied to the promulgation of the notion of "good wives and wise mothers." As one female contributor to *Funü zazhi* stated, "Is it not a woman's greatest natural duty to help her husband and to teach her son? Is it not the intention of the journal to respect this duty and make the majority of women wise wives and good mothers for the nation?"[29] Another female contributor also noted, "If there is a wise mother in the family and a good wife in the household, then the family will thrive. As the family thrives, the nation will do the same accordingly."[30] Xu Yibing 徐一冰, an expert on physical education, wrote in *Funü shibao* that a good wife was indispensable to a happy family. He maintained that cultivating good wives and wise mothers was a common objective in all the projects on women's education.[31]

The ideal of "wise mothers and good wives" (*xianmu liangqi* 賢母良妻; or sometimes taking the forms of *liangqi xianmu* 良妻賢母 and *xianqi liangmu* 賢妻良母) resonated in discussions of womanhood and motherhood in the Republican era.[32] Although the two terms *xianmu* and *liangqi* had appeared in Chinese texts as far back as the first century BCE, combining them in this way was new.[33] It had its origins in an early twentieth-century translation from the

27 Qing Meng 傾孟, "Dui yu nüzi canzheng zhi yanjiu 對於女子參政之研究 [On Women's Participation in Politics]," *Funü shibao* 8 (1912).

28 In addition to *Funü shibao* and *Funü zazhi*, *Zhonghua funüjie* also declared that a major task was to provide female students and housewives with knowledge on household tasks, such as sewing and cooking and how to raise and educate children. See "*Zhonghua funüjie* guanggao 中華婦女界廣告 [Announcement from *Chung Hwa Women's Magazine*]," *Zhonghua funüjie* 1 (1915).

29 婦女最大之天職，豈非在相夫教子？而雜誌發刊之本意，又豈非遵此職志為國中造多數之賢妻良母耶？ Liang Lingxian 梁令嫻, "Jingshu wujia jiude wei funü zazhi zhu 敬述吾家舊德為婦女雜誌祝 [Respectfully Presenting My Family Morals to *Ladies' Journal*]," *Funü zazhi* 1 (1915): 6.

30 家有賢母，室有良妻，家庭必隨之而盛昌。一家然，一國亦然。 Zhao Yuan 趙媛, "Jiating jiaoyu lu 家庭教育論 [On Family Education]," *Funü shibao* 1 (1911): 10.

31 Xu Yibing 徐一冰, "Lixiang zhong de xin jiating 理想中的新家庭 [The Ideal New Family]," *Funü shibao* 4 (1911).

32 The term *Xianmu liangqi* was first used in 1906 in a Japanese-owned Chinese newspaper published in Tianjin, *Shuntian shibao* 順天時報 [*Shuntian Times*]. See Bailey, *Gender and Education in China*, 33 and n127.

33 *Xianmu* was first used in *Zhan Guo Ce* 戰國策 [*Annals of the Warring States*] and *Liangqi* first appeared in "Wei shijia 魏世家 [History of the Wei Family]," a chronology of the

Japanese *ryôsai kenbo* 良妻賢母 (good wife and worthy mother), which was first coined in the 1880s to express the Meiji educational ideal of the modern housewife whose versatile skills in household management and child welfare made her very different from traditional upper- and lower-class women in Japan's past.[34] Because this ideology successfully connected women and the nation, familial and national duties, domestic labor and women's formal education, while highlighting the role of wife and mother, it gradually appealed to some conservative Qing officials and educators in their discussions of formal education for Chinese women.[35] However, this Japanese ideal of good wives and wise mothers did not gain currency in the first decade of the twentieth century, as the Chinese concept of "mothers of citizens" made the connection between motherhood and nationhood more explicit.

The notion of "wise mothers and good wives" came back into vogue in the new Republic. It not only gained prominence in popular discourse but also became a new ideology in the formal education for Republican women. For example, the guidelines on women's secondary education issued by the Ministry of Education in 1912 stressed that the teaching of domestic science, or "household affairs" (*jiashi ke* 家事科), was the most important component of the curriculum.[36] Another prominent new element of this Republican concept was that it took inspiration from the American republican "cult of domesticity"—a social ethic that accentuated women's roles at homes as essential to the success of families and the state. Beginning in the eighteenth century, a surge of literature in the United States focused on women's domesticity, with topics

---

aristocratic family of Wei in Sifma Qian's *Shiji* 史記 [*Records of the Grand Historian*]. Lü Meiyi 呂美頤, "Ping Zhongguo jindai guanyu xianqi liangmu zhuyi de lunzheng 評中國近代關於賢妻良母主義的論爭 [A Review of the Debates on the Ideology of Good Wives and Wise Mothers in Modern China]," *Tianjin shehui kexue* 天津社會科學 5 (1995); For an examination of the concept as a modern construct in Japan, Korea, and China, see Chen Zhengyuan 陳姃湲, "Jianjie jindai yazhou de *xianqi liangmu* sixiang—cong huigu Riben, Hanguo, Zhongguo de yanjiu chengguo tanqi 簡介近代亞洲的"賢妻良母"思想——從回顧日本、韓國、中國的研究成果談起 [A Brief Introduction to the Idea of 'Good Wives and Wise Mothers' in Modern Asia: Research Findings from Japan, South Korea, and China]," *Jindai Zhongguo funü shi yanjiu* 近代中國婦女史研究 10 (2002).

34 On the gender ideology embedded in the Japanese *ryôsai kenbo* ideal, see Sharon L. Sievers, *Flowers in Salt: The Beginnings of Feminist Consciousness in Modern Japan* (Stanford: Stanford University Press, 1983), 11–13, 22–23.

35 For a detailed discussion on how this concept traveled to China in the late Qing dynasty, see Judge, *The Precious Raft of History*, 110–114. Paul Bailey also shows how this concept was employed by the Chinese intellectuals at this time, in *Gender and Education in China*, 32–33.

36 Bailey, *Gender and Education in China*, 67–69.

ranging from mothers' responsibilities, to the principles of child rearing, women's education, and women's manners in public.[37]

Contributors to the women's journals constantly referred to this American ideal of womanhood to legitimate their imaginaries of Chinese Republican ideal wives and mothers. Yu Tiansui 余天遂, a teacher at a middle school in Shanghai, published an article in *Funü zazhi* to offer his views on women's education. He bemoaned the fact that "Chinese women's education did not focus on expanding women's knowledge but [rather] paid too much attention to women's rights." He appealed to ordinary Chinese women to develop their domestic talents, which he deemed as not incompatible with both traditional Chinese tenets on women's domesticity and Western customs. In his attempt to win over his readers by describing what he had witnessed in American families, he asserted that the development of women's rights did not conflict with women's domestic role. Even in the United States, where women's rights were the most advanced, he maintained, women also regarded helping their husbands as their fundamental duty. Evoking the traditional Chinese literati ideal of companionship, he conceptualized a romanticized American feminine ideal: "When assisting her husband in studying, she is like a good teacher; when taking good care of her husband, she is like a loving mother; when supporting her husband in life, she is like a beloved friend."[38]

Another male writer, Wang San 王三, also claimed that women's natural duty was to perform the role of "wise mothers and good wives." When criticizing extravagant, lazy women who showed little interest in domesticity, he invoked the classical female virtues of frugality, diligence, and dedication to educating their offspring. He criticized women who wanted to become members of a parliament, members of a political party, nurses, or businesswomen. He contended that these roles were limited and available to only a very small number of women. The primary responsibility for the majority of women was to learn cooking, sewing, bookkeeping, and childrearing.[39]

Whereas male writers such as Yu Tiansui and Wang San discouraged women from assuming a political and public role when promoting women's domestic virtues and responsibilities, female writers regarded the cultivation of "wise

37 Nancy F. Cott, *The Bonds of Womanhood: "Woman's Sphere" in New England, 1780–1835* (New Haven: Yale University Press, 1977), 63–64.

38 對其夫為學業上之補助，則如良師；身體上之愛護，則如慈母；生活上之扶持，則如愛友。 Yu Tiansui 余天遂, "Yu zhi nüzi jiaoyu guan 余之女子教育觀 [My Views on Women's Education]," *Funü zazhi* 1 (1915).

39 Wang San 王三, "Funü zhi tianzhi 婦女之天職 [Women's Natural Duty]," *Funü zazhi* 2 (1915).

mothers and good wives" as an alternative, effective means in place of political participation to serve the big project of national strengthening. As Liu Sheng wrote in the "Inaugural Statement" for *Funü zazhi*,

> In the past twenty years, communication between China and foreign countries has vastly increased, yet China has gradually proved inferior to other countries. [We realize that what] made Europe and America powerful in the world is not merely their strong boats and powerful guns. It is their education that cultivated wise mothers, good wives, and ladies[40] who managed the domestic realm and became the backup force for the citizenry.[41]

In more radical rhetoric, one female author made an unmistakable connection between the ideology of "wise mothers and good wives" and national salvation. In her reasoning, wise mothers and good wives could redeem their sons and husbands from the depths of immorality. Attributing the nation's economic weakness to the underdevelopment of the family economy, the author exhorted Chinese women to be frugal and productive housewives and regarded the cultivation of wise mothers and good wives as the most direct way to revitalize the nation.[42]

Whereas male authors emphasized that housewives should focus on household duties, female authors stressed the necessity for women to gain knowledge and skills beyond the domestic realm. A female student named Wu Bingyun 吳秉筠 wrote that, in addition to acquiring the practical knowledge and skills for managing a household such as sewing and cooking, female students, who would be the future "wise mothers and good wives," should not shy away from takin up other subjects such as the English language and science. Wu warned that women's future would be at risk if they did not attend to these subjects.[43]

---

40 近二十年，中外大通，形見勢絀。乃知歐美列強縱橫於世界，非徒船堅礮利也。實由賢母良妻淑女之教，主持於內為國民之後盾也。 From the 1830s to the 1840s, American magazines oriented toward "ladies" multiplied rapidly, featuring essays, stories, and suggestions with a similar domestic slant. See Cott, *The Bonds of Womanhood*, 64.

41 Liu, "Fakanci er," 3.

42 Wan Xiu 晚秀, "Xianmu liangqi zhuyi yu jiuguo wenti 賢母良妻主義與救國問題 [The Ideology of 'Wise Mothers and Good Wives' and National Salvation]," *Funü shibao* 18 (1916).

43 Wu Bingyun 吳秉筠, "Nüxue yi zhuzhong fengren pengtiao lun 女學宜注重縫紉烹調論 [The Education for Women Should Emphasize Sewing and Cooking]," *Funü zazhi* 4 (1915).

Despite these differences, both male and female writers of commercial women's journals were committed to providing specific and practical knowledge so that the ideology of "wise mothers and good wives" could be put into practice just as it had in the Confucian household manuals and instruction books for women over the course of Chinese history.[44] For example, women's virtues, such as frugality and productivity in managing the household, and the specific methods that women should employ in nursing and instructing their children continued to be featured prominently, but with a new slant. These contributors' prescriptions differed from traditional household manuals in terms of their attempts to create a new modern household doctrine underpinned by modern Western scientific knowledge. Following scientific principles in household management and education was crucial for being a modern good wife and wise mother. From the time it began publication, *Funü zazhi* featured a column on "household management" (*jiazheng* 家政), offering scientific guidance and techniques for women to manage their household more effectively and rationally.[45] In household education, scientific knowledge was just as important as household management. Joan Judge points out that *Funü shibao* unequivocally advocated a new mode of science-based family pedagogy. Both male and female authors underscored mothers' essential role in inculcating their children with scientific knowledge based on concrete experiences.[46]

The Republican concept of "wise mothers and good wives" paralleled the late Qing formulation of "mothers of citizens" in that they both underlined the centrality of women as mothers in fostering high-quality citizens. But the ways in which these two ideals were advocated varied significantly. Whereas the late Qing promoters of "mothers of citizens" tended to frame it in the terms of grand, abstract nationalist aspirations, the contributors to the Republican women's journals focused more on concrete, practical ways to realize the wise

44 On the long-held Confucian tradition of using family advice manuals and instruction books to train future wives and mothers in Chinese history, see Ebrey, *The Inner Quarters*, 118–20; Susan Mann, "Grooming a Daughter for Marriage: Brides and Wives in the Mid-Qing Period," in *Chinese Femininities/Chinese Masculinities*, ed. Susan Brownell and Jeffrey N. Wasserstrom (Berkeley: University of California Press, 2002), 95–96; Bailey, *Gender and Education in China*, 15.

45 Helen M. Schneider argues that the dissemination of scientific knowledge and women's acquisition of scientific skills enabled them to rationalize home economics in early Republican China, in *Keeping the Nation's House: Domestic Management and the Making of Modern China* (Vancouver: The University of British Columbia, 2012), 82–110.

46 Joan Judge, "Everydayness as a Critical Category of Gender Analysis: The Case of *Funü shibao* (The Women's Eastern Times)," *Jindai Zhongguo funü shi yanjiu* 近代中國婦女史研究 20 (2012): 17–24.

mothers and good wives ideal. This is not to say that the Republican ideal of virtuous motherhood and wifehood was divorced from the exigencies of social reform or national renewal; rather, its connection with national aspirations was mediated and manifested through everyday concerns and practices.[47] An unprecedented number of articles in women's journals instructed that wise mothers and good wives should adopt scientific and hygienic methods, such as bookkeeping, gardening, nutrition, and sanitization, to run their daily households.[48] Writings and discussions about women's personal hygiene and health also grew dramatically: special columns were created to offer medical advice on female reproduction such as menstruation, miscarriage, and childbirth; female readers were invited to submit questions or fill out surveys about their menstrual experience. In addition to the how-to articles and guides by medical experts and professionals, laypeople also discussed various kinds of biomedically-based knowledge to help improve women's health.

3 Women and *Weisheng* in the Household

Among the various forms of scientific knowledge, the science of hygiene (*weisheng* 衛生; lit., guarding the life) was of particular significance in the process of cultivating a good wife and wise mother. Although the term *weisheng* had existed in the Chinese classical text *Zhuangzi* 莊子 (*The Book of Master Zhuang*, third century BCE), the modern use constitutes what Lydia Liu defines as "a return graphic loan," a classical Chinese term used by the Japanese to translate the Western notion of "hygiene."[49] In her seminal study of the

47 Joan Judge points out that the concept of "experience" was central to the quotidian epistemology on which *Funü shibao*'s editorial agenda was premised and that contributors to the journal used everyday experience to connect women's daily practices with social and reform aspirations, in *Republican Lens*, 79–114.

48 Binbin Yang notes that gentry women in the late imperial period already employed medical knowledge as a practical skill to deal with their families' health issues, and, in so doing, these gentry women attempted to contribute to reforming the national body and reclaiming their centrality in China's transformation into a modern nation. Yang notes that these gentry women usually used family letters to record their day-to-day work in household management. See her "Guardians of Family Health in Qing China: From the Exemplary Wife to the Reformer," *Modern China* 40, no. 4 (2014).

49 A Japanese medical administrator in the Meiji period [1868–1912] first adopted *eisei*, a translation of *weisheng* from the Chinese Daoist classic *Zhuangzi*, to signify the system of expansive governance and administration of public health in Western countries, in which a variety of words were used to denote this system: *santé* in French; *sanitary* in English; and *Gesundheitspflege*, *Sanitäts-wesen*, or *öffentliche Hygiene* in German. See Ruth Rogaski, *Hygienic Modernity: Meanings of Health and Disease in Treaty-Port China*

changing meaning of health and disease in modern China, Ruth Rogaski points out that *weisheng* had different meanings before and after the twentieth century. Before the twentieth century, *weisheng* primarily meant maintaining one's internal balance and preserving individual well-being through disciplined behavior and a moderate regimen. However, in the early twentieth century, the connotation of *weisheng*, through the translation of countless Western scientific tracts and texts, was expanded from individual self-cultivation to public health and hygiene. The term was then used to denote state power, medical administration, and the health of the national body, becoming one of the significant ways to name China's modern conditions. Rogaski suggests "hygienic modernity" as a working translation of this new scientifically inflected concept of *weisheng*.[50]

Although *weisheng* began to develop new meanings at this juncture, the earlier understanding of the term did not disappear overnight. Lei Hsiang-lin notes that Chinese supporters of the Western notions of bacteriology and pathology still valued the importance of Chinese *weisheng*. Although they embraced the Western concept of the physical body as a medical object, they also held that the well-being of a human life not only included physical hygiene but also mental and emotional health.[51] *Weisheng* thus operated as a multivalenced concept that not only emphasized a close connection between individual health and a sanitary state but also encompassed a series of Chinese health practices employed to "guard life." *Weisheng* came to connote hygiene, health, public health, hygienic practices, self-cultivation, nutrition, and proper regimens of diet, sleeping, and physical activity.

This understanding of *weisheng* as a newly imported notion of hygiene linked to the realm of the scientific and indigenous health practices associated with the ancient Chinese notion of "guarding or maintaining one's health" was evident in the commercial women's journals. For example, *Nüzi shijie* 女子世界 (*Women's World*, 1914–1915) featured a column called "Weisheng" in all six issues, which discussed personal hygiene, practices related to health care for women and children, and specific regimens to cultivate mental

---

(Berkeley: University of California Press, 2004), 136. On *weisheng* as a "return graphic loan," see Liu, *Translingual Practice*, 290.

50 Rogaski, *Hygienic Modernity*, 1–22.

51 LeiHsiang-lin,"Weishengweihebushibaoweishengming?—Minguoshiqilingleideweisheng ziwo yu jibing 衛生為何不是保衛生命——民國時期另類的衛生、自我、與疾病 [Why Weisheng is Not about Guarding Life: Alternative Conceptions of Hygiene, Self, and Illness in Republican China]," *Taiwan shehui yanjiu jikan* 台灣社會研究季刊 54 (2004).

health.[52] *Weisheng* became a new gauge that redefined one's daily existence in the domestic arena. Many writings on *weisheng* tried to inject the scientific knowledge about health and hygiene into the households, while stressing the necessity of adhering to the ancient Chinese practice of *weisheng*. In the opening of an article titled "Jiating weisheng lun 家庭衛生論 (Household Hygiene)," the author, Song Butian 宋補天, passionately drew a picture of an ideal hygienic family in an imaginary civilized metropolis:

> In the civilized city, piles of splendid flowers are blooming, western-style houses are layered up, and mansions are closely linked with one another like clouds. These buildings are magnificent and exquisitely engraved. Bright windows and clean desks are free of fine dust. Surrounded by flowers and trees, the boulevards are as smooth as whetstones; the fresh air comes from the sky.
>
> Dressed in sleeveless clothes and high collars, the people who live in this city overflow with health and spirits. [They] eat fine grains and meat and have flourishing offspring. The young wives are contented at home; the children are waiting at the door to greet them. Sleeping, eating, and living follow a schedule—and they all take on an air of harmony and joviality. The gutters outside the walls of the houses are frequently swept and cleaned to prevent disease. When the sun sets, the electrical lights brighten all the houses—this view is more magnificent than one can draw! Ah! Isn't this exactly what a hygienic family should look like?[53]

52 These articles included: "Furu weisheng wuzhong 婦孺衛生五種 [Five Ways of Maintaining Hygiene For Women and Children]" and "Huoshi weisheng si zhong 伙食衛生四種 [Four Ways of Maintaining Hygiene Through Eating and Drinking]" in no. 1; "Furu weisheng yixihua 婦孺衛生一夕話 [Some Words on Women's and Children's Hygiene]," "Xiaoer zhi weisheng 小兒之衛生 [Young Children's Hygiene]," and "Ying'er weisheng 嬰兒衛生 [Hygiene for Infants]" in no. 2; "Ying'er weisheng 嬰兒衛生 [Infants' Hygiene]" and "Lun xiaoer jingfeng 論小兒驚風 [Fright Epilepsy among Young Children]" in no. 3; "Kanhu yinghai zhi fangzhen 看護嬰孩之方針 [Methods of Infant Care]" and "Xinli weisheng 心理衛生 [Mental Hygiene]" in no. 4; "Niuru yu weisheng 牛乳與衛生 [Cow Milk and Hygiene]" in no. 5; "Ru'er weisheng tan 乳兒衛生談 [On Infants' Hyiene]" and "Shiwu zhi ziran weisheng 食物之自然衛生 [Foods That Are Naturally Good for Hygiene]" in no. 6, *Nüzi shijie* 女子世界 1–6 (December 1914–July 1915).

53 文明之都，花團錦簇，洋樓層疊，大廈雲連，建築宏偉，雕刻優美，明窗淨几，不染纖塵。道平如砥，環植花木，清新之氣，來自天空。此中人士，禿袖高襟，風采奕奕。食粱肉，長子孫，少婦歡於室，稚子候於門。眠食起-居有時，咸帶一種雍和愉悅之色。墻外溝洫，　不時泗掃，以防疫於未至。殘暉既墜，電光齊然，氣象光昌，逾於畫焉！嘻！此非衛生家之現象耶？ Song

For Song, *weisheng* embodied civilization and modernity, encompassing various aspects of one's everyday life, from a clean living environment and healthy lifestyle to modern facilities. More important, this imaginary hygienic family produced robust offspring. The desire for a hygienic family in a modern civilized wonderland reflected concern over the prevailing unhygienic conditions in China at the time and intellectuals' struggle to achieve a hygienic modernity.

Song gave detailed instructions on how a family could achieve a hygienic state. All routine daily practices, such as eating, drinking, dressing, bathing, exercising, and even smoking and putting on makeup, had to comply with *weisheng* principles. He contended that, although the ideal of *weisheng* was a new invention from Western countries, China had ancient wisdom such as "taking care of one's health in harmony with Heaven" (*yiyang tianhe* 頤養天和) and "preventing unhealthful habits at the outset" (*fangweidujian* 防微杜漸).[54] Combining modern Western hygienic philosophy with Chinese concepts of "nurturing life" (*yangsheng* 養生), Song affirmed that a family's hygienic condition ultimately rested on women's practice of *weisheng*.

Song thus prescribed a series of *weisheng* practices, including diet, bathing, adornment, exercise, and ways of avoiding unhealthful habits. Song addressed these practices in relation to women in general and pregnant women in particular. For instance, he asserted that frequent bathing would improve pregnant women's blood circulation and vitality and recommended that they apply alum lotion to their nipples after bathing to reduce the pain caused by future breastfeeding. In the section titled "Ornaments with Regard to *Weisheng*," he called women's use of cosmetics as unhygienic because the rouge and powder inhibited the blood circulation in their faces and blocked vessels through which their vital energy flowed. Because of the consequent weakness in their blood, women were compromising their health and their ability to have healthy and bright children who would benefit the Chinese nation and race.[55] This pervasive fear of deficiency in women's blood was also reflected in the extensive advertisements on products that "nourished blood (*buxue* 補血)."[56]

Butian 宋補天, "Jiating weisheng lun (yi) 家庭衛生論 (一) [On Family Hygiene (1)]," *Funü shibao* 10 (1913): 6.

54 Song, "Jiating weisheng lun," 10.

55 Song, "Jiating weisheng lun," 9.

56 Another popular product for strengthening blood that was frequently advertised in the commercial women's press at this time was "manmade blood" [*renzao zilai xue* 人造自來血], a tonic invented by a Chinese pharmacist and sold in Western-style bottle with a Chinese label. For a discussion of this product and its marketing strategies in China, see Sherman Cochran, *Chinese Medicine Men: Consumer Culture in China and Southeast Asia* (Cambridge: Harvard University Press, 2006), 71–74.

For example, Dr. Williams' Pink Pills for Pale People, a blood-fortifying patent medicine manufactured in Canada in the late nineteenth century, were advertised in most issues of *Funü shibao*.[57] Using a testimonial advertising technique, Dr. Williams' Pink Pills targeted women as their main audience and promised good wives and wise mothers that they would become physically vibrant.

Whereas Song Butian devoted great attention to the physical aspects of women's daily practice of *weisheng*, a female contributor to the "Household Hygiene" column had a different focus. Writing under the name of Mu Lan 慕蘭 (a homophone of the name of the woman warrior Hua Mulan), this author emphasized the need to pay attention to the psychological and mental aspects of women's hygiene. She wrote that, unlike men who could have pastimes outside the home, women were confined to the domestic arena and were more susceptible to depression. She thus called for women to avoid books and activities that would cause anxiety or negative emotions.[58]

Both male and female contributors to women's commercial journals highlighted the importance of *weisheng* for women in fulfilling their domestic roles as mothers, wives, and caretakers for the elderly, but with evident differences in their writing and modes of thinking. For example, an article by a male contributor to the second issue of *Funü shibao* explained the necessity and exigency of having housewives study medicine in order to protect the well-being of family members, especially their children. The male author Feng Shi 風石 encouraged women to understand both the principles of *weisheng* and the properties of medicine because understanding the former helped to prevent

57 Dr. Williams' Pink Pills claimed to cure a wide variety of ailments such as stomachache, physical weakness, postpartum symptoms, and irregular menstruation. In Chinese medicine, the underlying cause of all of these physical complaints was weak "blood." Chinese medicine's long-standing preoccupation with tonics that "boosted blood" made China a readymade market for Pink Pills.

In the early twentieth century, Dr. Williams' Pink Pills were extensively advertised and marketed not only in Western countries but also in China. By the 1920s, imports of the product to China had doubled. See Emily Baum, "Health by the Bottle: The Dr. Williams' Medicine Company and the Commodification of Well-Being in *Liangyou*," in *Liangyou: Kaleidescopic Modernity and the Shanghai Global Metropolis, 1926–1945*, ed. Paul G. Pickowics, Shen Kuiyi, and Zhang Yingjin (Leiden: Brill, 2013), 83–84. On the creator of this patent medicine, see Lori Loeb, "George Fulford and Victorian Patent Medicine Men: Quack Mercenaries or Simlesian Entrepreneurs?" *Canadian Bulletin of Medical History* 16 (1999). For an analysis of Dr. Williams' Pink Pills advertisements in Chinese newspapers in the 1920s, see Rogaski, *Hygienic Modernity*, 227–230.

58 Mu Lan 慕蘭, "Jiating weisheng lun (er) 家庭衛生論 (二) [On Family Hygiene (2)]," *Funü shibao* 10 (1913).

disease at its inception whereas knowing the latter would cure disease after it was contracted. Using the language of biomedicine, the author asserted that "the study of food hygiene" (*shiwu weishengxue* 食物衛生學) was an urgent task for housewives, as it constituted a key part of nursing and childrearing. "Sixty or 70 percent of diseases are caused by the food one eats," Feng Shi stated. "After impurities and microorganisms combine in the blood, they become the vehicle for disease."[59] Feng Shi thus encouraged women to specialize in gynecology, obstetrics, and pediatrics and pay particular attention to diseases of the reproductive system.

Whereas Feng Shi spoke prescriptively in his call for women to practice household hygiene and wrote from the premise that most women were ignorant of scientific knowledge and skills concerning hygiene, some female contributors challenged such views. They not only provided detailed scientific instructions on the topic of household hygiene but also represented women as ideal practitioners of *weisheng* knowledge and philosophy. One of these contributors was Wang Jieliang, a frequent writer in *Funü shibao*.[60] Wang was a graduate of the Chengdong Girls' School in Shanghai and then worked as teacher at an elementary school in Nantong, Jiangsu province. Wang wrote several essays instructing women to assume the role as guardian of family hygiene and health. One of her essays, for example, offered women specific scientific advice on selecting foods for the health of the family with a set of techniques and dietetic regimens.[61] Claiming that improper or unscientific diet was one of the major external factors that gave rise to diseases, she identified different categories of foods that were beneficial to one's health and advised moderation and seasonality in the foods consumed:

---

59 Feng Shi 風石, "Nüzi yi zhuzhong yixue shuo 女子宜注重醫學說 [Women Should Focus on Medicine]," *Funü shibao* 2 (1911).

60 Wang published eight essays in *Funü shibao* from 1911 to 1912, touching on a wide array of topics, including women's education, professions, and women's hygiene and reproductive health. She was the second-most-published female writer after Jiang Renlan 江紉蘭, whose publications included poetry, lyrics, and polemical essays. See Chiou Chun-ming 邱俊明, " 'Jia you xianmu, shi you liangqi': *Funü shibao* (1911–1917) jiating jiaoyu chutan 「家有賢母，室有良妻」:《婦女時報》(1911–1917) 家庭教育討論初探 ['A Wise Mother in the Home, A Good Wife in the Room': A Preliminary Examination of the Discussion of Family Education in *Funü shibao*, 1911–1917]" (M.A. Thesis: Taiwan University, Department of History, 2010), 26; Judge, *Republican Lens*, 73–77.

61 Wang Jieliang 汪傑樑, "Lixiang de jiating mofan 理想的家庭模範 [Ideal Family Model]," *Funü shibao* 5 (1912).

> Drinking and eating are fundamental for life. If one does not moderate but [rather] indulge in an insatiable desire for food, disease will invade the body and even be harmful. Therefore, one should be careful to choose different kinds of foods and moderate mealtimes, to avoid damaging one's health. Among [non-meat] products, the five grains, vegetables, and fruit are sufficient for bodily health; among animal products, meat and milk are sufficient for nourishment. The major ingredients needed for nourishment are simply protein, fat, and starch. Protein is the most important of the three … mealtime must be consistent and must not exceed three times a day. A mother must eliminate things that are incompatible with hygiene and reject children's insatiable requests.[62]

This passage incorporated knowledge on the Chinese notion of *yangsheng*, which Rogaski defines as "a set of techniques that were specifically developed to prevent disease, harmonize body vitalities, and prolong life,"[63] and scientific knowledge on food and health imported from the West, as evidenced by Wang's use of terms such as "protein," "fat," and "starch." Wang thus instructed housewives to learn about edible ingredients in a scientific way in order to prevent the family from contracting diseases.

Wang also wrote two essays that expounded on the scientific and hygienic rules that a mother should follow in taking care of her children. The first essay, titled "Xiaoer bayu fa 小兒保育法 (How to Take Care of Young Children)," addressed a wide range of important issues concerning child care, including the advantages of breastfeeding, the choice of cow's milk, foods, and clothing, and the appropriate sleeping hours for infants. Wang was an ardent advocate of breastfeeding and contended that milk from a wet nurse would undermine a child's development. Wang further argued that breastfeeding benefited not only the child but also the mother, which, she wrote, had been proven by Western doctors. Wang also listed the nutritional components of cow's milk and

62 故飲食者，人之生活根原也。但若猥迷於口腹之欲而不知成慎，則疾病隨之而至，甚至猶傷害其生命者。故食物之種類，不可不選擇。而食物之時間，亦不可不節制。使於生理上無所妨害。曰五穀，曰蔬菜，曰果實，植物中之足以滋養身體者也。曰肉類，曰乳汁，動物中之足滋養身體者也。而此滋養之原料，不外蛋白質、脂肪、小粉三-種而已。三者之中，又以蛋白質為最要......其時間宜限定一致，每日以三次為度。其他如不合於衛生之事項，兒童無厭之請求，務宜擯斥。 Wang, "Lixiang de jiating mofan," 4.

63 Rogaski, *Hygienic Modernity*, 25.

deemed it supplementary to human milk.[64] The second essay, "Xiaoer jibing kanhu fa 小兒疾病看護法 (How to Care for Sick Children)," offered concrete suggestions on taking care of sick children. She identified over ten kinds of diseases that young children tend to contract and provided detailed descriptions of the symptoms of each disease. She advised mothers to adopt scientific measures and technologies, such as using a mercury thermometer to take a temperature and ensuring that their infants received vaccinations.[65]

Another female writer named Zhao Yuan 趙媛 also outlined concrete and strict guidelines for women to follow so as to ensure the well-being of their children. For example, she painstakingly recorded the parameters of daily frequency in a mother's feeding of her baby: a mother should breastfeed every two hours, and each feeding session should last approximately twenty minutes. When the baby was able to eat rice, then each meal should not be over half a bowl, and the rice must be soft. Mothers should moderate the duration of children's rest: the maximum number of hours for children to sleep should not exceed twelve hours. In particular, a mother was responsible for inculcating in her children knowledge of hygiene so that they could develop hygienic habits and respect their own bodies.[66]

The ways in which mothers and wives practiced *weisheng* in the home might have been similar to what many individuals did in order to be healthy before the twentieth century, but now they were instructed to practice *weisheng* for a fundamentally different end. The objective of their practice of *weisheng* was to strengthen the health of the family, which was foundational for the well-being of the Chinese nation and the attainment of Chinese modernity. This *weisheng* was no longer an individual's pursuit of health, separate from the social or political context but, rather, signified China's modern condition through the improvement of family hygiene. As Mu Lan declared, "*Weisheng* cannot be obtained only through one person's ability, it has to be followed and practiced by the entire family. In so doing, the efficacy of *weisheng* becomes pronounced."[67] Mothers and wives thus played a mediating role in facilitating the family's ability to achieve a hygienic state.

Under the new rubric of the modern science of hygiene, Chinese women were simultaneously required to be practitioners of domestic hygiene and

---

64 Wang Jieliang, "Xiaoer bayou fa 小兒保育法 [How to Take Care of Young Children]," *Funü shibao* 2 (1911).

65 Wang Jieliang, "Xiaoer jibing kanhu fa 小兒疾病看護法 [How to Care for Sick Children]," *Funü shibao* 3 (1911).

66 Zhao, "Jiating jiaoyu lun," 9.

67 Mu, "Jiating weisheng lun," 11.

transmitters of knowledge of hygiene to their children. Consistent with the concept of mothers of citizens, the cultivation of Republican wise mothers prioritized the strengthening of the female body in order to strengthen the race. Beginning in the late nineteenth century, countless texts directly tied the mothering of able-bodied citizens to women's physical cultivation. In the early Republican commercial women's journals, the development of mothers' physical health centered on the science of hygiene and was closely woven into the fabric of women's everyday life. Women were mobilized to engage in a wide variety of practices such as women's personal hygiene, dietary routines, and exercise in their daily lives to produce strong citizens. One author, Hui Yuan 悔原, lamented that Chinese women's unhygienic habit of infrequent bathing had affected the production of fit and healthy descendants.[68] He asserted that only if women kept their bodies clean and hygienic could they generate strong citizens and further strengthen the race. "Children inherit only 2 percent from their father's blood, but they inherit over 90 percent from their mother's blood," the writer claimed. "It is impossible for their sons to be clean and robust if women reek and are emaciated."[69] Another author, Shu Zi 叔子, maintained that women had an obligatory duty to produce healthy progeny. The improvement in women's reproductive health thus should be elevated as a national task.[70]

A mother's hygiene habits would also impart to her children correct ideas about hygiene and have an imperceptible impact on the formation of their character. As one author asserted, "Practicing hygiene in everything is the beginning of family education" (凡事衛生, 即家庭教育之發軔也).[71] The emphasis on hygiene in family education pedagogy required a mother to be a moral instructress as well as a teacher of science and hygiene. By practicing the science of hygiene as well as inculcating her children with the knowledge on how to be hygienic, she would raise not only upright sons but also healthy and hygiene-conscious modern citizens.

4 Women's Hygiene and Reproductive Health

Although concern about women's reproductive health and medical specialization in diseases affecting women had developed in imperial China, it was

68 Hui Yuan 悔原, "Lun funü weisheng shang bixu zhi yingye 論婦女衛生上必須之營業 [Rules That Must Be Followed on Women's Hygiene]," *Funü shibao* 10 (1913).

69 Hui, "Lun funü weisheng," 24.

70 Shu Zi 叔子, "Furen zhi wesheng 婦人之衛生 [Women's Hygiene]," *Funü zazhi* 8 (1915): 6.

71 Song, "Jiating weisheng lun," 10.

the sweeping import of Western biomedicine that led Chinese intellectuals to accept a medicalized view of the female body in the early twentieth century.[72] By the 1910s, "women's hygiene" (*funü weisheng* 婦女衛生) had emerged as a new arena for discourse on women's reproductive health and bodies. Discussions on women's reproductive health under the rubric of "women's hygiene" abounded in commercial women's journals. Male and female authors, including medical practitioners and lay people, actively employed the knowledge of Western biomedicine and sanitary science to offer technical know-how on matters ranging from menstrual cramps and bleeding to choices in sanitary napkins, childbirth, and prenatal and postpartum care.

The existing scholarship shows that, in the context of imperialist aggression and global biomedical reform in the late nineteenth century, the meaning of the Chinese term *weisheng*, which primarily referred to maintaining healthy by following certain ways of living in accordance with seasonal and environmental variations, began to shift from "personal hygiene" to "public health," in which the individual body became an integral part of the national body.[73] In this context, women's reproductive health was closely linked to the prosperity of the Chinese national body, and the protection and cultivation of the female reproductive body was not just a medical or moral imperative, as it had been in the late imperial period, but more importantly a political and nationalist imperative.[74]

In the early Republican period, a notable shift took place, however. Although women's reproductive health was still promoted as a linchpin in the epic, grand project of national strengthening, the ways in which it was talked about began to change substantially. It was now woven into the fabric of women's everyday life, with much emphasis on women's individual bodily experience. Discussions on women's reproductive health and bodies were filled with scientific

---

72 Charlotte Furth, "Rethinking van Gulik: Sexuality and Reproduction in Traditional Chinese Medicine," in *Engendering China: Women, Culture and the State*, ed. Christina K. Gilmartin, Gail Hershatter, Lisa Rofel, and Tyrene White (Cambridge: Harvard University Press, 1994), 125–146. For more discussion on how the introduction of western medical science reformulated the ideologies of gendered bodies in modern China, see Frank Dikötter, *Sex, Culture and Modernity in China: Medical Science and the Construction of Sexual Identities in the Early Republican Period* (London: Hurst 1995).

73 Rogaski, *Hygienic Modernity*.

74 On the well-being of women's reproductive body as a long-standing medical and moral imperative in China, see Angela Ki Che Leung, "Recent Trends in the Study of Medicine for Women in Imperial China," *Nan Nü: Men, Women and Gender in China* 7, no. 2 (2005); Yi-li Wu, *Reproducing Women: Medicine, Metaphor, and Childbirth in Late Imperial China* (Berkeley: University of California Press, 2010).

terminologies and ideas from Western biomedicine, such as the principles of germ theory, anatomy, and physiology. The increased interest in applying biomedical knowledge to the discussion of the female body also marked a distinct departure from the late Qing intellectuals' discourse on women's physical culture. Denise Gimpel notes that late Qing nationalist intellectuals were more concerned about imbuing women's physical development with moral and political urgency than providing specific measures in scientific terms for women to realize an ideal healthy physical state.[75] You Jianming also points out that the promotion of women's physical cultivation in the late Qing largely served as a synecdoche of China's national health and strength. Discourses on women's physical health were often more about the "purposes of women's physical cultivation" than about the cultivation of the female body per se.[76]

For contributors to the early Republican commercial women's journals, the female body, however, was a biological entity that could be legitimately exposed to public discussion and medical scrutiny. Scientific and biomedical knowledge provided women with concrete and pragmatic means, rather than abstract theories, to find out about their own gendered bodies. Moreover, these understandings of the female body were based on women's specific, individual daily experiences and involved the self-care activities needed to manage their personal health. The intensive writing and discussion surrounding the topic of "women's hygiene" attested to this increased public attention on women's individual health, working to generate an alternative conception of the female body—that is, the protection and well-being of the female body was not only essential to the creation of a hygienic modern nation but of paramount significance in their own right.

Both *Funü shibao* and *Funü zazhi* emphasized the need to improve women's reproductive health. As discussed at the beginning of this chapter, Bao

75 See, e.g., in her discussion of the noted nationalist and feminist writer Chen Xiefen's 1903 article "Lun nüzi yi jiang tiyu 論女子宜講體育 [Women Should Pay Attention to Physical Cultivation]," Denise Gimpel argued that "physical culture," rather than "physical cultivation," was a more appropriate English translation for *tiyu* because Chen did not really touch on any of the curricular activities to which "physical education" usually refers. See her "Freeing the Mind through the Body: Women's Thoughts on Physical Education in Late Qing and Early Republican China," *Nan Nü: Men, Women and Gender in China* 8, no. 2 (2006); For similar views on Chen's article, see Fan Hong, *Footbinding, Feminism and Freedom: The Liberation of Women's Bodies in Modern China* (London: Frank Cass, 1997), 89–90.

76 You Jianming 游鑑明, *Yundongchang nei wai: jindai Huadong diqu de nüzi tiyu, 1895–1937* 運動場內外: 近代華東地區的女子體育（1895–1937） [*On and Off the Playing Fields: A Modern History of Physical Education for Girls in Eastern China, 1895–1937*] (Taipei: Zhongyang yanjiuyuan jindaishi yanjiusuo, 2009).

Tianxiao stipulated that women's obstetrical health was one of the primary concerns on his editorial agenda. Articles on women's reproduction and health frequently appeared in *Funü zazhi* and were often grouped under the regular columns of "Jiazheng men 家政門 (Gate of Domestic Science)" and "Xueyi men 學藝門 (Study of Skills)." The two journals published contributions not only by medical practitioners who worked in the fields of obstetrics and gynecology and were dedicated to China's biomedical reform but also by lay people who had little formal medical education or training but were keen to offer advice on women's health. Women also actively participated in public discussions of matters related to women's reproduction, but, except for a few, most of them had no medical training.

Both male and female contributors valorized biomedical expertise in their discussions about women's reproductive health and bodies, but they often took distinctive approaches. Male writers, most of whom were medical practitioners or students, tended to use medical terms and vocabulary, sometimes in English, to explicate the causes and symptoms of female conditions such as menstruation, pregnancy, and childbirth, whereas female writers employed a more accessible medical language and shared their personal experiences or observations regarding the management of these conditions with their readers. Another notable characteristic of men's writing was that they often prescribed solutions in an authoritative and assertive tone and portrayed Chinese women as ignorant of and reticent about their own ailments. Female authors made no comment on men's portrayal of these matters, but their candid and detailed writings about women's gendered bodies defied men's negative representation and testified to women's agency in creating their own discourse and defining their gendered bodies.[77]

4.1 *Menstruation*

The first important concern in women's reproductive health was menstruation. Late imperial texts about gynecology and "women's medicine" (*fuke* 婦科) had already emphasized the vital role of menstruation in indicating the overall economy of women's bodily vitality. Menstruation was understood as one of the most prominent manifestations of *xue* 血 (Blood), a primary bodily vitality often paired with *qi* 氣 (vital energy).[78] Late imperial discourse regarded

77 Joan Judge makes a similar observation about the tension between men's and women's views about female reproductive bodies in *Funü shibao*, in *Republican Lens*, 115–117.

78 In Chinese medicine, Blood (*xue*) was understood as bodily vitality that could not be reduced to a material fluid. It is different from the biomedical idea of blood as a red liquid that circulates in vessels from the heart throughout the body; rather, it is the *yin* aspect

regular menstruation as the most visible indicator of a woman's general health and held that that the regulation of women's menses required intensive attention to both women's physical and emotional well-being.[79] Republican commentators continued to stress the importance of menstrual regulation and designed regimens to correct irregular menstrual cycles, as late imperial physicians had done, but they referred to biomedicine and openly discussed the methods and techniques in managing women's menses.

One of most vocal advocates of the importance of women's menstrual care was Qu Jun 瞿鈞 (1888–1960), a well-trained physician who specialized in gynecology and obstetrics. Qu graduated from Osaka Senior Medical School in Japan in 1916 and spent much time popularizing medical knowledge about women's reproductive health under the rubric of "women's hygiene."[80] In his article "Funü weisheng zhi yiban 婦女衛生之一斑 (Some Views on Women's Hygiene)," published in *Funü shibao* in 1911, he devoted great attention to the importance of managing women's menstruation scientifically.[81] At the beginning of the essay, he rebuked the deep-seated custom that considered women's menstrual discharges "dirty and polluting" (*huizhuo* 穢濁). He noted that Chinese women were reticent to broach the topic of menstruation even to their female friends, let alone to their husbands or doctors. Stating that menstruation was a natural physiological phenomenon of the female body that occurred every four weeks, Qu encouraged women to take special care of their bodies during their menstrual periods. He provided a detailed list of the physical and emotional conditions specific to menstruating women, including low back pain, abdominal pain, headache, toothache, breast swelling and pain, excessive emotionality, and irritability.

What marked Qu's discussion of menstruation was his meticulous advice on the management of women's menstrual flows. Whereas late imperial gynecologists were collectively silent about the disposal of menstrual fluids, Qu

---

of bodily *qi*, a basic quality of the energy material that exists all human beings. Blood is particularly crucial in the health problems of women. See Charlotte Furth, "Blood, Body and Gender: Medical Images of the Female Condition in China, 1600–1850," *Chinese Science* 7 (1986); idem, *A Flourishing Yin: Gender in China's Medical History, 960–1665* (Berkeley: University of California Press, 1998).

79 Wu, *Reproducing Women*, 89.

80 For an analysis on how Qu integrated Chinese women's menstruation histories into the existing global biomedical knowledge of women's hygiene, see Judge, *Republican Lens*, 132–134.

81 Qu Jun 瞿鈞, "Funü zhi weisheng yiban: yuejing zhi zhuyi/renshen zhi baoyang 婦女之衛生之一斑：月經之注意/妊娠之保養 [Some Views on Women's Hygiene: Paying Attention to Menstruation/Care During Pregnancy]," *Funü shibao* 3 (1911).

prescribed practical and hygienic instructions for women to follow. He instructed them to abandon the coarse and unhygienic paper that they often used to collect their menstrual blood and instead use absorbent and sanitary cotton. He also suggested that Chinese women place the absorbent, sterilized cotton in front of, rather than inside, their vulva so as to avoid infection. The most effective way of managing menstrual flow, Qu Jun advised, was to use the "cloth menstrual pads" (*yuejing dai* 月經帶) that were popular among Western women. Cloth pads had rubber on one side and cloth filled with cotton on the other. Such menstrual pads, he stated, would cause little harm to women's health.[82]

Another article by Qu in *Funü shibao* focused on the need to devote particular attention to the psychological well-being of menstrual women. He pointed out that menstruating girls were susceptible to negative and excessive emotions and were prone to "hysteria" (*xi si dai yi* 希死代伊).[83] Hysteria was a modern European medical term used to describe extreme mental disorders such as hypersensitivity, emotional instability, a tendency to frequent depression, and all kinds of deviant behavior.[84] Whereas in classical Chinese medical thinking, emotional pathology was considered a symptom of the entire body-spirit, the modern European notion of hysteria suggested a separate psyche whose emotional disorders were expressed in displaced bodily manifestations.[85] Warning against the dangers of female hysteria, Qu Jun suggested that one should be particularly vigilant and provide correct emotional and moral guidance for girls who were pursuing studies away from home when they had their first menstrual cycle.[86]

In addition to portraying Chinese women as silent about and incapable of dealing with the physical discomfort incurred by menstruation in general, Qu Jun also believed that women lacked the knowledge and competence to manage their menstrual emotions. His instructions on caring for pregnant women made even more explicit the necessity of male intervention. He stated that

82 Qu, "Funü zhi weisheng yiban," 26–27.

83 The term was written as "Hpstherie" in the article. Qu Jun, "Furen zhi weisheng zahua 婦人之衛生雜話 [Miscellaneous Comments on Women's Hygiene]," *Funü shibao* 4 (1911).

84 On discussions of hysteria as a gendered disorder in the Republican era, see Dikötter, *Sex, Culture and Modernity in China*, 48–51; Emily Baum, *The Invention of Madness: State, Society, and the Insane in Modern China* (Chicago: University of Chicago Press, 2018), 168–170.

85 For a discussion on the difference between Chinese medical ideas on the body and emotion and Western psychosomatic illnesses, see Furth, *A Flourishing Yin*, 87–91.

86 Qu, "Furen zhi weisheng zahua," 18.

husbands should provide their childbearing wives with emotional support and comfort and not blame their wives even when they made mistakes.[87] Although Qu prescribed "how-to" knowledge and practices for women to properly manage their menses, it also appears that the readers he actually wanted to address were men. After all, men were more likely to understand the dense biomedical vocabulary in Qu's essay and then instruct their wives in hands-on hygienic practices and techniques.

Women were far from being silent about or ignorant of matters related to women's reproductive health, as Qu Jun had suggested, however. For example, "Funü weisheng tan 婦女衛生談 (On Women's Hygiene)," published in 1915 in *Funü zazhi*, suggests that the female contributor Shen Fang 沈芳 was savvy about the modern medical understandings of women's reproductive health. In anatomical and biomedical terms, she remarked that exposure to cold wind while they were menstruating might cause women to suffer from inflammation of the uterus and that thorough sterilization should be enforced while a woman was in childbirth. In great detail, she offered concrete routine health practices for women during menstruation, pregnancy, and childbirth, including how to eat, sleep, dress, bathe, maintain breast health, and regulate sexual intercourse.[88] All the information on each practice was offered in an accessible way. The author directly addressed female readers at the beginning of the essay, as she called on them to master knowledge on women's hygiene.[89]

Female contributors also actively wrote about the use of scientific methods to manage women's health during pregnancy. For example, a female author named Chen-Yao Zhiping 陳姚稺屏 gave detailed scientific descriptions of the gestational process, fetal development, changes in the gestational body, and daily routine practices for pregnant women.[90] She also suggested medications to treat illnesses that were common in pregnancy. Chen-Yao provided the names of medications in both Latin and transliterated Chinese and offered a pregnancy wheel to help women calculate their due dates (Figure 4). Chen-Yao's use of both specialized medical language and a chart suggests that she aspired to speak publicly with scientific authority while remaining accessible to her female audience.

---

87 Qu, "Furen zhi weisheng zahua," 26.

88 Shen Fang 沈芳, "Funü weisheng tan 婦女衛生談 [Discussion of Women's Hygiene]," *Funü zazhi* 1 (1915).

89 Shen, "Funü weisheng tan," 2.

90 Chen-Yao Zhiping 陳姚稺屏, "Renshen yixi tan 妊娠一夕談 [Some Views on Pregnancy]," *Funü zazhi* 5 (1916).

FIGURE 4 Pregnancy Wheel. Chen-Yao Zhiping, "Renshen yixi tan 妊娠一夕談 (Some Views on Pregnancy)," *Funü zazhi* 5 (1916): 11.
According to Chen-Yao, the due date is calculated in two parts: the expected month of labor can be calculated by adding nine months or subtracting three months from the month of the last menstrual period; the date is determined by adding the days shown in the wheel (i.e., five, six, or seven days depending on which week of the month the last day falls on) to the first day of the last menstrual period. For example, if a woman's last menstrual period began on December 1 (a date between the third week of November and the second week of December, hence adding six days to the first day of the last menstrual period), then the expected due date should be September 7.
SOURCE: SHANGHAI LIBRARY COLLECTION

4.2 *Childbirth*

Another prominent topic that concerned women's reproduction was childbirth. Contributors writing on the subject unanimously called for adopting a biomedical approach to childbirth. For example, an author named Wang Chuanying 王傳英 wrote an essay entitled "Xin dasheng pian 新達生篇 (A New Treatise on Easy Childbirth)" for *Funü zazhi* in 1918.[91] The author declared that, although *Treatise on Easy Childbirth*, a popular text on childbirth published in China in the eighteenth century,[92] had some useful knowledge, it also had some outdated practices that were not in accordance with biomedical principles, such as the use of "old-style midwives" (*wenpo* 穩婆). A new treatise on childbirth, Wang proclaimed, thus aimed to correct the erroneous practices of old-style midwifery and provide ordinary women with useful and accessible scientific knowledge and techniques. Wang emphasized the urgency of replacing old-style midwives, who knew nothing about sterilization, with "experienced nurses who are familiar with knowledge on biology and physiology" (熟於生理，實驗有素之看護婦).[93]

Midwifery reform was often foregrounded by both men and women commentators as the first priority of early Republican childbirth reform. Qu Jun, for instance, lamented China's lack of specialized midwifery schools, which were common in Western countries and gradually established in Japan. He pointed out that professional and well-trained midwives were needed not only in childbirth but also during pregnancy. New-style educated midwives (*chanpo* 產婆), Qu claimed, would prevent women in labor from developing serious illnesses such as puerperal fever.[94]

Chen-Yao Zhiping also denounced the dangerous and unsanitary practices of ignorant and uneducated old-style midwives.[95] She noted that midwives in Western countries and Japan were required to undergo at least a year of professional training and to register, whereas Chinese midwives were simply made up of "three kinds of old aunties and six kinds of old grannies" (*sangu liupo*

91 Wang Chuanying 王傳英, "Xin dasheng pian 新達生篇 [A New Treatise on Easy Childbirth]," *Funü zazhi* 2 (1918): 1–4; 6 (1918): 4–8.

92 *Dasheng bian* 達生編 was an amateur text on childbirth first published in 1715 by an anonymous low-level literatus. The text was reproduced many times after its first appearance and continued to be reprinted well into the twentieth century. For a discussion of the treatise and its medical impact, see Wu, *Reproducing Women*, 67–83.

93 Wang, "Xin dasheng pian," *Funü zazhi* 6 (1918): 4.

94 Qu, "furen zhi weisheng zahua," 28.

95 Chen-Yao Zhiping, "Zhongguo jinri yi yangcheng chanpo lun 中國今日宜養成產婆論 [On the Necessity of Cultivating New-Style Midwives in Today's China]," *Funü zazhi* 4 (1916).

三姑六婆), who had no knowledge of physiology or anatomy. These old grannies, Chen-Yao criticized, cared only about how to make a profit from delivering babies and often resorted to brutal methods that caused the tragic death of many infants and their mothers. Chen-Yao proposed two types of reform in midwifery: the first was to establish midwifery schools and train new-style midwives and the second was to retrain old-style midwives. She suggested that the new-style midwives be taught knowledge and skills about how to deliver a baby, take care of the mother and the newborn, and sterilize equipment. Chen-Yao further advised that these new-style midwives complete a two-year course and pass examinations before they could become licensed midwives. Her advocacy of comprehensive midwifery reform preceded the Nationalist government's effort to train and register midwives during the Nanjing decade (1927–1937) by about eleven years.[96]

In writing about childbirth reform, both male and female contributors demonstrated their biomedical knowledge, albeit in varying degrees, but some female writers included personal accounts of experience in their writing to reinforce their discursive and medical authority. Qiu Ping, discussed at the beginning of this chapter, explained that she was committed to new midwifery practices because she had witnessed the death of classmates and friends from difficult births. She called her article "a miscellaneous record based on what I have seen and heard as well as stories and observations shared by my friends."[97]

Qiu Ping used her own observations in Japan to emphasize the importance of preparation for childbirth. She had once visited a noble and wealthy Japanese count, noting that he had taken all the necessary medical equipment from storage the moment his wife began to show signs of going into labor. The count was so well-equipped that he had a stretcher ready to carry his wife to a safe place in the event of a natural disaster such as an earthquake or fire. Three different kinds of lamps were prepared for use at night. The count not only was in charge of all the equipment but also devoted close attention to his wife after the baby was delivered. His attentive care was rewarded: she remained healthy and strong even after having had four children.[98] In the passage following this story, Qiu Ping discussed in detail how to manage women's postpartum

96 On the Nationalist government's efforts at midwifery reform, see Ka-che Yip, *Health and National Reconstruction in Nationalist China: The Development of Modern Health Services, 1928–1937* (Ann Arbor, MI: Association of Asian Studies, 1995), 58–59, 165–172.

97 我就見聞所及，并得諸友人所談者，拉雜誌之。 Qiu, "Chanfu xinde ji shiyantan," 17.

98 Qiu, "Chanfu xinde ji shiyantan," 17–18.

hygiene such as preventing breast infection. Her use of terms such as "bacteria" (*weijun* 微菌) suggests that she was familiar with germ theory.[99]

Although Qiu Ping praised the Japanese man's full preparation for his wife's delivery, she also stressed the necessity of medical intervention by specialized doctors, sharing a story of breech birth. A woman in the ninth month of pregnancy and about to have her second child was having massive labor pains. A midwife was summoned and found that the baby was in a breech position (i.e., feet first). The woman in labor was bleeding heavily, and she had dilated sufficiently for the umbilical cord to drop out. The midwife was unable to deliver the baby, and a specialist was called in. Using sterile cotton, the doctor gently repositioned the fetus and saved the life of both mother and child. Qiu Ping continued to list examples in which a medical professional was urgently needed, such as in cases of premature birth, premature rupture of the amniotic sac, breech birth, umbilical cord prolapse, excessive labor pain, and the prolapse of all four limbs of the fetus.[100]

Xiao Yun 笑芸, another female author, also wrote about how to care for women who had just given birth.[101] She began by stating that she had heard many stories about women who had died in and just after childbirth. Out of sympathy for these women, she searched for useful knowledge, gathered accounts of experience, and consulted medical texts so as to provide them with advice. She used less biomedical terms than Qiu Ping and described both scientific know-how and traditional Chinese medical practices to help women before, during, and after giving birth. For example, she advised midwives to closely follow the rules on cleaning and sterilization when taking care of women in labor. She explained that lack of sterilization would leave these women prey to "dangerous viruses" (*weixian bingdu* 危險病毒). She outlined the correct steps in sterilization: a piece of soft cotton that had been soaked in boiled water should be used to wipe the birth mother's wounds and, then, a piece of soft cotton soaked in 30 to 100 percent carbolic acid should be used on any wounds to be bandaged. Any unclean objects should be kept away from the woman after having given birth.[102]

Xiao Yun also detailed a variety of precautions that were in accordance with Chinese medical principles, such as proper exercise, rest, bathing, and diet. She stressed the importance of adequate rest and quiet for both the body and

---

99 Qiu, "Chanfu xinde ji shiyantan," 18.
100 Qiu, "Chanfu xinde ji shiyantan," 19.
101 Xiao Yun 笑芸, "Nüzi fenmian hou zhi kanhu 女子分娩後之看護 [Care for Women Who Have Given Birth]," *Funü shibao* 18 (1916).
102 Xiao, "Nüzi fenmian hou zhi kanhu," 54.

spirit. Xiao Yun wrote that talking about domestic matters in front of a postpartum woman was proscribed because she was in a vulnerable mental state after giving birth. Extreme and negative emotions, such as fear, anger, and resentment, or any nerve-wracking activities should be avoided.[103]

Xiao Yun's emphasis on the psychological well-being of pregnant women creates an interesting comparison with Qu Jun's advocacy of prenatal care. In his 1911 article on women's hygiene, Qu Jun contended that the cultivation of psychological health, such as maintaining calm and positive emotions, not only was important for the gestating woman but had a positive influence on the fetus, which was integral to the ancient practice of fetal education (*taijiao* 胎教).[104] For Qu Jun, managing the pregnant mother's emotional and psychological state was not so much about achieving self-cultivation for its own sake as about cultivating the fetus for the natalist, eugenicist goals of the Republican state.[105] Xiao Yun, by contrast, warned against any outside environment or stimuli that were detrimental to the new mother's psychological cultivation.

For the contributors to commercial women's journals, their promulgation of women's hygiene and reproductive health was not achieved through the enunciation of abstract, enlightened principles on strengthening women's health, as the late Qing intellectuals had done. Rather, these early Republican commentators turned to employ newly emergent scientific and biomedical knowledge to call for a modern obstetrical reform and prescribed concrete and practical instructions for general Chinese women to manage their reproductive health. The modern scientific discourse on women's hygiene and reproductive health created an alternative epistemology of the female body: women's hygiene was not only about preventing female reproductive ailments but also signified the ability of individual women to understand and manage bodies in their daily existence.

5 Conclusion

The mixed-gender public space in the early Republican commercial women's journals, marked by the tension between male editorial agency and female

103 Xiao, "Nüzi fenmian hou zhi kanhu," 54.

104 Qu, "Furen zhi weisheng zahua," 26.

105 Nicole Richardson points out that, in the 1930s, discussions on *taijiao* drew upon the new idea of eugenics and on Western science, and fetal education was for the eugenicist and natalist goals of producing healthy Chinese citizens. For a discussion of the modern discourse of *taijiao* in Republican China, see Nicole Richardson, "The Nation *in Utero*: Translating the Science of Fetal Education in Republican China," *Frontiers of History in China* 7, no. 1 (2012).

authorial subjectivity, served as a fertile ground on which both male and female contributors could employ modern scientific knowledge to promote the Republican ideal of "wise mothers and good wives." Drawing upon Western ideas on biomedicine and traditional Chinese medical principles and practices, these commentators prescribed women's new roles as scientifically informed housewives and mothers who also possessed Confucian female virtues such as frugality and diligence in modern homes. Women were reconfigured not only as effective practitioners of domestic hygiene to ensure the health of the modern family but also as transmitters to their children of the knowledge and skills of the science of hygiene. Moreover, both male and female writers valorized a biomedical approach, based on germ theory and an understanding of anatomy, to Republican women's reproductive health. Using the discourse of "women's hygiene," these writers not only stressed the imperative of modernizing childbirth, as evinced by their impassioned call for midwifery reform, but also devoted great attention to vernacularizing medical knowledge to help women deal with their reproductive ailments such as menstruation, pregnancy, childbirth, and postpartum care.

Although male and female writers both centralized the important role of modern science in fashioning new Republican womanhood, they took divergent approaches to each of the prominent topics discussed in this chapter and the difference in their modes of thinking when writing on the same topic was also conspicuous. Whereas male writers relegated Republican women to the role of "wise mothers and good wives," female writers saw it as an alternative way for women to contribute to the project of national strengthening. While male commentators portrayed women as ignorant of scientific and biomedical knowledge in managing both the household and their bodies, female writers forcefully subverted the men's representations in their own writing on personal and family hygiene, menstruation, midwifery reform, and modern childbirth practices. Another notable difference was that, other than relying on medical expertise, female contributors gave descriptions of women's bodily experiences in their writing on women's reproductive health. These experiences were not only specific to individual women but also revealed a gendered approach to women's health and bodies in the early Republican era.

The proliferation of writings on the new connection between women and modern science in the women's journals also suggests that early Republican intellectuals took a different approach to the woman question from their late Qing predecessors—for example, in the discussion of the female body. Although early Republican writers held that the development of the female body was integral to the well-being of the national body, they focused more on providing concrete scientific and technical know-how for general women to manage their individual bodies in their everyday lives, rather than discussing improvement in women's physical health in relation to the nation by invoking abstract theories and emancipatory discourse. As this chapter shows, the know-how was deeply grounded in everyday experience and held individual women responsible for both their own health and that of the nation.

CHAPTER 5

Policing Girl Students

When the contributors to early Republican women's journals ardently promoted the ideal of "wise mothers and good wives," they specifically addressed girl students (*nü xuesheng* 女學生) as the target audience with the greatest potential to grow up and become this ideal.[1] For example, Shao Piaoping 邵飄萍 (1886–1926), a renowned journalist of the time, declared in a 1915 article in *Funü zazhi* that "Today's girl students are tomorrow's good wives and wise mothers."[2] Another author writing for the journal also suggested that "wise mothers and good wives should be sought at girls' schools."[3]

Despite their potential to be future "wise mothers and good wives," the status quo of "today's girl students" was far from satisfactory, however. Shao observed that the social attitudes toward girl students in the past had shifted over the years from curiosity to fear and, ultimately, to disdain. Those who had once shown faith in women's education were now disenchanted. Whereas some girl students indeed demonstrated excellence in both their studies and conduct, wrote Shao, there were also some "black sheep" (*haiqunzhima* 害群之馬;

1 The women's journals were reading materials at some girls' schools. For example, a female teacher reported that *Funü zazhi* was used as extracurricular reading for her students. See Chen Yiqin 陳亦秦, "Yu zhi xuexiao shenghuo 余之學校生活 [My School Life]," *Funü zazhi* 11 (1915); A female principal of a girls' school listed *Funü zazhi* as of a must-read for the self-cultivation of girl students. See Zhu-Zhou Guozhen 朱周國真, "Nü xuesheng zixiu yongshu zhi yanjiu 女學生自修用書之研究 [Books for the Self-Cultivation of Girl Students]," *Funü zazhi* 5 (1915); Joan Judge points out that *Funü shibao* counted female students and teachers among its most devoted readers and contributors, in *Republican Lens*, 179. Zhou Xuqi 周敘琪 also notes that female students comprised a majority of the readership of *Funü zazhi* from 1915 to 1919, in *1910–20 niandai duhui xin funü shenghuo fengmao—yi Funü zazhi wei fenxi shili* 一九一○~一九二○年代都會新婦女生活風貌——以《婦女雜誌》為分析實例 [*Aspects in the Life of Urban New Women in the 1910s and 1920s: Taking* Funü zazhi *as An Example*] (Taipei: Taiwan University, 1996), 42–46; idem, "Yuedu yu shenghuo: Yun Daiying de jiating shenghuo yu *Funü zazhi* zhi guanxi 閱讀與生活——惲代英的家庭生活與《婦女雜誌》之關係 [Reading and Life: The Relationship between Yun Daiying's Family Life and *Funü shibao*]," *Si yu yan* 思與言 43, no. 3 (2005): 113–117.

2 女學生者，今日為學生，即他日為賢妻良母。 Piaoping nüshi 飄萍女史 [Shao Piaoping 邵飄萍], "Lixiang zhi nü xuesheng 理想之女學生 [Ideal Girl Students]," *Funü zazhi* 3 (1915): 3.

3 Wang San, "Jinggao quanguo nü xuexiao 敬告全國女學校 [Respectfully Addressing All the Girls' Schools in China]," *Funü zazhi* 9 (1915): 1.

 | DOI:10.1163/9789004438545_007

lit., "the horse that harms the herd") who prevented female students from gaining respectability. These miscreants spoke enthusiastically of freedom, equality between men and women, and politics, but they were economically dependent and spendthrift. They wore flashy and extravagant clothing, were obsessed with foreign products, and, worst of all, possessed little knowledge about and even less interest in household matters.[4]

Shao Piaoping was not alone in expressing concerns about the studies and behavior of girl students. Although *nü xuesheng* had been a subject of public interest and intellectual concern since the waning years of the Qing dynasty, in the early years of the Republican era, these concerns "attained fever pitch in the periodical and women's press."[5] In the pages of the women's journals of the 1910s, criticism of *nü xuesheng* was prevalent and usually appeared under two rubrics. Female students were either cited as negative examples embodying the undesirable repercussions of modern women's education, or they were represented as negative foils for "wise mothers and good wives." In any case, they were specifically referred to as young, restless schoolgirls, whose presence in public meant trouble or even threatened the existing social order. The persistent association of *nü xuesheng* with a figure of identifiable feminine adolescence, unseemly and transgressive through her affiliation with modern schooling, has rendered "girl student," rather than the generic "female student," a more pertinent translation for the term *nü xuesheng* during this period.[6]

4 Shao, "Lixiang zhi nü xuesheng."

5 Bailey, *Gender and Education in China*, 83. For more analyses on the controversies surrounding female students from the late Qing to the early Republican era, see Paul J. Bailey, "Unharnessed Fillies: Discourse on the 'Modern' Female Student in Early Twentieth-Century China," in *Wusheng zhi sheng (III): Jindai zhongguo de funü yu wenhua (1600–1950)* 無聲之聲 III：近代中國的婦女與文化（1600–1950）[*Voices amid Silence III: Women and Culture in Modern China, 1600–1950*], ed. Luo Jiurong 羅久蓉 and Lü Miaofen 呂妙芬 (Taipei: Zhongyang yanjiuyuan jindaishi yanjiusuo, 2003); idem, "Women Behaving Badly: Crime, Transgressive Behavior and Gender in Early Twentieth Century China," *Nan Nü: Men, Women and Gender in Early and Imperial China* 8, no. 1 (2006); see also Joan Judge, "The Culturally Contested Student Body: *Nü Xuesheng* at the Turn-of-the-Twentieth Century," in *Performing Nation: New Gender Constructs in Literature, the Visual and the Performing Arts of Modern China and Japan*, ed. Joshua Mostow, Catherine Vance Yeh, and Doris Croissant (Leiden: E.J. Brill 2008).

6 In their edited volume on global images of "the Modern Girl" in the 1920s and 1930s, Alys Eve Weinbaum et al. note the multifaceted meanings connoted by the word "girl." They argue that, unlike the term "woman," the word "girl" reveals the "contested status of young women and their unstable and sometimes subversive relationship to social norms relating to heterosexuality, marriage and motherhood." Perry Link also notes that "girl student" was a term that "carried within it the interest of a paradox," and this special category of young women often implied a tendency to go beyond proper women's roles. Drawing upon these interpretations, I suggest that "girl student" is a more faithful translation of *nü xuesheng* in the early

This chapter explores how writers in the early Republican women's periodical press approached the woman question by imposing a regulatory discourse on girl students. It first traces how girl students shifted from being objects of government regulation, intellectual debate, and public interest in the late Qing to become a new representational category in the early Republican era. The Republican girl student was a distinct departure from the late Qing girl students, who were portrayed as passive objects viewed by others and subjected to public gaze and scrutiny. Rather, Republican girl students appeared as active viewers themselves, gazing fiercely back at the public. The chapter then focuses on how the policing of Republican girl students as a representational project was carried out differently by both men and women commentators in the women's press. While men's criticism of girl students might derive from observed fact—writings about girl students' undesirable qualities and the dangers of their public presence had circulated since the late Qing—it also served as an effective rhetorical strategy for men to assert their intellectual authority in guiding the nation's progress in general and modern women's education in particular. Although some women's criticisms of girl students were aligned with men's, they reflected more concern for girl students' own development and cultivation per se. More significant, a number of women writers provided detailed accounts of their own personal experiences at girls' schools, which forcefully challenged the stereotypical and negative images of girl students created by their critics. These female contributors' writings thus mitigated the power of the regulatory discourse on girl students.

1 Female Students in the Late Qing

Attempts to regulate the behavior of female students proceeded in tandem with the development of modern women's education in China. In addition to nationalist intellectuals' espousal of advancing modern women's education, the Qing government also saw women's education as a useful vehicle for strengthening the ailing Chinese nation and refashioning the traditional virtues and domestic skills for women. When the Ministry of Education of the Qing court sanctioned women's formal education in 1907, the memorials explicitly stated

---

Republican era. See Alys Eve Weinbaum, Lynn M. Thomas, Priti Ramamurthy, Uta G.Poiger, Madeleine Yue Dong, and Tani E. Barlow, ed., *The Modern Girl around the World: Consumption, Modernity, and Globalization* (Durham: Duke University Press, 2008), 9; Link, *Mandarin Ducks and Butterflies*, 220.

that it was not incompatible with the ancient ethical teachings for women.[7] The conventional Confucian way of educating girls still played an influential role in the new educational principles and curriculum guidelines. Although female students were exposed to an unprecedented range of new fields of study, such as physics, mathematics, geography, and gymnastics, they were also expected to carry on the traditional feminine virtues such as the "four womanly attributes": womanly virtue (*fude* 婦德), womanly speech (*fuyan* 婦言), womanly carriage (*furong* 婦容), and womanly work (*fugong* 婦功).[8] Moral cultivation had particular significance. For example, the memorial on regulations for normal schools for girls and women considered "self-cultivation" (*xiushen* 修身) a priority in the curriculum and provided a list of ancient didactic texts, such as *Lienü zhuan* 列女傳 (*Biographies of Exemplary Women*) and *Nei ze* 內則 (*Regulations of the Inner Sphere*), as recommended textbooks in the new female education.[9] New textbooks for female students' moral instruction also appeared, with titles such as *Nüzi xiushen duben* 女子修身讀本 (*Readers for Women's Moral Cultivation*).[10] Moreover, the regulations on girls' schools stated that female students were strictly prohibited from participating in politics, freely choosing their husbands, and engaging in social intercourse with men. Female students were also exhorted to avoid superficial adornments such as fancy clothes and make-up.[11] Girls' schools were thus made into a protective domain where female students were expected to be quiet, frugal, and moral.

---

7 The Ministry of Education published regulations for primary and normal girls' schools: "Xuebu zouding nüzi xiaoxue tang zhangcheng 學部奏定女子小學堂章程 [Memorial to Create Regulations for Women's Primary Schools by the Ministry of Education]" and "Xuebu zouding nüzi shifan xuetang zhangcheng zhe 學部奏定女子師範堂章程折 [Memorial to Create Regulations for Women's Normal Schools by the Ministry of Education]." For these regulations, see Zhu Youhuan 朱有瓛, ed., *Zhongguo jindai xuezhi shiliao* (di'er ji) 中國近代學制史料（第二輯） [*Historical Materials on China's Modern Education System*, second collection], 2 vols. (Shanghai: Huadong shifan daxue chubanshe, 1987), 2: 657–666, 666–674.

8 The four womanly attributes were first prescribed in the *Zhouli* 周禮 [Rites of Zhou] and later elaborated by Ban Zhao 班昭 (ca. 49–ca. 120). They were the core concepts in the conventional Confucian education for women. See Susan Mann, "Learned Women in the Eighteenth Century," in Christina K. Gilmartin, Gail Hershatter, Lisa Rofel, and Tyrene White, *Engendering China*, 27–46.

9 "Xuebu zouding nüzi shifan xuetang," 669.

10 For example, in 1906, Xu Jiaxing 許家惺 composed a reader for female students, *Zuijin nüzi xiushen jiaokeshu* 最近女子修身教科書 [*Newest Textbooks for the Moral Cultivation for Girls and Women*]. This reader combined ancient Chinese ethical texts for women and excerpts from ethical books for women from other countries. For a discussion of textbooks for women's education at the turn of the twentieth century, see Judge, *The Precious Raft of History*, 20–23.

11 "Xuebu zouding nüzi shifan xuetang," 666.

At a practical level, however, these regulations faced constant challenge, as an ever-expanding public space was opened for female students, whose numbers expanded dramatically in the final years of the Qing dynasty.[12] "Public space" had multilayered meanings for different groups of female students. As discussed in Chapter 2, at the turn of the twentieth century, a small number of female students ventured out into the public space by studying abroad, participating in social and political activities, and initiating feminist movements. Specifically, they availed themselves of the new print medium—the women's press—to articulate and construct a *nüjie*, an imagined community signifying new spatial and temporal potential for Chinese women. These progressive female students transcended not only geographical boundaries but also the gendered spheres subject to the long-held Confucian doctrines on the conventional segregation between the inner and outer domains. For these female students, as Weikun Cheng has succinctly argued, the notion of "public" could "suggest a gender gap, a new terrain of competition and the development of a feminist movement."[13] At a deeper level, their "going public" was justified and enhanced by their ability to write and articulate their own ideas, as evidenced in their various writing practices in the women's press. Their writing itself also signaled the opening of new imaginary public spaces.

But for the majority of female students who did not enjoy the privilege of "going public" via writing, public spaces were more physical and related to everyday life, hence more susceptible to the government's policing and scrutiny. Early in 1904, Zhang Zhidong, the governor-general of Hunan and Hubei as well as the primary designer of the national female education reform program, explicitly expressed his concerns about the potential threats that might emerge from young girls' "going public." He deemed it highly inappropriate for "young girls to enter schools in large groups and wander about the streets."[14]

12 Before the era of public support for formal women's education, missionaries founded schools for Chinese girls in the 1840s. The first Chinese-run girls' school was established in 1898 (see Chapter 1). On the history of women's education in the late Qing, see Bailey, *Gender and Education*, 1–66. The number of female students (including those who studied abroad) rose exponentially from 468 in 1904 to 26,465 in 1909 and continued to amount to 141,130 in 1912 as the new Republic was founded. There were no reports from 1910 to 1911 because of the 1911 Revolution. See Ida Belle Lewis, *The Education of Girls in China* (New York: Columbia University Press, 1919), 34.

13 Cheng, "Going Public Through Education," 108.

14 Zhang Zhidong, Zhang Baixi 張百熙, and Rongqing 榮慶, "Zouding mengyangyuan zhangcheng ji jiating jiaoyu fa zhangcheng 奏定蒙養院章程及家庭教育法章程 [Memorial to Create Regulations for Kindergartens and Family Education]," in Zhu, *Zhongguo jindai xuezhi shiliao*, 2: 573.

The Ministry of Education's 1907 regulations on girls' schools declared that female students wear light or dark blue colored cotton gowns and no face powder, rouge, or any other kind of adornment. Wearing silk clothing or Western-style dress was strictly prohibited.[15] These mandates became more detailed and rigid in 1910 when the Ministry of Education proposed to enforce an appropriate dress code for female students.[16] The regulations included an elaborate list of things that female students "must" and "must not" do with regard to appropriate clothing styles. For example, the regulations stipulated that all female students, except those in primary schools, always wear uniforms at school. Uniforms had to be long gowns (*changshan* 長衫) below the knees, with a hemline two inches above the ground with no slits, and one-inch borders on the sleeves and in the front; they had to be made of cotton or linen and domestically produced, rather than imported. Female students had to wear a badge on their chests as a marker of identification and were not permitted to wear hairpins or flowers in their hair or to wear their hair loose. They were not allowed to adopt any foreign attire, Japanese or Western.[17]

At the same time, the growing visibility of female students also attracted widespread public attention, interest, and, most of all, curiosity. The late Qing women's journals, along with some prominent national daily newspapers, frequently ran columns or articles on female students' involvement in a wide range of activities that were considered beneficial for society and the nation. Despite the official prohibitions on female students' involvement in politics, these articles foregrounded female students as the representatives of "women's world" and encouraged them to engage in politics and national affairs.[18] Nonetheless, much of the late Qing newspaper and periodical press had ambivalent attitudes toward the female students' presence in public. In both textual and visual representations, the female student was constantly watched, judged, and severely criticized. A 1907 illustration in a pictorial newspaper best encapsulates the spectacle of a female student's presence in public (Figure 5). The image depicts a female student riding a horse through the streets, and a group of men, except for one who turns his back on the female student, look

15 "Xuebu zouding nüzi shifan," 674.

16 "Xuebu zou zunni nüxue fuse zhangcheng (bing dan) 學部奏遵擬女學服色章程（並單）[Memorial to Create Regulations for Female Students' Dress Code, with Regulations Attached]," in Zhu, *Zhongguo jindai xuezhi shiliao*, 2: 675–676.

17 "Xuebu zou zunni nüxue fuse zhangcheng," 676.

18 For example, in 1907 *Dagong bao* and *Shuntian shibao* published a considerable number of articles on female students' active involvement in public and national affairs. See Bailey, " 'Unharnessed Fillies' "; see also Judge, "The Culturally Contested Female Body."

FIGURE 5 "Nüshi zouma (A Young Lady Riding a Horse)," *Xingqi huabao* 22 (March 1907)
SOURCE: TOYO BUNKO (THE ORIENTAL LIBRARY)

at her with great interest and curiosity. The caption to the image states that a spectator criticized the female student's public appearance by commenting that "women should occupy themselves with affairs from the inner chambers rather than parading their skills or abilities like this way [riding a horse]." The caption further reads that the author of the illustration refuted the spectator's views as coming from "stubborn minds." He compared the female student favorably with ancient women warriors such as Hua Mulan, who rode horses on the battlefield.[19] Despite the author's attempt to assuage social anxiety about seeing female students active in public, the female student remained a passive object of public viewers' gaze, as illustrated by her demurely lowered head and eyes.

Female students were also vulnerable to malicious slander or criticism from the public. For example, a 1907 article in *Zhongguo ribao* 中國日報 noted that,

19 "Nüshi zouma 女士走馬 [A Young Lady Riding a Horse]," *Xingqi huabao* 星期畫報 22 (March 1907).

if a female student walked along the street wearing Shanghai-style fancy silk clothing and leather shoes, she would readily attract slanderous remarks and her reputation would be questioned. The author commented that the slanderous spread of unfounded accusations about female students would hinder the development of women's education because parents would refuse to send their daughters to school out of fear that their daughters' good reputation might be tarnished. The author thus called for reform in female students' dress codes to rectify this situation. He suggested that all girls' schools adopt uniforms as a marker of differentiation and that each uniform be numbered with a secret mark; if there were indeed unruly, misbehaving female students, they should be punished or expelled with the help of the police.[20]

In his examination of the public attitudes toward women's education in the late Qing popular pictorials, Chen Pingyuan shows that female students were subject to public scrutiny and male gaze, which usually had sexual overtones. For example, rules such as forbidding female students to go to school in groups or to parade in the street and markets might have been intended to protect the frail female students from harm, but they simultaneously disclosed the male voyeurism that may have been caused by female students' visibility in public spaces. "For male readers," Chen notes, "the concept of 'female student' acted as a cultural signpost encompassing attributes of 'fashion' and 'sex' that were ripe with playful possibilities."[21] For instance, the scene of a troop of female students walking in the street with guns over their shoulders was decidedly sensational for the public viewing it. All aspects of female students' physical form—their faces, deportment, uniforms, and three-inch bound feet—could incite voyeuristic desire.[22] Likewise, the illustrations of female students also engaged readers in the voyeurism, nourishing a popular taste for the spectacle of the female students' public presence.

It is clear that from the beginning of the promotion of women's education, female students played a dual role. On the one hand, they were integrated into the modernization agenda, which made them the ideal carriers and

---

20 "Xuejie yi su shefa yi baoquan nüxue zhi mingyu 學界宜速設法以保全女學之名譽 [Education Authorities Should Quickly Seek Ways to Protect the Reputation of Women's Education]," *Zhongguo ribao* (4 September, 1907), reprinted in Li and Zhang, *Jindai Zhongguo nüquan yundong shiliao*, 2: 1163–1165. On the prevalent criticism of female students' wayward behavior in newspapers at this time, see also Paul Bailey, "Women Behaving Badly."

21 Chen Pingyuan, "Male Gaze/Female Students: Late Qing Education for Women as Portrayed in Beijing Pictorials, 1902–1908," in Qian, Fong, and Smith, *Different Worlds of Discourse*, 345.

22 Chen, "Male Gaze/Female Students," 346.

transmitters of traditional virtues and new knowledge in a national order. On the other hand, the growing public visibility of female students destabilized the long-standing Confucian strictures of gender segregation and posed new threats to the social order. The threatening aspects of female students would continue to be heatedly discussed in the early years of the new Republic. Yet, at the same time, the Republican images of female students became varied and more contested.

2 The Republican Girl Student

Facilitated by the expansion of girls' schools as well as the loosening of regulations on separation of the sexes, female students grew in record numbers, as the Republic was founded in 1912.[23] They emerged as a significant social category and became more visible in public spaces such as school campuses, street demonstrations, public parks, and boulevards. At the same time, portrayals of the Republican girl student also abounded in imaginary public spaces such as new fiction and popular periodicals.[24] In those representations, she often appeared as a young, adolescent schoolgirl whose behavior tended to be unruly and posed a challenge to the established social order, whose presence often aroused public controversy, and who was an avid consumer of foreign commodities and aesthetics. In some ways, the Republican girl student can be understood as the harbinger of the Modern Girl, a figure that was widely circulated and gained prominence in 1930s urban China, because they both demonstrated reckless behavior and habits of wasteful consumption and were

---

23 Many schools were forced to adopt a co-education policy because of the lack of resources before 1912. Based on incomplete data, there were 15,324 female students at 434 girls' schools in 1907, when the Qing government formally sanctioned women's public education. In 1912 and 1913, the number of female students rose to 141,130 and that of girls' schools to 2,389. See Bailey, *Gender and Education in China*, 34–36, 83–89. It is noteworthy that only the number of primary school students greatly increased; higher education was still not accessible to women at this time. See Bailey, " 'Unharnessed Fillies'," 332; Harriet T. Zurndorfer, "Gender, Higher Education, and the 'New Woman': The Experiences of Female Graduates in Republican China," in *Women in China: the Republican Period in Historical Perspective*, ed. Mechthild Leutner and Nicola Spakowski (Münster: Lit, 2005), 450–481.

24 For a study on the theme *nü xuesheng* in literary genres such as "scandal novels" [*heimu xiaoshuo* 黑幕小說] and tabloid newspapers during this period, see Huang Xiangjin 黃湘金, *Shishi yu chuanqi: Qingmo Minchu xiaoshuo nei de nü xuesheng* 史事與傳奇：清末民初小說內的女學生 [*History and Legend: Female Students in Late Qing and Early Republican Fiction*] (Beijing: Beijing daxue chubanshe, 2016), esp. 244–301.

constantly considered a threat to personal morality and national strength. Furthermore, like the Modern Girl, the Republican girl student not only became a symbol that was the subject of heated discussion, engendering social tensions, but she also became an embodiment of what women should not be, a warning about where young school girls might go wrong.[25]

The Republican girl student thrived in visual representations in commercial women's journals such as *Funü shibao* and *Funü zazhi*. But, in contrast to her late Qing predecessor who was often represented as the object of public gaze, the Republican girl student began to reject the viewers' gaze and, instead, gaze right back at the public, which Joan Judge suggests shows "a new subject position of women as viewers rather than viewed, as knowers rather than known."[26]

Two cover pictures of *Funü shibao* exemplify this new dynamic between the girl student and "the gaze" during the 1910s.[27] Unlike the late Qing female student image that involves men viewers, neither of the cover images depicts the presence of any male figures.[28] The girl students are displayed as appearing independently or with her female companions in the public spaces, such as schools and other non-domestic locations. The cover of the inaugural issue presents a photo of two girl students holding a copy of *Funü shibao* (Figure 6).

---

25 On discussions of the Modern Girl figure, see Tani Barlow, "Wanting Some: Commodity Desire and the Eugenic Modern Girl," in Leutner and Spakowski, *Women in China*, 312–350; Madeleine Yue Dong, "Who Is Afraid of the Chinese Modern Girl," in Weinbaum et al., *The Modern Girl around the World*, 194–219; Sarah E. Stevens, "Figuring Modernity: The New Woman and the Modern Girl in Republican China," *NWSA Journal* 15, no. 3 (2003); Antonia Finnane, *Changing Clothes in China: Fashion, History, Nation* (New York: Columbia University Press, 2008), 167–168; on the social and political anxieties around the Modern Girl, see Louise Edwards, "Policing the Modern Woman in Republican China," *Modern China* 26, no. 2 (2000).

26 Judge, *Republican Lens*, 1.

27 The illustrator of these two cover images of *Funü shibao* was Xu Yongqing 徐詠清 (1880–1953), a noted watercolorist who created covers for ten issues (1–4 and 11–16) of the journal. Xu was also the creator of covers of the first twelve issues of *Funü zazhi*. For discussions on Xu's biography and his career as a watercolor artist, see Judge, *Republican Lens*, 22–25, 81–84; Ellen Johnston Laing, *Selling Happiness: Calendar Posters and Visual Culture in Early Twentieth Century Shanghai* (Honolulu: University of Hawai'i Press, 2004), 115–138.

Joan Judge provides an analysis of the cover images of *Funü shibao* in comparison with the traditional Chinese artistic genre of "beauties," in *Republican Lens*, 81–88.

28 For a similar observation on the absence of an identifiable male gaze in illustrations of modern beauties in this period, see Louise Edwards, *Citizens of Beauty: Drawing Democratic Dreams in Republican China* (Seattle: University of Washington Press, 2020), 155–171.

The two girls on the cover have typical looks and attire of girl students at the time: the "top-and-trousers" (*shanku*衫褲 or *aoku*襖褲) ensemble was often worn by girl students; their cotton hip-length jackets with side slits are worn over their trousers, and they both wear their hair in a long single braid.[29] What makes this image distinctive is that the two girls' likenesses also appear on the cover of the journal they are holding. At first glance, as both the girl students and their own portraits are on display, their act of looking at themselves might suggest their complicity in the act of display.[30] But the image carries a more complex meaning here. Whereas Figure 5 shows that the demure late Qing female student is looked at by the pictorial's male readership in general and men spectators in the street in particular, this self-reflexive image suggests the creation of a female audience or even a "female gaze."[31] Although these two girl students might also be viewed by male readers, the girl students' self-referential gaze, however, signals a clear sense of self-possession and their act of turning

29 Although the *shanku* was often worn by students, it also influenced general fashion trends in this period and was widely donned by young urban women, prostitutes, and respectable married women. On typical girl students fashion and clothing in the first years of the Republic, see Finnane, *Changing Clothes in China*, 87; on more on women's vestimentary transformations in modern China, see also Antonia Finnane, "What Should Chinese Women Wear? A National Problem," Modern China 22, no. 2 (1996); Ellen Johnston Laing, "Visual Evidence for the Evolution of 'Politically Correct' Dress for Women in Early Twentieth Century Shanghai," *Nan Nü: Men, Women, and Gender in Early and Imperial China* 5, no. 1 (2003); Henrietta Harrison, *The Making of the Republican Citizen: Political Ceremonies and Symbols in China, 1911–1929* (Oxford: Oxford University Press, 2000), 49–60.

30 In his now-classic book *Ways of Seeing* (New York: Viking Press, 1973), 50–51, the prominent art critic John Berger discusses the category of Renaissance oil paintings in which nude women are shown looking at themselves through mirrors. Berger suggests that the mirror, a symbol of female vanity, performs the function of conniving the naked woman in treating herself as a sight, and the naked woman herself thus also becomes a spectator. Here, the illustration of the girl students' own images also partly serves as a mirror, but the girl students depicted here are different from the nude women in that the former do not evoke explicit erotic pleasure or desire, as the latter usually do.

31 "The female gaze" is a theoretical notion in response to film scholar Laura Mulvey's conception of "the male gaze," a phenomenon in which women are viewed and objectified by their male creators or from male perspectives. By contrast, the female gaze counters this male voyeuristic viewing and presents the work from a female perspective, whether because of the creator's gender or because the work is directed at a female audience. In the cover image under examination, the girl students' holding of a copy of *Funü shibao* and their act of looking at it could be understood as a clear expectation of a female audience. On the concept of the male gaze, see Laura Mulvey, "Visual Pleasure and Narrative Cinema," *Screen* 16, no. 3 (1975): 6–18; for thoughtful discussions on the role of the female gaze in contemporary media, see Lorraine Gamman and Margaret Marshment, ed., *The Female Gaze: Women as Viewers of Popular Culture* (London: Women's Press, 1988).

back to the reader indicates resistance to the male gaze. For a female reader of the journal at the time, this illustration was drawn in a way that would invoke identification and empathy, rather than admiration or desire. Moreover, the girl students' intense gaze on themselves—as fashionably dressed, young civilized girls—could also be read as their awareness of viewing themselves as an embodiment of Chinese modernity.[32]

On the cover of the second issue is another photo of a girl student. The girl is wearing a white jacket with a light-green checkered pattern and tight-fitting trousers (Figure 7). She wears cotton-topped shoes with cloth soles, and her feet are clearly not bound. Carrying a small bookbag with one hand and a large umbrella with the other hand, she is about to enter the school. Yet she pauses and turns back, looking directly outward at the viewer in a distance. In contrast to the demure, sideways glance of the female student in Figure 5, in this cover image the girl student's gaze back at the viewer discloses her refusal to be passively viewed, which creates a dynamic relationship with the viewer—"she looks back at us looking at her."[33] She is aware of being watched, and she gazes right back at the viewer, as if rejecting the possible pleasures the viewer would take in looking at her. Her stern gaze may also suggest that, rather than being judged by the viewer in a passive way, she turns the viewer into an object that she is examining. Moreover, unlike the previous cover photo of two girl students, this girl student is shown alone, unaccompanied by her fellow girl students or escorted by servants. This implies her independence as a young modern woman and her increasingly prominent role in the public space.

In addition to these two images, *Funü shibao* published several other cover images of the girl student in subsequent issues.[34] She is often portrayed outdoors or in action, or both. For example, whereas the girl student in Figure 7 is standing quietly in front of her school, the girl student on the cover of the fifth

32 Antonia Finnane argues that the cover girls in *Funü shibao* were idealized girls in a progressive, civilized China (*Changing Clothes in China*, 91–93).

33 This quotation comes from Berger's discussion of the naked women's gaze, in *Ways of Seeing*, 50.

34 The cover images in *Funü shibao* primarily featured two kinds of women: young women and married women. Three of the cover images of young women are those of girl students, based on the school settings or the school-related objects they carry, such as books or schoolbags. The rest of the young women are portrayed performing different tasks and occupations. The scenes included young girls playing tennis, knitting by a window, fishing, or enjoying the cool air on a summer night. Despite the different settings, these young women are shown wearing similar clothing with hairstyles similar to those of the clearly identified girl students. It is highly possible that even those outside the school setting were also intended to be girl students.

FIGURE 6 Cover of the first issue of *Funü shibao* (June 1911)
SOURCE: SHANGHAI LIBRARY COLLECTION

FIGURE 7 Cover of *Funü shibao* 2 (July 1911)
SOURCE: SHANGHAI LIBRARY COLLECTION

issue of *Funü shibao* (Figure 8) is shown in the midst of a tennis game. She is wearing a casual tight-fitting, high-collared jacket, her trousers are narrow, and her shoes show her natural feet. She is raising her racket, with a determined look, as if she is getting ready to return her opponent's shot. All her body movements and gestures suggest that she is fully in motion, liberating herself with sports in an outdoor setting. Similarly, the cover of the ninth issue depicts two girl students crossing a bridge walking hand in hand (Figure 9). The bookbags indicate that they may be on their way to school in the morning or heading home after school. They have the same hairstyle—a long braid down their backs with bangs. Like the two girls in Figure 6, these girl students turn their back to the viewer. Instead of fixing their sight on a particular object, both of them are looking at the vast landscape before them, complete with boats, which signal the enlarging spaces they begin to occupy.

The 1910s was a time when girl students emerged as fashion trendsetters in cities such as Shanghai, where prostitutes and courtesans had previously led fashion trends.[35] As photos on the covers mentioned above demonstrate, all the girl students are dressed to emphasize modesty and simplicity. As plain as their clothing may seem, it was far from unfashionable. Some scholarship has discerned that the checkered pattern of the girl students' jackets is recognizably Western, which characterized Chinese fashion in the 1910s.[36] An article in *Funü zazhi* in 1915 noted the popularity among the girl students of adopting Western fashion: "In our country, there are a good number of women studying English, but those who consider themselves to have a good command of it all opt for Western fashions and elect to wear Western clothing."[37] Although this

---

35 Yu Xingmin 于醒民 and Tang Jiwu 唐繼無, *Shanghai: jindaihua de zaochan er* 上海：近代化的早產兒 [*Shanghai: A Premature Child of Modernization*](Taipei: Jiuda wenhua, 1992), 275. On the role that prostitutes and courtesans played in fashion reforms in urban Shanghai, see Luo Suwen 羅蘇文, "Lun Qingmo Shanghai dushi nüzhuang de yanbian (1880–1910) 論清末上海都市女裝的演變, 1880–1910 [On Changes in Urban Women's Clothing in Late Qing Shanghai]," in *Wusheng zhi sheng II: jindai Zhongguo de funü yu shehui* (1600–1950) 無聲之聲 II：近代中國的婦女與社會（1600–1950） [*Voices amid Silence II: Women and Culture in Modern China, 1600–1950*], ed. You Jianming (Taipei: Zhongyang yanjiuyuan jindaishi yanjiusuo, 2003); Catherine Vance Yeh, *Shanghai Love: Courtesans, Intellectuals, and Entertainment Culture, 1850–1910* (Seattle: University of Washington Press, 2006); Hershatter, *Dangerous Pleasures*; On courtesans as fashion leaders represented in literature, see also Paola Zamperini, "Clothes that Matter: Fashioning Modernity in Late Qing Novels," *Fashion Theory: The Journal of Dress, Body & Culture* 5, no. 2 (2001).

36 Chin, "Translating the New Woman," 504.

37 我國女子學西文者，頗不乏人，　但語言文字稍精者，莫不改西裝，衣西衣。 Ren Yanyou 任妍幽, "Lun jiating yi shi zhu zhi dang zhuyi 論家庭衣食住之當注意 [Important Matters on Eating, Clothing, and Housing]," *Funü zazhi* 5 (1915): 8.

FIGURE 8 Cover of *Funü shibao* 5 (January 1912)
SOURCE: SHANGHAI LIBRARY COLLECTION

FIGURE 9 Cover of *Funü shibao* 9 (February 1913)
SOURCE: SHANGHAI LIBRARY COLLECTION

commentary on girl students' wholesale embrace of Western fashions tended to be negative, it revealed the important role played by Western fashion in shaping girl students' own visions of being fashionable and modern. As Joan Judge has noted, in the first years of the Republic, foreign objects were often "lauded as progressive, enlightened, and exemplary as often as they were decried."[38] The pursuit of Western style was reflected not only in the clothing but also in the accessories. An article in *Shenbao* cataloged the must-have items for a fashionable woman in Shanghai:

> a pair of sharp-toed, high-heeled fine leather shoes
> a sable muff
> two or three diamond or gold brooches
> a white woolen string or a fur shawl
> a pair of new-style gold-rimmed spectacles
> a crescent-shaped ivory comb
> a silk scarf[39]

Not surprisingly, some girl students also flocked to follow such fashion trends. A critic wryly remarked, "Some girl students would wear gold-rimmed spectacles even if they are not near sighted and high-heeled leather shoes even when it is not raining."[40]

Similar criticism of girl students' showy and extravagant clothing soon prevailed in the periodical press, particularly in the women's journals. For example, Zhang-Zhu Hanfen 張朱翰芬, a female contributor to *Funü shibao*, complained about how students at primary and normal girls' schools in Shanghai squandered money on clothing. She observed that their clothing was made of silk not only from China but also imported from other countries. These students sought novelty in styles as well as in fabrics. What concerned the author more than their conspicuous consumption and relentless competition was that this flashy clothing worn by girl students demonstrated little distinction from that of prostitutes:

---

38 Judge, *Republican Lens*, 61–62.

39 尖頭高底上等皮鞋一雙，紫貂手筒一個，金剛鑽或寶石金扣針二三只，白絨繩或皮圍巾一條，金絲邊新式眼鏡一付，彎形牙梳一只，絲巾一方。"Ziyou tan: Shimao pai 自由談：時髦派 [Free Talk: Fashion Clique]," *Shenbao* (January 6, 1912).

40 Shao, "Lixiang zhi nü xuesheng," 3. In "Chinese Life and Fashions," *XXth Century* 4, no. 1 (1943): 59, Eileen Chang 張愛玲 (1920–1995) also noted the inextricable connection between Western products and modernity: "The indiscriminate importation of things foreign went to such an extent that society girls and professional beauties wore spectacles for ornament since spectacles were a sign of modernity."

> Shanghai is gathering place for prostitutes, and it is a universally acknowledged view that the clothing of prostitutes is outlandish and ostentatious. But nowadays even enlightened girl students imitate prostitutes by wearing this kind of clothing. Under such complicated and confusing conditions, who can distinguish between girl students and prostitutes?[41]

Zhang-Zhu's concern about the supposed difficulty in distinguishing between girl students and prostitutes was directed not at women's education but at girl students' taste in fashion. In other words, what produced this ambiguity was not the public space opened by women's education but, rather, indecent sartorial choices and behavior by the girl students, which blurred the line between reputable and disreputable women.[42]

Zhang-Zhu's criticism reiterated one of the most debated topics in the late Qing through the Republican period: the feared permeability of the social worlds between girl students and prostitutes. Since the late Qing, critics of women's education had either frequently repeated a similar story about debauched, licentious prostitutes dressing like girl students and vice versa or condemned girls' schools as dubious sites for illicit mixing of the sexes.[43] The anxieties about the dangerous and confusing lines between prostitutes and girl students were still evident well into the early Republican era. For example, a female author named Shen Shuzhen 沈淑貞 was adamantly opposed to a proposal to open a school for prostitutes to attend in Shanghai. Calling prostitutes "vermin" and "parasites," she was particularly fearful that they would undermine the credibility of women's education:

> Prostitutes cause a great deal of harm, so how can they be placed in the world of women's education? The harm they have caused is far more than this—they have long tainted the reputation of women's education! Why do we say this? It is because the majority of prostitutes are adopting the attire of girl students and passing themselves off as girl students. When

41 上海為妓女薈萃之地，服裝之奇麗，久為社會所公認。今以文明之女學生，而亦尤而效之。試問迷離樸朔，又孰能辨其是為女生，是為妓女哉？ Zhang-Zhu Hanfen 張朱翰芬, "Lun Shanghai nüxuesheng zhi zhuangshu 論上海女學生之裝束 [On Shanghai Female Students' Clothing]," *Funü shibao* 11 (1913): 12.

42 Zhang-Zhu, "Lun Shanghai," 12–13.

43 For discussions on the difficulty of differentiating between prostitutes and female students and girls' schools as suspicious sites for illicit activities, see Judge, "The Culturally Contested Student Body"; idem, *The Precious Raft*, 77–78; Bailey, "Women Behaving Badly," 188–189; Huang, *Shishi yu chuanqi*, 303–307; On prostitutes dressing like female students, see also Hershatter, *Dangerous Pleasures*, 62.

> conservatives have seen this phenomenon, they do not only forbid young women to attend schools but also force those girl students already enrolled to drop out.[44]

Unlike their somewhat silent and passive late Qing counterparts, girl students in the Republican era appeared to be active, bold, and sometimes subversive. However, they remained contested figures and consistent targets of attempted control. As shown below, Republican girl students also became the subject of heated intellectual discussion in the mixed-gender public space of women's journals.

3 Debates on Girl Students

In the 1910s, the major women's journals, such as *Funü shibao* and *Funü zazhi*, began to engage in debates on what an ideal girl student should look like and the qualities she should possess. Article after article deplored the ubiquity of young female students walking in the street showing off their expensive clothes, devoting energy to learning foreign languages, and neglecting knowledge of domestic science. Worse still, these girl students completely disregarded their household duties. Although these comments could be read as part of a rhetorical strategy to herald the ideal of "wise mothers and good wives," they also attested to the fact that girl students had gone beyond what the reformist intellectuals expected from women's education. Shao Piaoping envisioned the ideal girl students as needing to improve themselves in six ways: personal hygiene, national learning, clothing, showing respect to teachers and classmates, household management, and contributing to society and the nation. Although Shao was sympathetic in prescribing solutions to perceived problems of the girl students, he barely concealed his disdain. For example, at the beginning of the article, he derisively commented, "After girl students have only learned the basics of the English alphabet, they start writing love letters so that their parents will not be able to read them; even those who can read in Chinese use it for improper purposes."[45]

---

44 妓女之害人實甚，豈可使之置身於學界哉？非特此也，吾女學界之名譽，被其敗壞者，亦已甚矣！何者？蓋彼等妓女，大半數效女學生之裝束，且假冒女學生之名，令守舊家見之，不獨不許女子入學，即已入學之女子，亦中止也。 Shen Shuzhen 沈淑貞, "Hushang nishe jinü xuexiao lun 滬上擬設妓女學校論 [Proposal of Establishing Schools for Prostitutes in Shanghai]," *Funü shibao* 7 (1912): 46.

45 Shao, "Lixiang zhi nü xuesheng," 1.

Once again, the clothing worn by girl students was at the forefront of Shao's concerns. He observed that they indulged in extravagant and outlandish clothing and competed with each other in pursuing these external trappings. "School uniforms," he sadly lamented, "are like discarded worn-out shoes."[46] He also disapproved of girl students' preference for foreign products over those made in China. Shao pictured the ideal girl student as follows:

> [She] always wears cotton school uniforms either when she is at school or when she goes out. She should value the cleanliness of her clothing, rather than the extravagance of it, and the decency of her dress, rather than the frivolity of it. Her skirt should not be too long nor her jacket too short. When there are family gatherings or banquets, she could wear beautiful clothes that are domestically manufactured. She must make her own footwear and sew her own clothes.[47]

Whereas the "sartorial correctness" of the female student was government imposed in the late Qing, it was now the intellectuals dictating the dress code for the Republican girl student. Critics often drew a causal link between what they saw as inappropriate clothing with indecent conduct in public spaces. One of the most important strictures on girl students was the wearing of simple and decent dress, which symbolized the virtues expected of them: thrift, industriousness, and proper conduct.

Critics often castigated girl students for their excessive attention to outward appearance—a sign of hedonism—and reiterated the importance of virtue and morality. For reformist writers, only girl students who rejected exterior adornment and valued inner qualities such as morality and virtue could be considered ideal girl students. For example, Cheng Zhanlu 程瞻廬 (1879–1943), a popular writer in Shanghai, penned a short story to address the importance for girl students of cultivating inner qualities over exterior decoration. The story begins with a female teacher grading her students' essays on the topic "It Is Better to Cultivate the Interior Than to Decorate the Exterior" (飾容不如飾心說). The teacher soon frowned upon one girl student's argument that "one's exterior cannot be left unadorned, yet one's inner qualities cannot be left unattended" (容故不可不飾，而心亦不宜獨放). She instantly recollected that

46 Shao, "Lixiang zhi nü xuesheng," 2.

47 在校則布服而着校衣，出外亦然。求其清潔而不求其華麗，求其端重而不求其飄忽。裙不過長，衣不過短。或－親戚宴會，則衣雖美而必用國貨。履必自制，衣必自縫。 Shao, "Lixiang zhi nü xuesheng," 3.

the author of this argument had a proclivity for self-adornment. Calling this argument "frightful," the teacher began to reflect on her own experience. In order to promote women's education, she had abandoned all adornment and accessories and endured immeasurable hardships. She was determined to cultivate respectable girl students who "are not contaminated by old customs, not vainglorious, and do not value Western products over Chinese ones."[48] At the end of the story, readers learn that the teacher successfully corrected the girl student's improper inclination toward external trappings.

Girl students also had their motives in pursuing studies questioned. In another essay published in *Funü zazhi* in 1915, Cheng Zhanlu wrote that girl students usually approached education only for two reasons: first, to follow the trend because going to school was fashionable and, second, to become schoolteachers in the future. To Cheng, both motives were narrow and myopic. He bemoaned that, because of the prevalence of the first purpose, for many women education was a merely decorative and vainglorious activity. Even those who did not go to school attempted to imitate the girl students' clothing and behavior and this was why society tended to associate the term "girl student" with negative connotations and deemed it a vain name unwarranted by any real learning.[49] In his effort to address the problems, Cheng exhorted girl students to pay more attention to practical knowledge and domestic affairs. He contended that the objective of women's education was not to inculcate girl students with advanced and sophisticated knowledge; rather, it was to develop wise mothers and good wives. He wrote, "Which of these types are needed in the women's world: women of letters, female scientists, or wise mothers and good wives? All would agree that it is wise mothers and good wives that are needed."[50] Cheng further suggested that girls' schools impose strict rules to help cultivate girl students' behavior and improve their knowledge in domestic science. The basic goal of women's education was to ensure that girl students could perform the tasks required of a housewife, rather than pursue advanced studies as male students did.[51]

Hu Jichen 胡寄塵 (1886–1938), another well-known traditional-style writer, also serialized a story to demonstrate the ideal life trajectory for a girl student. His "Mufan nü'er zhuan 慕凡女兒傳 (Tale of Mufan)" recounts the life story

48 Cheng Zhanlu 程瞻廬, "Yi xiaoshi zhi sichao 一小時之思潮 [Thoughts in One Hour]," *Funü zazhi* 2 (1915).

49 Cheng Zhanlu, "Duiyu zhuchi nüxue zhe zhi zhiyan 對於主持女學者之卮言 [Suggestions for Education Authorities]," *Funü zazhi* 6 (1915): 1–2.

50 Cheng, "Duyu zhuchi nüxue zhe," 2.

51 Cheng, "Duyu zhuchi nüxue zhe," 2–3.

of a girl student named Mu Fan, an intended pun on the word *mofan* 模範 (model). Born to a peasant family in a small village in the Jiangnan area, Mu Fan was clever of mind and skillful in hand. For instance, she was capable of maintaining both a clean household and a good record at school. More important, she masterfully applied the knowledge from school to her daily life. After graduation, she became a teacher at a girls' school, for she aspired to cultivate more respectable girl students. The whole story is divided into eighteen chapters, each of which depicts one of her laudable characteristics. The last chapter ends with Mu Fan's happy marriage and a decision to establish a girls' school with her husband.[52] Like many other stories featuring ideal girl students, this story also replicates the stereotypical image of model girl students called for by reformist writers. As her name suggests, Mu Fan was merely a physical shell designed to embody all the desirable characteristics of an ideal girl student.

Female contributors also joined men in criticizing girl students, but compared to male writers' derisive and prescriptive tones, they often spoke exhortatively and sympathetically as women and placed much emphasis on providing concrete solutions. Rui Hua 瑞華, the principal of a girls' school in Wuxi County, Jiangsu Province, drew a stark contrast between girl students' fine dresses and their loosening morals and unseemly conduct. She noted that the so-called girl students went to school by car, wore silk clothes and long skirts, tied up their hair, and looked around them with an air of haughtiness. They seemed serious about their study but, in fact, they only gained the most superficial knowledge. Despite their fashionable attire, they were in effect shallow and frivolous and abused the real meaning of freedom.[53] The author commented that these badly-behaved girl students were reducing the credibility of women's education. She proposed concrete rules for girl students to observe. For example, she suggested that a third person always be present when girl students were interacting with men who were not family members. She also exhorted girl students to rid themselves of any frivolous behavior when speaking to men. The reason that girl students' behavior needed to be rectified and regulated, Rui Hua declared, was that the women's world at the time was plunged in darkness and women's rights had been lost. The author thus exhorted girl students to reflect on their conduct so that they could be above reproach and controversy, which would in turn facilitate the development of women's education for the sake of China's national survival.

---

52 Hu Jichen 胡寄塵，"Mu Fan nü'er zhuan 慕凡女兒傳 [A Tale of Mu Fan],"*Funü zazhi* 1–11 (1916).

53 Rui Hua 瑞華, "Jinggao nü xuesheng 敬告女學生 [Respectfully Exhort Girl Students]," *Funü zazhi* 7 (1915).

A female writer named Xia Zhen 遐珍 also employed her own personal experiences to offer advice for girl students. Xia Zhen wrote that she had been a girl student and was a passionate proponent of women's education. But she was the only girl in her family to have received education because her family no longer believed that the knowledge and skills a girl student learned at a girls' school would benefit the family. Contending that domesticity, marriage, and motherhood were primary goals of women's education, Xia Zhen criticized girl students' general disregard of practical knowledge and ignorance of domestic matters. Asserting that she was familiar with the mentality of girl students, she discerned four groups of girl students. The first she called "the group of excellence" (*youliang pai* 優良派). Girl students in this category saw the study of domestic economics as the primary task and did not aim to pursue more advanced knowledge. Xia Zhen argued that girl students of this kind were the most badly needed. The second was "the group of letters" (*xuewen pai* 學問派). Girl students in this group were obsessed with studying science and yet careless about the study of domestic economics. The author believed that the majority of girl students belonged to this group. The third one was "the group of arrogance" (*zijin pai* 自矜派). These girl students were egotistical and immodest in their opinions. They were disrespectful toward teachers and flaunted their "knowledge" before their husbands. The fourth was "the group of vanity" (*fuxiao pai* 浮囂派). These girl students saw women's education as a decorative activity undertaken as a recreation. They had a bad influence on both the girls' schools and society. Xia Zhen thus exhorted girl students to look to "the group of excellence" for role models and cultivate themselves for the benefit of the family and the nation.[54]

While Rui Hua and Xia Zhen tended to repeat the criticism of girl students by men when offering advice, Wei Hongzhu 魏宏珠, a female contributor to *Funü shibao*, fiercely refuted this criticism and defended girl students by drawing upon her own experience. She argued that the prevalent accusations of moral turpitude among girl students were unjustified. As a former girl student, she contended that it was understandable that girl students aspired to enjoy more freedom:

> After they are granted the same rights to education as men, girl students are like caged birds that have broken out of their confines, prisoners who have escaped from the jail. This unexpected freedom and release enable

---

54 Xia Zhen, "Yu zhi zhonggao yu nü xuesheng 余之忠告於女學生 [My Advice for Girl Students]," *Funü zazhi* 4 (1915).

> the girl students to express their high spirits vigorously and develop their dispositions freely. Even flying birds cannot be as free as they are.[55]

Wei declared that those who were ill-informed tended to slander such expressions of freedom as debauchery. Criticizing them as "ignorant and unreasonable," Wei beseeched girl students to enhance their self-cultivation and be more careful in their behavior. Although the author noticed that "girl students nowadays loosen their hair, tighten their clothes, narrow their sleeves, wear gold-rimmed spectacles and leather shoes, carry leather bags, and blatantly seek publicity on the street,"[56] she was more concerned about the consequences of this ostentation rather than of the act itself. Wei frequently used her own experience to suggest the proper behavior and desirable qualities for girl students. For example, she wrote about enjoying sightseeing and exploring scenic places and went to places of interest even though male and female tourists usually mixed there. Asserting that sightseeing and excursions generated a positive spirit and rid one of negativity, she advised girl students to enjoy these activities.

Wei exhorted girl students to fully devote themselves to pursuing knowledge, which she saw as an end in itself. Unlike most commentators, she did not emphasize the study of household management as a key component of women's education. In contrast, she saw domestic affairs as a hindrance and burden that prevented her from devoting more time and energy to the pursuit of knowledge. She recounted her own experience as a wife and mother, complaining that household tasks occupied most of her time and that she regretted not having studied earlier and learned more about other types of knowledge when she was a student. Noting that women had shorter study periods than men, yet they had greater responsibilities, she advised girl students to make the best use of their time while at school and commit themselves to gaining as much knowledge as possible. Possessing a certain level of knowledge, she maintained, "is the prerequisite for a person (woman) to achieve independence."[57]

---

55 一旦興學設教育，視同男子，為女生者，如久困之鳥，驟脫樊籠，久拘之囚，遽離犴狴。意外之遭，盡情之喜，其志氣飛揚，性情發暢，自有一種天際飛鴻不可方物之槩。 Wei Hongzhu 魏宏珠, "Duiyu nü xuesheng zhi zhiyan 對於女學生之卮言 [Suggestions for Girl Students]," *Funü shibao* 4 (1911): 10.

56 Wei, "Duiyu nü xuesheng zhi zhiyan," 11.

57 Wei, "Duiyu nü xuesheng zhi zhiyan," 13. In 1915, an article by Xu Qing 許清, "Jinggao nü xuesheng 敬告女學生 [Respectfully Exhort Female Students]," *Zhonghua funüjie* 1, no. 7 (1915), was strikingly similar to Wei Hongzhu's essay, in content and language, to the point that Xu could be suspected of plagiarizing Wei. In this article, Xu also recollected her

4 Personal Accounts from Girl Students

In addition to offering intellectual debates on girl students, the women's journals also featured personal accounts by former girl students of teaching or study experiences at girls' schools. Authors of these accounts of experience neither rejected the intellectuals' criticisms and derision about girl students nor spoke in favor of the girl students. Instead, they devoted much attention to providing records of their own observations or experiences of the life of girl students, which inadvertently challenged the critics' discursive power over and control of the image of the girl student. For example, in 1915 *Funü zazhi* published an article by Chen Yiqin 陳亦秦, who had been a former student at a girls' normal school in Sichuan province and later became the principal at a girls' primary school in her hometown.

In describing her teaching life, Chen began by providing a detailed account of her students' class schedule and extracurricular reading and activities. According to her account, the school where she taught had eighty-seven girl students, divided into three classes. Chen was one of the two female teachers; the other had been her classmate at the normal school. Chen taught ethics, Chinese, and arithmetic for one class, and music, art, and gymnastics lessons for all three classes.[58]

Chen proceeded to recount the daily routine that she and her students had followed. Every morning she arrived at school by 7:30 and checked whether students had cleaned the classroom and put their belongings in order and whether their clothing was clean and tidy. Chen lectured from 8:00 a.m. until noon and from 2:00 to 4:00 p.m. She observed that during the break after each session, her students either asked her questions about the lecture or read newspapers and periodicals on their own. During the lunch break, the students gathered together and read extracurricular books on education and psychology (Figure 10), and after school was over, they continued reading newspapers and periodicals. Chen wrote that the school assigned senior students to accompany junior students in going home after school, and she and the other instructor also followed them to ensure her students' safety on their way home.[59]

At the end of her essay, Chen described her teaching methods and philosophy. She advised teachers to be open-minded and teach girl students to devote

experience as a student from the vantage point of a school teacher, whereas Wei was a housewife when she recalled her school experience.

58 Chen, "Yu zhi xuexiao shenghuo," 1–3.

59 Chen, "Yu zhi xuexiao shenghuo," 2.

況茲將余一日活動及所閱書報。列舉如後。

時間	午前五—七	七—八	八—十二	午後一—二	二—四	四—五	六—九
勤務	理家事	到校	授課	閱教育書	授課	閱報	準備明日課事及讀文看書

憩息時間之活動。已詳前。不再及。

教育書之種類
教育學
教育史
教授法
單級教授法
二部教授法
管理法
心理學

新聞雜誌之種類
婦女雜誌
教育雜誌
中華教育界
學生雜誌
教育公報
東方雜誌
國民公報

FIGURE 10 Table of girl students' class schedule and extracurricular texts. Chen Yiqin, "Yu zhi xuexiao shenghuo (My School Life)," *Funü zazhi* 11 (1915): 2.
SOURCE: SHANGHAI LIBRARY COLLECTION

to the cultivation of virtues such as diligence, perseverance, and respect for teachers and fellow students. According to Chen, a teacher should inculcate her students with practical knowledge and skills such as letter writing, use of an abacus, and bookkeeping, so that they would not become an object of public criticism due to their ignorance of these affairs. Chen also stated that a teacher should be fully prepared for each lecture and make the best use of her time during vacations to improve their knowledge and teaching ability. She specifically stressed the importance of gaining actual experience in the real world, not just relying on knowledge in textbooks.[60]

In 1916, Ji Zonglan 計宗蘭, a female author, contributed the long article "Wo zhi xuexiao shenghuo 我之學校生活 (My School Life)" to the second issue of *Funü zazhi*.[61] Ji had graduated from the Beijing Girls' Normal School (Jingshi nüzi shifan xuetang 京師女子師範學堂) before becoming a teacher at a girls' school. Unlike Chen, whose article focused on her students' school life, Ji wrote about her own eight-year study experience, with a full and vivid description of herself as a girl student and her school life. Ji did not directly comment on or respond to the criticism of girl students in women's journals, but her account stood in sharp contrast to the derogatory portrayals of girl students as extravagant and degenerate by presenting an image of a diligent, hardworking, and unflashy girl student.

Ji wrote that her school life began in 1908, when she was first admitted to the Beijing Girls' Normal School. Before then, she had spent most of the time learning how to read and write with her brothers at home in Jiangnan. After becoming a student, she was surrounded by brilliant and talented classmates, which made her determined to study harder in order to catch up with them. While she prepared for an important qualification test that would decide whether she could remain at school to continue her studies, Ji followed a rigorous study plan. Not only did she take notes on every lecture—so meticulously that she took down almost every word spoken by the instructors—but she reviewed these notes repeatedly after class. She was so dedicated that she "could not sleep peacefully and enjoy good food" (寢不安枕，食不甘味).[62] In the end, she passed her test with high grades, and still she did not slack off. She continued to study unflaggingly and won a scholarship for academic excellence only six months after she began her studies.

Ji detailed her experience in applying to her daily life the knowledge and skills of domestic science that she learned in the classroom. When she and some of her fellow classmates spent their first winter break at school, the dean generously gave them various kinds of food for them to cook. Ji reasoned that cooking entailed practice and correct culinary knowledge. Whereas ordinary cooks only cooked food based on their experience and had scant knowledge about gastronomy, Ji wrote, she and her classmates had learned about cooking at school, so they knew how to cook dishes that were not only delicious but

60 Chen, "Yu zhi xuexiao shenghuo," 2–3.

61 Ji Zonglan 計宗蘭, "Wo zhi xuexiao shenghuo 我之學校生活 [My Life at School]," *Funü zazhi* 1 (1916).

62 Ji, "Wo zhi xuexiao shenghuo," 45.

also healthful. She thus highlighted practice (*shixi* 實習) as a new pedagogical imperative in the study of academic subjects such as home economics. Unlike contributors who were prescriptive in tone when encouraging girl students to be attentive to domestic tasks, Ji Zonglan told readers about her actual experience in combining cooking theory with practice.[63]

Ji Zonglan also wrote about mourning the death of a classmate, which provides a rare window into the private social and affective life of girl students at the time. Ji described that she was grief-stricken when she learned of her classmate's death, and she and other classmates held a memorial service for her. Like Ji, the classmate was from Southern China and pursued studies in faraway Beijing. This death had a profound impact on Ji, as she became depressed and lost weight—worse still, she lost her passion for studies. Ji revealed that it took a few months for her to recover, both physically and psychologically.

Ji concluded her article by saying how proud she felt to have studied at the Beijing Girls' Normal School. Her study experience not only taught her the importance of women's education but also confirmed her decision to teach and cultivate more young girls so as to contribute to the nation.[64]

5 Conclusion

Nü xuesheng had been a topic of sustained intellectual and popular interest since the emergence of a new female education in the late Qing period. Although the late Qing reformers attempted to refashion female students as effective carriers of new spheres of knowledge in the new national order, they simultaneously expressed profound concerns about the potential threat that female students posed to society and public spaces. In the popular representation and imagination, *nü xuesheng* were constantly subject to social scrutiny and incited titillation provided by the public surrounding sexuality and gender roles. However, as girl students emerged as a prominent representational category in the early Republican era, they demonstrated qualities that marked them as substantially different from those of their late Qing predecessors. In the women's periodical press, the Republican girl student emerged as an active subject who viewed and examined both herself and the public, rather than a mere aesthetic object of being viewed. This new image not only challenged the late Qing visual mode in which female students were often

63 Ji, "Wo zhi xuexiao shenghuo," 46.
64 Ji, "Wo zhi xuexiao shenghuo," 46–48.

depicted as demure, the viewed, but also revealed the new ways in which the public presence of early Republican girl students was empowered by their own act of seeing.

The constant discussion of girl students' proper deportment and behavior in the women's journals discloses how early Republican intellectuals attempted to address the woman question through discursive regulation. Such disciplining of girl students would soon find strong resonance in the wake of the May Fourth Movement, as evidenced by the pervasive intellectual policing of the figures of the New Woman and the Modern Girl throughout the 1920s and the 1930s.[65] The heated debates on early Republican girl students thus illustrate how social and intellectual anxieties were first addressed around the harbinger of the modern woman.

This chapter also demonstrates the different ways in which male and female contributors approached the phenomenon of girl students. Whereas men often spoke prescriptively when circumscribing and defining appropriate roles for girl students, women's criticism was often based on their shared experience as having been girl students and was exhortative. Most significant, a number of former girl students' accounts of personal observations or experiences of school life further provide prime examples of this gendered approach. These detailed accounts, which appeared in the mixed-gender public space of women's journals alongside heated debates about girl students, offer alternative images of girl students that contrast with stereotypical images constructed by critics of them. Although these female authors never directly refuted male writers' portrayals and criticisms, their writings limited their male counterparts' discursive authority and power.

65 Edwards, "Policing the Modern Woman."

Conclusion

In this book, I have adopted a new approach that foregrounds the prominent and yet unrecognized mixed-gender public space in the study of the early Chinese women's periodical press. This approach is particularly useful for addressing both the complexity of the "gender" question central to the women's press and the multiauthored and polyvocal nature of this print genre. This study highlights both men's and women's significant roles and the dynamic between them in the discursive space and public domain afforded by the women's press. Four distinct forms of mixed-gender public space testified to this dynamic. The first woman's journal, *Nü xuebao*, constituted a mixed-gender public space in which reformist men and women were intellectually active in contributing to the publication of the journal and the definition of its agenda. In the feminist women's press, the mixed-gender public space was derived from men's and women's writing activity both across specific journals and in the broader context of Chinese feminism. The two pro-Manchu women's journals afforded a mixed-gender public space where men and women sometimes directly encountered one another on their pages. In the early Republican commercial women's journals, the mixed-gender public space was defined by the active interplay between "male editorial agency" and "female authorial subjectivity."

In these different forms of mixed-gender public space, except for some rare instances, women seldom had direct discursive encounters with or openly argued against men in their discussions of the same topic or theme. Instead, some strategically modified and negotiated with the discursive contours delineated by men while articulating their own ideas and agendas, and others went on to develop their own approaches without responding to or criticizing men. In any case, women consistently strove to enlarge their intellectual authority and scope for action in the public space. Their active writing engagements challenged and limited men's discursive power over and control of a wide range of prominent issues related to the Chinese woman question examined in this book.

Recognizing the mixed-gender public space in the early Chinese women's periodical press reveals new approaches to the woman question from the late Qing to the early Republican era. This book demonstrates the complex ways in which men and women offered their gendered articulations on a variety of important topics surrounding the woman question. In the discussion of women's literary heritage and popular education in *Nü xuebao* in 1898, both male and female intellectuals agreed that civic female literacy was integral to the building of a modern Chinese nation-state. Male reformists such as Liang Qichao

 | DOI:10.1163/9789004438545_008

and Yan Fu took a radical approach to erasing Chinese women's past literary accomplishments when envisioning modern women's education. Although some female contributors subscribed to male intellectuals' ideas, disruptive voices were also heard. Xue Shaohui, the chief editor of *Nü xuebao*, forcefully defended women's literary heritage and saw it as compatible with the development of women's popular education for the sake of China's national strengthening. More significant, the majority of female contributors' endorsement of their own traditional female learning took practical form. They skillfully appropriated their literary traditions to advocate the new nationalist demands.

Male and female feminists had distinct approaches to addressing the woman question in the mixed-gender public space of the feminist press, which spread across several feminist journals. While male feminists defined all Chinese women as an oppressed collectivity yoked to the confines of nationalism, as evidenced by their construction of the concept of *nüjie*, female feminists drew upon this term to develop their own agendas and construct a new collective female identity within and beyond the context of nationalism. Two influential women's journals, Yan Bin's *Zhongguo xin nüjie zazhi* and He-Yin Zhen's *Tianyi*, exemplified the innovative ways in which female feminists reconfigured women's roles as citizens and agents of absolute gender equality. Although men's voices receded on the pages of these two journals, women feminists constantly positioned their writings against the broader feminist backdrop behind the male-invented concept of *nüjie*.

The mixed-gender public space carved out by two Manchu women's journals opens a rare window onto the intersection between the woman question and ethnicity, a topic that has received little scholarly attention. Both men and women made sense of the Manchu woman Huixing's suicide and the questions of gender and ethnicity that surrounded it. Whereas male Manchu nationalists made use of the event to serve their political purpose of constructing a distinct racial identity, Manchu women showed less interest in identifying themselves in ethnic terms. Instead, they saw themselves as part of the subjugated category of "women" and allied themselves with the Han women in gender terms, rather than with their male Manchu counterparts in racial terms.

Revealing the mixed-gender public space afforded by the early commercial women's press questions a widely circulated scholarly interpretation, which held that men assumed a predominant role in setting editorial agendas and creating and defining the topics about women in these journals. Instead, this book emphasizes the dynamic tension between "male editorial agency" and "female authorial subjectivity," arguing that the male editors and female contributors to commercial women's journals such as *Funü shibao* and *Funü zazhi* co-delineated and co-defined the discursive contours of a series of topics essential to the woman question in the early Republican era. Both men and women expounded on the ideal of "wise mothers and good wives," women's role in household hygiene, and women's reproductive health. But as discussed in Chapter 4, they had different ways of addressing these topics: whereas men often spoke prescriptively, with intellectual and medical authority, when writing for the same topic, women wrote exhortatively, by invoking their gender-specific experiences. Without directly refuting men's ideas or views, female authors offered powerful alternatives to the themes and topics initiated and determined by men.

The mixed-gender public space in the commercial journals reveals how early Republican intellectuals first approached the woman question through discursive regulation. The ways in which men and women commentators disciplined the figure of the girl student in the 1910s resonated with urban intellectuals' collective policing of the modern woman image in the 1920s and 1930s. Furthermore, while the existing scholarship shows that female intellectuals aligned themselves with their male counterparts in disciplining the modern woman,[1] this book suggests that this alliance might reflect historical contingency rather than continuity. As discussed in Chapter 5, women either held sympathetic attitudes toward young female students or provided their own gendered accounts of experience that inadvertently challenged men's negative representation of them.

The mixed-gender public space approach also reconstructs a partial but usable history of the early Chinese women's periodical press. It makes possible a systematic examination of various types of women's journals across different critical historical moments. Most important, it allows us to see how the prominent topics comprising the Chinese woman question first emerged and were discussed by both men and women and how women persistently made effort to articulate their own ideas and pushed to broaden the scope of their action in the public space that was newly available to them.

1 For example, Louise Edwards notes that male and female intellectuals demonstrated no obvious gendered difference in terms of modes of reasoning in the policing of the modern woman in the 1920s and 1930s. See Edwards, "Policing the Modern Woman."

Works Cited

Allen, Young J. "Quandi wudazhou nüsu tongkao xu qiyi 全地五大洲女俗通考序其一 [Preface to *Women in All Lands*]." *Wanguo gongbao* 萬國公報 29 (1903).

Anderson, Benedict. *Imagined Communities: Reflections on the Origin and Spread of Nationalism.* New York: Verso, 1983.

Bailey, Paul J. "Chinese Women Go Global: Discursive and Visual Representations of the Foreign 'Other' in the Early Chinese Women's Press and Media." *Nan Nü: Men, Women and Gender in China* 19, no. 2 (2017): 213–262.

Bailey, Paul J. *Gender and Education in China: Gender Discourses and Women's Schooling in the Early Twentieth Century.* London: Routledge, 2006.

Bailey, Paul J. "Unharnessed Fillies: Discourse on the 'Modern' Female Student in Early Twentieth-Century China." In *Wusheng zhi sheng III: Jindai zhongguo de funü yu wenhua (1600–1950)* 無聲之聲 III：近代中國的婦女與文化（1600–1950） [*Voices amid Silence (III): Women and Culture in Modern China, 1600–1950*], ed. Luo Jiurong 羅久蓉 and Lü Miaofen 呂妙芬, 327–357. Taipei: Zhongyang yanjiuyuan jindaishi yanjiusuo, 2003.

Bailey, Paul J. *Women and Gender in Twentieth-Century China.* Basingstoke: Palgrave Macmillan, 2012.

Bailey, Paul J. "Women Behaving Badly: Crime, Transgressive Behavior and Gender in Early Twentieth Century China." *Nan Nü: Men, Women and Gender in Early and Imperial China* 8, no. 1 (2006): 156–197.

Barlow, Tani. "Theorizing Woman: *Funü, Guojia, Jiating* (Chinese Women, State, and Family)." In *Body, Subject and Power in China,* ed. Angela Zita and Tani E. Barlow, 253–290. Chicago: University of Chicago Press, 1994.

Barlow, Tani. *The Question of Women in Chinese Feminism.* Durham: Duke University Press, 2004.

Baum, Emily. "Health by the Bottle: The Dr. Williams' Medicine Company and the Commodification of Well-Being in *Liangyou*." In *Liangyou: Kaleidescopic Modernity and the Shanghai Global Metropolis, 1926–1945,* ed. Paul G. Pickowicz, Shen Kuiyi, and Zhang Yingjin, 71–93. Leiden: Brill, 2013.

Baum, Emily. *The Invention of Madness: State, Society, and the Insane in Modern China.* Chicago: University of Chicago Press, 2018.

Beahan, Charlotte. "Feminism and Nationalism in the Chinese Women's Press, 1902–1911." *Modern China* 1, no. 4 (1975): 379–416.

"Benguan gaobai 本館告白 [Announcement from This Journal]," *Nü xuebao* 女學報 1 (1898).

Berger, John. *Ways of Seeing.* New York: Viking Press, 1973.

"Bianjishi 編輯室 [Editorial Office]." *Funü shibao* 婦女時報 2 (1911): 56.

"Bianjishi 編輯室 [Editorial Office]." *Funü shibao* 6 (1912): 88.

Bray, Francesca. *Technology, Gender and History in Imperial China: Great Transformations Reconsidered.* London: Routledge, 2013.

Bray, Francesca. *Technology and Gender: Fabrics of Power in Late Imperial China.* Berkeley: University of California Press, 1997.

Britton, Roswell S. *The Chinese Periodical Press, 1880–1912.* Shanghai: Kelley & Walsh, 1933.

Brokaw, Cynthia J., and Kai-wing Chow, ed. *Printing and Book Culture in Late Imperial China.* Berkeley: University of California Press, 2005.

Carlitz, Katherine. "The Daughter, the Singing-Girl, and the Seduction of Suicide." *Nan Nü: Men, Women and Gender in China* 3, no. 1 (2001): 22–46.

Carlitz, Katherine. "The Social Uses of Female Virtue in Late Ming Editions of the *Lienü zhuan*." *Late Imperial China* 12, no. 2 (1991): 117–148.

Chan, Ching-kiu Stephen. "The Language of Despair: Ideological Representations of the 'New Women' by May Fourth Writers." *Modern Chinese Literature and Culture* 4 (1988): 19–38.

Chang, Eileen. "Chinese Life and Fashions." *XXth Century* 4, no. 1 (1943): 54–61.

Chang, Kang-i Sun. "Gender and Canonicity: Ming-Qing Women Poets in the Eyes of the Male Literati." *Hsiang Lectures on Chinese Poetry* 1 (2001): 1–18.

Chen, Yiqin 陳亦秦. "Yu zhi xuexiao shenghuo 余之學校生活 [My School Life]." *Funü zazhi* 婦女雜誌 11 (1915): 1–3.

Chen, Zhengyuan 陳姃湲. "Jianjie jindai yazhou de *xianqi liangmu* sixiang—cong huigu Riben, Hanguo, Zhongguo de yanjiu chengguo tanqi 簡介近代亞洲的"賢妻良母"思想——從回顧日本、韓國、中國的研究成果談起 [A Brief Introduction to the Idea of 'Good Wives and Wise Mothers' in Modern Asia: Research Findings from Japan, South Korea, and China]." *Jindai Zhongguo funü shi yanjiu* 近代中國婦女史研究 10 (2002): 199–219.

Chen-Yao, Zhiping 陳姚穉屏. "Renshen yixi tan 妊娠一夕談 [Some Views on Pregnancy]." *Funü zazhi* 5 (1916): 5–11.

Chen-Yao, Zhiping. "Zhongguo jinri yi yangcheng chanpo lun 中國今日宜養成產婆論 [On the Necessity of Cultivating New-Style Midwives in Today's China]." *Funü zazhi* 4 (1916): 7–9.

Cheng, Eileen J. "Gendered Spectacles: Lu Xun on Gazing at Women and Other Pleasures." *Modern Chinese Literature and Culture* 16, no. 1 (2004): 1–36.

Cheng, Weikun. "Going Public through Education: Female Reformers and Girls' Schools in Late Qing Beijing." *Late Imperial China* 21, no. 1 (2000): 107–144.

Cheng, Zhanlu 程瞻廬. "Duiyu zhuchi nüxue zhe zhi zhiyan 對於主持女學者之巵言 [Suggestions for Education Authorities]." *Funü zazhi* 6 (1915a): 1–4.

Cheng, Zhanlu. "Yi xiaoshi zhi sichao 一小時之思潮 [Thoughts in One Hour]." *Funü zazhi* 2 (1915b): 1–2.

Chiang, Yung-chen. "Womanhood, Motherhood and Biology: The Early Phases of *The Ladies' Journal*, 1915–1925." *Gender & History*, 18, no. 3 (2006): 519–545.

Chin, Carol C. "Translating the New Woman: Chinese Feminists View the West, 1905–1915." *Gender & History* 18 (2006): 490–518.

Chiou, Chun-ming 邱俊明. "'Jia you xianmu, shi you liangqi': *Funü shibao* (1911–1917) jiating jiaoyu chutan 「家有賢母，室有良妻」:《婦女時報》（1911–1917）家庭教育討論初探 ['A Wise Mother in the Home, A Good Wife in the Room': A Preliminary Examination of the Discussion of Family Education in *Funü shibao*, 1911–1917]." M.A. thesis, Taiwan University, 2010.

Ch'iu, Chung-Lin 邱仲麟. "Bu xiao zhi xiao: Sui Tang yilai gegu liaoqin xianxiang de shehuishi chutan 不孝之孝: 隋唐以來割股療親現象的社會史初探 [Filial Piety of the Unfilial: A Socio-Historical Study of the Phenomenon of 'Cutting Flesh to Heal Parents' from the Sui and Tang Dynasties to Modern China]." *Xin shixue* 新史學 6 (1995): 49–94.

Cochran, Sherman. *Chinese Medicine Men: Consumer Culture in China and Southeast Asia.* Cambridge: Harvard University Press, 2006.

Cott, Nancy F. *The Bonds of Womanhood: "Woman's Sphere" in New England, 1780–1835.* New Haven: Yale University Press, 1977.

Crossley, Pamela Kyle. *A Translucent Mirror: History and Identity in Qing Imperial Ideology.* Berkeley: University of California Press, 1999.

Dikötter, Frank. *The Discourse of Race in Modern China.* Hong Kong: Hong Kong University Press, 1992.

Dikötter, Frank. *Sex, Culture and Modernity in China: Medical Science and the Construction of Sexual Identities in the Early Republican Period.* London: Hurst, 1995.

Ding, Chuwo 丁初我. "*Nüzi shijie* songci 女子世界頌詞 [Ode to *Women's World*]." *Nüzi shiji* 女子世界 1 (1904): 5–8.

Ding, Chuwo. "Shuo nümo 說女魔 [On the Evils of Women]." *Nüzi shiji* 2 (1904): 1–6.

Dooling, Amy. *Women's Literary Feminism in Twentieth Century China.* New York: Palgrave Macmillan, 2005.

Du Jikun 杜繼琨. "Zai tan *Nü xuebao* 再談女學報 [A Continued Discussion of *Nü xuebao*]." *Tushuguan* 圖書館 4 (1963): 55–56.

Ebrey, Patricia Buckley. *The Inner Quarters: Marriage and Lives of Chinese Women in The Sung Period.* Berkeley: University of California Press, 1993.

Edwards, Louise. "Chin Sung-ts'en's '*A Tocsin for Women*': The Dexterous Merger of Radicalism and Conservatism in Feminism of the Early Twentieth Century." *Jindai Zhongguo funüshi yanjiu* 近代中國婦女史研究 2 (1992): 117–40.

Edwards, Louise. *Citizens of Beauty: Drawing Democratic Dreams in Republican China.* Seattle: University of Washington Press, 2020.

Edwards, Louise. *Gender, Politics, and Democracy: Women's Suffrage in China.* Stanford: Stanford University Press, 2008.

Edwards, Louise. "Policing the Modern Woman in Republican China." *Modern China* 26, no. 2 (2000): 115–147.

Edwards, Louise. "Transformations of The Woman Warrior Hua Mulan: From Defender of The Family to Servant of the State." *Nan Nü: Men, Women, and Gender in China* 12, no. 2 (2010): 175–214.

Edwards, Louise. *Women Warriors and Wartime Spies of China.* Cambridge: Cambridge University Press, 2016.

Elliott, Mark C. *The Manchu Way: The Eight Banners and Ethnic Identity in Late Imperial China.* Stanford: Stanford University Press, 2001.

Elliott, Mark C. "Manchu Widows and Ethnicity in Qing China." *Comparative Studies in Society and History* 41, no. 1 (1999): 33–71.

Elvin, Mark. "Female Virtue and State in China." *Past and Present* 104 (1984): 111–152.

Epstein, Maram. *Competing Discourses: Orthodoxy, Authenticity, and Engendered Meanings in Late Imperial Chinese Fiction.* Cambridge: Harvard University Asia Center, 2001.

"Fakanci 發刊詞 [Inaugural Statement]." *Funü shibao* 1 (1911): 1.

Feng, Shi 風石. "Nüzi yi zhuzhong yixue shuo 女子宜注重醫學說 [Women Should Focus on Medicine]." *Funü shibao* 2 (1911): 11–13.

Finnane, Antonia. *Changing Clothes in China: Fashion, History, Nation.* New York: Columbia University Press, 2008.

Finnane, Antonia. "What Should Chinese Women Wear? A National Problem." *Modern China* 22, no. 2 (1996): 99–131.

Fong, Grace. *Herself an Author: Gender, Agency, and Writing in Late Imperial China.* Honolulu: University of Hawai'i Press, 2008.

Fong, Grace. "Signifying Bodies: The Cultural Significance of Suicide Writings by Women in Mid-Qing China." *Nan Nü: Men, Women and Gender in China* 3, no. 1 (2001): 105–142.

Foying 佛英. "Yanshuo guodu shidai zhi nüzi 演說過渡時代之女子 [A Speech on Women in the Transitional Era]." *Huixing nüxue bao* 惠興女學報 2 (June 1908): 6–8.

Foying. "Yanshuo nü xuetang zhi guanxi 演說女學堂之關係 [A Speech on the Benefits of Girls' Schools]." *Huixing nüxue bao* 1 (May 1908): 7–8.

Furth, Charlotte. "Blood, Body and Gender: Medical Images of the Female Condition in China, 1600–1850." *Chinese Science* 7 (1986): 45–66.

Furth, Charlotte. *A Flourishing Yin: Gender in China's Medical History, 960–1665.* Berkeley: University of California Press, 1998.

Gamman, Lorraine, and Margaret Marshment, ed. *The Female Gaze: Women as Viewers of Popular Culture.* London: Women's Press, 1988.

Gao, Mingkai 高名凱, and Liu Zhengtan 劉正埮. *Xindai hanyu wailai ci yanjiu* 現代漢語外來詞研究 [*A Study of the Loanwords in Modern Chinese*]. Beijing: Wenzi gaige chubanshe, 1958.

Gilmartin, Christina K., Gail Hershatter, Lisa Rofel, and Tyrene White, ed. *Engendering China: Women, Culture and the State*. Cambridge: Harvard University Press, 1994.

Gimpel, Denise. "Freeing the Mind through the Body: Women's Thoughts on Physical Education in Late Qing and Early Republican China." *Nan Nü: Men, Women and Gender in China* 8, no. 2 (2006): 316–358.

Guilin 貴林. "Hangfang Yulihui qingzhu lixian yanshuo 杭防豫立會慶祝立憲演說 [A Celebratory Speech on the Establishment of a Constitutional System, by the Preparatory Society for Constitution in the Hangzhou Banner Garrison]." *Huixing nüxue bao* 8 (December 8, 1908): 6–8.

Guilin. "Hangzhou qi cheng wei Huixing nüshi kai zhuidaohui yanshuo 杭州旗城為惠興女士開追悼會演說 [A Speech at the Memorial for Ms. Huixing in the Hangzhou Banner Garrison]." *Huixing nüxue bao* 1 (1908): 10; *Huixing nüxue bao* 2 (1908): 9–10.

Guilin. "Huixing nüshi xunxue zhounian jinianhui yanshuo 惠興女士殉學週年記念會演說 [A Speech at the First Anniversary Memorial for Huixing's Sacrifice for Education]." *Huixing nüxue bao* 3 (July 1908): 9–10.

Guilin. "Huixing xiansheng xunxue disi zhounian yanshuo 惠興先生殉學第四週年演說 [A Speech for the 4th Anniversary of Huixing's Martyrdom]." *Huixing nüxue bao* 21 (1909): 2–3.

Guilin. "Sanyue ershi liu ri Huixing nüxuexiao zongban Guilin zai Guangdelou xiguan zhi yanshuo 三月二十六日惠興女學校總辦貴林在廣德樓戲館之演說 [A Speech Delivered at the Guangde Theater on 26th March by Guilin, the Superintendent of Huixing Girls' School]." *Beijing nübao* 北京女報 (May 11, 1907).

Guo, Yanli 郭延禮. "Ershi shiji chu nüxing zhenglun zuojia qunti de dansheng 20世紀初女性政論作家群體的誕生 [The Birth of Female Political Polemical Writers in Early Twentieth-Century China]." *Zhongguo xiandai wenxue yanjiu congkan* 中國現代文學研究叢刊 3 (2009): 90–102.

"Hangzhou Huixing nüshi wei xue xunshen jielüe 杭州惠興女士為學殉身節畧 [A Brief Account of Ms. Huixing's Sacrifice for Education in Hangzhou]." *Huixing nüxue bao* 1 (May 1908): 9.

"Hangzhou Zhenwen nüxuexiao xiaozhang Huixing nüshi jueming yi zhong xuesheng shu 杭州貞文女學校惠興女士絕命遺眾學生書 [A Suicide Note to Students of Hangzhou Zhenwen Girls's School from its Principal Ms. Huixing]." *Huixing nüxue bao* 1 (May 1908): 9–10.

Harrison, Henrietta. *The Making of the Republican Citizen: Political Ceremonies and Symbols in China, 1911–1929*. Oxford: Oxford University Press, 2000.

He-Yin Zhen 何殷震. "Nüzi fuquanhui jianzhang 女子復權會簡章 [Bylaws of Society for the Restoration of Women's Rights]." *Tianyi bao* 1 (1907).

He-Yin Zhen. "*Tianyi bao* jianzhang 天義報簡章 [Bylaws of *Natural Justice*]." *Tianyi bao* 1 (1907): 7–8.

Hershatter, Gail. *Dangerous Pleasures: Prostitution and Modernity in Twentieth-Century Shanghai.* Berkeley: University of California Press, 1997.

Hershatter, Gail. *The Gender of Memory: Rural Women and China's Collective Past.* Berkeley: University of California Press, 2011.

Hershatter, Gail. *Women in China's Long Twentieth Century.* Berkeley: University of California Press, 2007.

Ho, Clara Wing-chung, ed. *Biographical Dictionary of Chinese Women: The Qing Period, 1644–1911.* Armonk, NY: M. E. Sharpe, 1998.

Hong, Fan. *Footbinding, Feminism and Freedom: The Liberation of Women's Bodies in Modern China.* London: Frank Cass, 1997.

Howe, Christopher, ed. *Shanghai, Revolution and Development in an Asian Metropolis.* Cambridge: Cambridge University Press, 1981.

Hu, Jichen 胡寄塵. "Mufan nü'er zhuan 慕凡女兒傳 [A Tale of Mu Fan]." *Funü zazhi* 1–11 (1916).

Hu, Ying. "Enemy, Friend, Martyr: Commemorating Liangbi (1877–1912), Contesting History." *Late Imperial China* 38, no. 1 (2017): 1–45.

Hu, Ying. *Tales of Translation: Composing the New Woman in China, 1899–1918.* Stanford: Stanford University Press, 2000.

Huang, Xiangjin 黃湘金. *Shishi yu chuanqi: Qingmo Minchu xiaoshuo nei de nü xuesheng* 史事與傳奇: 清末民初小說內的女學生 [*History and Legend: Female Students in Late Qing and Early Republican Fiction*]. Beijing: Beijing daxue chubanshe, 2016.

Hui Jian nüshi 慧劍女士. "Quan nüjie jiefei gou tielu gupiao xiaoqi 勸女界節費購鐵路股票小啓 [Announcement of Calling on Women to Conserve on their Expenses to Buy Railroad Stocks]." *Zhongguo xin nüjie zazhi* 中國新女界雜誌 4 (1907): 17–18.

Hui, Yuan 悔原. "Lun funü weisheng shang bixu zhi yingye 論婦女衛生上必須之營業 [Rules That Must Be Followed on Women's Hygiene]." *Funü shibao* 10 (1913): 22–25.

"Huixing nüxue bao fakanci 惠興女學報發刊辭 [Opening Statement for Journal of Huixing Girls' School]." *Huixing nüxue bao* 1 (April 15, 1908): 1–2.

"Huixing nüshi wei xue xisheng 惠興女士為學犧牲 [Ms. Huixing Sacrificed for Education]." *Shenbao* 申報 (December 30, 1905).

"Huixin nüshi xun xue ji 惠馨女士殉學記 [Account of Ms. Huixin's Sacrifice for Education]." *Dongfang zazhi* 東方雜誌 3, no. 5 (1906): 103–104.

"*Huixing nüshi zhuan* xinxi 《惠興女士傳》新戲 [A New Play Called *the Story of Ms. Huixing*]." *Huixing nüxue bao* 12–17 (1909).

Huters, Theodore. *Bringing the World Home: Appropriating the West in Late Qing and Early Republican China.* Honolulu: University of Hawai'i Press, 2005.

Idema, Wilt, and Beata Grant, ed. *The Red Brush: Writing Women of Imperial China.* Cambridge: Harvard University Asia Center, 2004.

Ji, Zonglan 計宗蘭. "Wo zhi xuexiao shenghuo 我之學校生活 [My Life at School]." *Funü zazhi* 1 (1916): 44–48.

Jiang, Weitang 姜緯堂, and Liu Ningyuan 劉寧元, ed. *Beijing funü baokan kao* 北京婦女報刊考, 1905–1949 [*A Study of Women's Journals and Newspapers in Beijing, 1905–1949*]. Beijing: Guangming ribao chubanshe, 1990.

Jin, Guantao 金觀濤 and Liu Qingfeng 劉青鋒. "Cong *tianxia, wanguo* dao *shijie*—wan Qing minzu zhuyi xingcheng de zhongjian huanjie 從「天下」、「萬國」到「世界」——晚清民族主義形成的中間環節 [From *tianxia, wanguo,* to *shijie*: Intermediary Links in the Formation of Nationalism in the Late Qing]." *Ershi yi shiji* 二十一世紀 94 (2006): 40–53.

Jin, Tianhe 金天翮. *Nüjie zhong* 女界鐘 [*The Women's Bell*], ed. Li Youning 李又寧. New York: Outer Sky Press, 2003.

Jin, Tianhe. "*Nüzi shijie* fakanci 女子世界發刊詞 [Inaugural Statement for *Women's World*]." *Nüzi shijie* 1 (1904): 9–11.

Judge, Joan. "Between *Nei* and *Wai*: Women Students in Japan in the Early Twentieth Century." In *Gender in Motion: Divisions of Labor and Cultural Change in Late Imperial and Modern China,* ed. Bryna Goodman and Wendy Larson, 121–143. Boulder, CO: Rowman and Littlefield, 2005.

Judge, Joan. "Blended Wish Images: Chinese and Western Exemplary Women at the Turn of the Twentieth Century." *Nan Nü: Men, Women, and Gender in Early and Imperial China* 6, no. 1 (2004): 102–135.

Judge, Joan. "Citizens or Mothers of Citizens? Gender and the Meaning of Modern Chinese Citizenship." In *Changing Meanings of Citizenship in Modern China,* ed. Elizabeth Perry and Merle Goldman, 23–43. Cambridge: Harvard University Asia Centre, 2002.

Judge, Joan. "The Culturally Contested Student Body: *Nü Xuesheng* at the Turn-of-the-Twentieth Century." In *Performing Nation: New Gender Constructs in Literature, the Visual and the Performing Arts of Modern China and Japan,* ed. Joshua Mostow, Catherine Vance Yeh, and Doris Croissant, 105–132. Leiden: E.J. Brill, 2008.

Judge, Joan. "Everydayness as a Critical Category of Gender Analysis: The Case of *Funü shibao* (The Women's Eastern Times)." *Jindai Zhongguo funüshi yanjiu* 20 (2012): 1–28.

Judge, Joan. "Expanding the Feminine/National Imaginary: Social and Martial Heroines in Late Qing Women's Journals." *Jindai Zhongguo funüshi yanjiu* 15 (2007): 1–33.

Judge, Joan. *The Precious Raft of History: the Past, the West, and the Woman Question in China.* Stanford: Stanford University Press, 2008.

Judge, Joan. *Print and Politics:* Shibao *and the Culture of Reform in Late Qing China.* Stanford: Stanford University Press, 1996.

Judge, Joan. *Republican Lens: Gender, Visuality, and Experience in Early Chinese Periodical Press*. Berkeley: University of California Press, 2015.

Judge, Joan. "Talent, Virtue, and the Nation: Chinese Nationalisms and Female Subjectivities in the Early Twentieth Century." *American Historical Review* 106 (2001): 765–803.

Judge, Joan, and Hu Ying, ed. *Beyond Exemplar Tales: Women's Biography in Chinese History.* Berkeley: Global, Area, and International Archive/University of California Press, 2011.

Judge, Joan, Barbara Mittler, and Michel Hockx, ed. *Women and the Periodical Press in China's Long Twentieth Century: A Space of Their Own?* Cambridge: Cambridge University Press, 2018.

Kang, Tongwei 康同薇. "Nüxue libi shuo 女学利弊说 [On the Advantages and Disadvantages of Women's Education]." *Nü xuebao* 7 (1898): 3a–3b.

Karl, Rebecca E. "Creating Asia: China in the World at the Beginning of the Twentieth Century." *American Historical Review* 103, no. 4 (1998): 1096–1118.

Karl, Rebecca E., and Peter Zarrow. *Rethinking the 1898 Reform Period: Political and Cultural Change in Late Qing China.* Cambridge: Harvard University Asia Center, 2002.

Kaske, Elisabeth. *The Politics of Language in Chinese Education, 1895–1919.* Leiden: Brill, 2007.

Kazuko, Ono. *Chinese Women in a Century of Revolution, 1850–1950*. Trans. Kathryn Bernhardt et al.; ed. Joshua A. Fogel. Stanford: Stanford University Press, 1989.

Ko, Dorothy. "The Body as Attire: The Shifting Meanings of Footbinding in Seventeenth-Century China." *Journal of Women's History* 8 (1997): 8–27.

Ko, Dorothy. *Cinderella's Sisters: A Revisionist History of Footbinding.* Berkeley: University of California Press, 2005.

Ko, Dorothy. *Teachers of the Inner Chambers: Women and Culture in seventeenth Century China.* Stanford: Stanford University Press, 1994.

Lackner, Michael, and Natascha Vittinghoff, ed. *Mapping Meanings: The Field of New Learning in Late Qing China*. Leiden: Brill, 2004.

Laing, Ellen Johnston. *Selling Happiness: Calendar Posters and Visual Culture in Early Twentieth Century Shanghai.* Honolulu: University of Hawai'i Press, 2004.

Laing, Ellen Johnston. "Visual Evidence for the Evolution of 'Politically Correct' Dress for Women in Early Twentieth Century Shanghai." *Nan Nü: Men, Women and Gender in China* 5, no. 1 (2003): 69–114.

Lean, Eugenia. "Recipes for Men: Manufacturing Make-up and the Politics of Production in 1910s China." *Osiris* 30, no. 1 (January 2015): 134–157.

Lean, Eugenia. "The Butterfly Mark: Chen Diexian, His Brand, and Cultural Entrepreneurism in Republican China." In *The Business of Culture: Cultural Entrepreneurs in China and Southeast Asia, 1900–65,* ed. Christopher Rea and Nicolai Volland, 36–62. Vancouver: UBC Press, 2015.

Lei, Hsiang-lin. "Weisheng weihe bushi baowei shengming? Minguo shiqi lingleide weisheng ziwo yu jibing 衛生為何不是保衛生命? 民國時期另類的衛生、自我、與疾病 [Why Weisheng is Not about Guarding Life: Alternative Conceptions of Hygiene, Self, and Illness in Republican China]." *Taiwan shehui yanjiu jikan* 台灣社會研究季刊 54 (2004): 17–59.

Leung, Angela Ki Che. "Recent Trends in the Study of Medicine for Women in Imperial China." *Nan Nü: Men, Women and Gender in China* 7, no. 2 (2005): 110–126.

Leutner, Mechthild, and Nicola Spakowski, ed. *Women in China: The Republican Period in Historical Perspective*. Münster: Lit, 2005.

Levenson, Joseph R. *Confucian China and Its Modern Fate: A Trilogy*. Berkeley: University of California Press, 1972.

Lewis, Ida Belle. *The Education of Girls in China*. New York: Columbia University Press, 1919.

Li, Guotong. *Migrating Fujianese: Ethnic, Family, and Gender Identities in an Early Modern Maritime World*. Leiden: E.J. Brill, 2016.

Li, Qinde 李勤德. "Nüshi kao 女史考 [An Investigation of the Term *Nüshi*]." *Xueshu yanjiu* 學術研究 1 (1992): 77–80.

Li, Wai-Yee. *Women and National Trauma in Late Imperial Chinese Literature*. Cambridge: Harvard University Asia Center, 2013.

Li, Xiaorong. *Women's Poetry of Late Imperial China: Transforming the Inner Chambers*. Seattle: University of Washington Press, 2012.

Li, Xizhu 李細珠. "Qing mo minjian yulun yu guanfu zuowei zhi hudong guanxi: yi Zhang Zengyang yu Qiu Jin an wei li 清末民間輿論與官府作為之互動關係——以張曾敭與秋瑾案為例 [The Interactions between Local Government and Public Opinion in the Late Qing: The Cases of Zhang Zengyang and Qiu Jin]." *Jindaishi yanjiu* 近代史研究 2 (2004): 1–44.

Li, Xizhu. "Qiu Jin nüxing gemingjia xingxiang de lishi jiangou 秋瑾女性革命家形象的歷史建構 [The Historical Construction of Qiu Jin's Image as a Female Revolutionary]." *Shehui kexue yanjiu* 社會科學研究 5 (2007): 147–152.

Li, Youning 李又寧. "*Zhongguo xin nüjie zazhi* de chuangkan ji neihan: *Zhongguo xin nüjie zazhi* chongkan xu 中國新女界雜誌的創刊及內涵：中國新女界雜誌重刊序 [The Publication and Significance of *Magazine of New Women's World of China*: Preface to the Reprint of *Magazine of New Women's World of China*]." In *Zhongguo funü shi lunwen ji* 中國婦女史論文集 [*Collections of Essays on Chinese Women's History*], ed. Li Youning 李又寧 and Zhang Yufa 張玉法, 1:179–241. Taipei: Taiwan shangwu yinshuguan, 1981.

Li, Youning 李又寧, and Zhang Yufa 張玉法, eds. *Jindai Zhongguo nüquan yundong shiliao 1842–1911* 近代中國女權運動史料 1842–1911 [*Historical Materials on Modern Chinese Women's Movements*], vols. 1 & 2. Taipei: zhuanji wenxueshe chuban, 1975.

Lian Shi 煉石 [Yan Bin 燕斌]. "Ben bao duiyu nüzi guomin juan zhi yanshuo 本報對于女子国民捐之演說 [A Public Speech on a Female Citizen's Fund]." *Zhongguo xin nüjie zazhi* 1 (1907): 41–50.

Lian Shi. "Ben bao wuda zhuyi yanshuo 本報五大主義演說 [Five Tenets of This Journal]." *Zhongguo xin nüjie zazhi* 2–4 (1907).

Lian Shi. "Bo'aizhuyi shixingjia Mode nüshi zhuan 博愛主義實行家墨德女士傳 [Biography of the Philanthropist Lucretia Mott]." *Zhongguo xin nüjie zazhi* 5 (1907): 41–50.

Lian Shi. "Fakanci 發刊詞 [Inaugural Statement]." *Zhongguo xin nüjie zazhi* 1 (1907): 1–2.

Lian Shi. "Lun nüjie yu guojia zhi guanxi 論女界與國家之關係 [On the Relationship between Women and the Nation]." *Zhongguo xin nüjie zazhi* 2 (1907): 1–3.

Lian Shi. "Nüquan pingyi 女權平議 [On Women's Rights]." *Zhongguo xin nüjie zazhi* 1 (1907): 4.

Liang, Lingxian 梁令嫻. "Jingshu wujia jiude wei funü zazhi zhu 敬述吾家舊德為婦女雜誌祝 [Respectfully Presenting My Family Morals to *Ladies' Journal*]." *Funü zazhi* 1 (1915): 6–8.

Liang, Qichao 梁啟超. "Bianfa tongyi: lun youxue 變法通議·論幼學 [A General Discussion of Reform—On Education for Children]." In *Yinbing shi heji: wenji* 飲冰室合集文集 [*Collected Writings from the Ice-Drinker's Studio*], ed. Liang Qichao, 1, 44–60. Shanghai: Zhonghua shuju, 1936.

Liang, Qichao. "Changshe nü xuetang qi 倡設女學堂啟 [Announcement of Establishing the Girls' School]." *Shiwu bao* 時務報 (1897): 7–9.

Liao Xiuzhen 廖秀珍, "Qingmo nüxue zai xuezhi shang de yanjin ji nuzi xiaoxue jiaoyu de fazhan, 1897–1911 清末女學在學制上的演進及女子小學教育的發展 (1897–1911) [The Evolution of the Schooling System for Women in the Late Qing (1897–1911)]." In *Zhongguo funu shi lunwen ji* 中國婦女史論文集 [*Collections of Essays on Chinese Women's History*], ed. Li Youning and Zhang yufa, 2: 203–255. Taipei: Taiwan shangwu yinshuguan, 1988.

Ling, Xi 靈希. "Meiguo da xinwenjia Asuoli nüshi zhuan 美國大新聞家阿索里女士傳 [Biography of the Great American Journalist Ms. Margaret Fuller Ossoli]." *Zhongguo xin nüjie zazhi* 1 (1907): 65–71.

Link, Perry. *Mandarin Ducks and Butterflies: Popular Fiction in Early Twentieth-Century Chinese Cities.* Berkeley: University of California Press, 1981.

Link, Perry. "Traditional-Style Popular Urban Fiction in the Teens and Twenties." In *Modern Chinese Literature in the May Fourth Era,* ed. Merle Goldman, 327–349. Cambridge: Harvard University Press, 1977.

Liu, Huiying 劉慧英. "Shengli shuo de laiyuan ji yansheng yu funü wenti "生利" 說的來源及衍生於婦女問題 [The Origins and Developments of the Theory of "Profit Making" and Its Impact on the Woman Question]." *Nankai xuebao* 南開學報 6 (2009): 1–8.

Liu, Lydia H. *Translingual Practice: Literature, National Culture, and Translated Modernity—China, 1900–1937*. Stanford: Stanford University Press, 1995.

Liu, Lydia H., Rebecca E. Karl, and Dorothy Ko, ed. *The Birth of Chinese Feminism: Essential Texts in Transnational Theory*. New York: Columbia University Press, 2013.

Liu, Renfeng 劉人鋒. *Zhongguo funü baokan shi yanjiu* 中國婦女報刊史研究 [*A Study on the Chinese Women's Periodical Press*]. Beijing: Zhongguo shehui kexue chubanshe, 2012.

Liu, Renlan 劉紉蘭. "Quan xing nüxue qi 勸興女學啓 [Letter on Advancing Women's Education]." *Nü xuebao* 4 (1898). In *Zhongguo jindai funü yundong lishi ziliao, 1840–1918* 中國近代婦女運動歷史資料，1840–1918 [*Historical Materials on Modern Chinese Women's Movements, 1840–1918*], ed. Xu Huiqi 徐輝琪, Liu Jucai 劉巨才, and Xu Yuzhen徐玉珍, 96–98. Beijing: Zhongguo funü chubanshe, 1991.

Liu, Sheng 劉壒. "Fakanci er 發刊詞二 [Inaugural Statement II]." *Funü zazhi* 1 (1915): 2–4.

Liu, Sheng. "*Zhonghua funüjie* zhuci 中華婦女界祝辭 [Congratulatory Speech for *Chung Hwa Women's Magazine*]." *Zhonghua funüjie* 中華婦女界 1, no. 1 (1915): 1–2.

Loeb, Lori. "George Fulford and Victorian Patent Medicine Men: Quack Mercenaries or Simlesian Entrepreneurs?" *Canadian Bulletin of Medical History* 16 (1999): 125–145.

Lü, Meiyi 呂美頤. "Ping Zhongguo jindai guanyu xianqi liangmu zhuyi de lunzheng 評中國近代關於賢妻良母主義的論爭 [A Review of the Debates on the Ideology of Good Wives and Wise Mothers in Modern China]." *Tianjin shenhui kexue* 天津社會科學 5 (1995): 73–79.

Lu, Weijing. *True to Her Word: The Faithful Maiden Cult in Late Imperial China*. Stanford: Stanford University Press, 2008.

"Lun Manzhou nüzi de duoluo 論滿洲女子的墮落 [On the Degeneration of Manchu Women]." *Beijing nübao* (October 18, 1905).

Luo, Suwen 羅蘇文. "Lun qingmo shanghai dushi nüzhuang de yanbian (1880–1910) 論清末上海都市女裝的演變, 1880–1910 [On Changes in Urban Women's Clothing in Late Qing Shanghai]." In *Wusheng zhi sheng II: jindai Zhongguo de funü yu shehui* (1600–1950) 無聲之聲 II：近代中國的婦女與社會（1600–1950）[*Voices amid Silence II: Women and Culture in Modern China, 1600–1950*], ed. You Jianming 游鑑明, 141–172. Taipei: Zhongyang yanjiuyuan jindaishi yanjiusuo, 2003.

Ma, Yuxin. *Women Journalists and Feminism in China, 1898–1937*. Amherst, NY: Cambria Press, 2010.

Mann, Susan. "Grooming a Daughter for Marriage: Brides and Wives in the Mid-Qing Period." In *Chinese Femininities/Chinese Masculinities*, ed. Susan Brownell and Jeffrey N. Wasserstrom, 93–119. Berkeley: University of California Press, 2002.

Mann, Susan. *Precious Records: Women in China's Long Eighteenth Century*. Stanford: Stanford University Press, 1997.

Mann, Susan. *The Talented Women of the Zhang Family.* Berkeley: University of California Press, 2008.

Mei, Zhu 梅鑄. "Faguo jiuwang nüjie Ruoan zhuan 法國救亡女傑若安傳 [Biography of Joan of Arc, a French Heroine Who Saved the Nation]." *Zhongguo xin nüjie zazhi* 3 (1907): 53–82.

Meyer-Fong, Tobie. *What Remains: Coming to Terms with Civil War in 19th Century China.* Stanford: Stanford University Press, 2013.

Mittler, Barbara. *A Newspaper for China? Power, Identity, and Change in Shanghai's News Media, 1872–1912.* Cambridge: Harvard University Press, 2004.

Morgan, Evan. *Chinese New Terms and Expressions with English Translations: Introduction and Notes.* Shanghai: Kelly & Walsh, 1913.

Mou, Zhengyun 牟正蘊. "Jiegou *funü*: jiuci xinlun 解構 "婦女": 舊詞新論 [Deconstructing *Funü:* New Interpretations of An Old Term]." *Jindai Zhongguo funüshi yanjiu* 6 (1998): 119–139.

Mu, Lan 慕蘭. "Jiating weisheng lun (er) 家庭衛生論 (二) [On Family Hygiene (2)]." *Funü shibao* 10 (1912): 10–12.

Mulan tongxiang 木蘭同鄉. "Gonghe xinnian 恭賀新年 [Best Wishes for a New Year]." *Zhongguo xin nüjie zazhi* 2 (1907): 27–33.

Mulvey, Laura. "Visual Pleasure and Narrative Cinema." *Screen* 16, no. 3 (1975): 6–18.

Nathan, Andrew J. *Peking Politics, 1918–1923.* Berkeley: University of California Press, 1976.

Nivard, Jacqueline. "L'évolution de la press féminine 1898 à 1949." *Études Chinoises* 5, nos. 1–2 (1986): 157–184.

Nivard, Jacqueline. "Women and the Women's Press: The Case of the Women's Journal (*Funü zazhi*) 1915–1931." *Republican China* 10, no. 1 (1984): 37–55.

"Nüshi zouma 女士走馬 [A Young Lady Riding a Horse]." *Xingqi huabao* 星期畫報 22 (March 1907).

"Nüzi wucai bianshi de bo 女子無才便是德駁 [A Rebuttal to 'Women without Talent are Virtuous']." *Zhongguo xin nüjie zazhi* 3 (1907): 27–29.

Ouyang, Yuqian 歐陽予倩. "Tan wenming xi 談文明戲 [On Civilized Drama]." In *Zhongguo huaju yundong wushinian shiliao ji* 中國話劇運動五十年史料集 [*Collection of Historical Sources of Fifty Years of Spoken Drama Movements in China*], ed. Tian Han 田漢 et al., 13–46. Beijing: Zhongguo xiju chubanshe, 1985.

Owen, Stephen. "Poetry in the Chinese Tradition." In *Heritage of China: Contemporary Perspectives on Chinese Civilization,* ed. Paul S. Ropp, 294–308. Berkeley: University of California Press, 1990.

Pan, Xuan 潘璇. "Lun *Nü xuebao* nanchu he Zhongwai nüzi xiangzhu de lifa 論女學報難處和中外女子相助的理法 [On the Difficulties of Founding the *Nü xuebao* and the Way of Mutual Help between Chinese and Western Women]." *Nüxue bao* 3 (1898): 2a–3a.

Pan, Xuan. "Shanghai *Nü xuebao* yuanqi (diyi jie): Lun yong *guanhua* 上海女學報緣起（第一節）：論用官話 [Forward to *Nü xuebao*, Part One: On the Use of Mandarin]." *Nü xuebao* 1 (1898): 2a–2b.

Pan, Xuan. "Shanghai *Nüxue bao* yuanqi (di'er jie): Lun ben bao wei nüxue qi jian 上海女學報緣起（第二節）：論本報為女學起見 [Forward to *Nü xuebao*, Part Two: For the Sake of Women's Education]." *Nü xuebao* 2 (1898): 2a–3a.

Porter, David C. "Manchu Racial Identity on the Qing Frontier: Donjina and Early Twentieth Century Ili." *Modern China* 44, no. 1 (2018): 3–34.

Qian, Nanxiu. "Borrowing Foreign Mirrors and Candles to Illuminate Chinese Civilization: Xue Shaohui's Moral Vision in the *Biographies of Foreign Women*." *Nan Nü: Men, Women and Gender in China* 6, no. 1 (2004): 60–101.

Qian, Nanxiu. *Politics, Poetics, and Gender in Late Qing China: Xue Shaohui and the Era of Reform*. Stanford: Stanford University Press, 2015.

Qian, Nanxiu. "Revitalizing the *Xianyuan* (Worthy Ladies) Tradition: Women in the 1898 Reforms." *Modern China* 29, no. 4 (2003): 399–454.

Qian, Nanxiu, Grace Fong, and Richard J. Smith, ed. *Different Worlds of Discourse: Transformations of Gender and Genre in Late Qing and Early Republican China*. Leiden: E.J. Brill, 2008.

"Qing jiang xunfu xunxue zhi nüshi 請獎殉夫殉學之女士 [A Petition to Award the Woman Who Martyred Herself for Her Husband and Education]." *Huixing nüxue bao* 16 (1909): 4.

Qing, Meng 傾孟. "Dui yu nüzi canzheng zhi yanjiu 對於女子參政之研究 [A Study of Women's Political Participation]." *Funü shibao* 8 (1912): 7–8.

Qing, Ru 清如. "Lun nüxue 論女學 [On Women's Education]." *Zhongguo xin nüjie zazhi* 2 (1907): 1–10.

"Qinü yi wei bi xingxue hu 旗女亦為彼興學乎 [Manchu Women also Promoted Education for Themselves?]." *Jingzhong ribao* 警鐘日報 (November 8, 1904).

Qiu, Jin 秋瑾. *Qiu Jin ji* 秋瑾集 [*Collected Works by Qiu Jin*], ed. Shanghai guji chubanshe 上海古籍出版社. Shanghai: Shanghai guji chubanshe, 1991.

Qiu, Ping 秋蘋. "Chanfu zhi xinde ji shiyan tan 產婦之心得與實驗談 [On Knowledge and Experience from Women Who Have Just Given Birth]." *Funü shibao* 1 (1911): 17–20.

Qiu, Yufang 裘毓芳. "Lun nü xuetang yu nan xuetang bingzhong 論女學堂與男學堂並重 [On the Equal Importance of Establishing Girls' and Boys' Schools]." *Nü xuebao* 7 (1898).

Qu, Jun 瞿鈞. "Funü zhi weisheng yiban: yuejing zhi zhuyi/ renshen zhi baoyang 婦女之衛生一斑 ：月經之注意/妊娠之保養 [Some Views on Women's Hygiene: Paying Attention to Menstruation/Care During Pregnancy]." *Funü shibao* 3 (1911): 25–29.

Qu, Jun. "Furen zhi weisheng zahua 婦人之衛生雜話 [Miscellaneous Comments on Women's Hygiene]." *Funü shibao* 4 (1911): 17–28.

Rankin, Mary Backus. "The Emergence of Women at the End of the Ch'ing: The Case of Ch'iu Chin." In *Women in Chinese Society,* ed. Margery Wolf and Roxanne Witke, 39–66. Stanford: Stanford University Press, 1975.

Rawski, Evelyn Sakakida. *Education and Popular Literacy in Ch'ing China.* Ann Arbor: University of Michigan Press, 1979.

Reed, Christopher A. *Gutenberg in Shanghai: Chinese Print Capitalism, 1876–1937.* Vancouver: University of British Columbia Press, 2004.

Ren, Yanyou 任妍幽. "Lun jiating yi shi zhu zhi dang zhuyi 論家庭衣食住之當注 [Important Matters on Eating, Clothing, and Housing]." *Funü zazhi* 5 (1915): 8–11.

Rhoads, Edward J. M. *Manchus and Han: Ethnic Relations and Political Power in Late Qing and Early Republican China, 1861–1928.* Seattle: University of Washington Press, 2000.

Richardson, Nicole. "The Nation *in Utero*: Translating the Science of Fetal Education in Republican China." *Frontiers of History in China* 7, no. 1 (2012): 4–31.

Rogaski, Ruth. *Hygienic Modernity: Meanings of Health and Disease in Treaty-Port China.* Berkeley: University of California Press, 2004.

Ropp, Paul. "Passionate Women: Female Suicide in Late Imperial China." *Nan Nü: Men, Women and Gender in China* 3, no. 1 (2001): 3–21.

Rui, Hua 瑞華. "Jinggao nü xuesheng 敬告女學生 [Respectfully Exhort Girl Students]." *Funü zazhi* 7 (1915): 6–8.

Ruixing 瑞興. "Baqi xieling gong cheng 八旗協領公呈 [Memorial from a Regiment Colonel]." *Beijing nübao* (July 9, 1906).

Sanduo 三多. "Ji Huixing nüjie wei xue xunshen shi 記惠興女傑為學殉身事 [An Account of the Female Hero Huixing's Sacrifice for Education]." *Dagong bao* (March 14, 1906).

Schneider, Helen M. *Keeping the Nation's House: Domestic Management and the Making of Modern China.* Vancouver: University of British Columbia, 2012.

Shan, Patrick Fuliang. "Elastic Self-Consciousness and the Reshaping of Manchu Identity." In *Ethnic China: Identity, Assimilation, and Resistance,* ed. Xiaobing Li and Patrick Fuliang Shan, 39–59. Lanham, MD: Lexington Books, 2015.

Shao, Piaoping 邵飄萍. "Lixiang zhi nü xuesheng 理想之女學生 [Ideal Girl Students]." *Funü zazhi* 3 (1915): 1–5.

Shen, Fang 沈芳. "Funü weisheng tan 婦女衛生談 [Discussion of Women's Hygiene]." *Funü zazhi* 1 (1915): 2–10.

Shen, Jie 沈潔. "Cong Guilin zhi si kan Xinren zhi ji de zhongzu yu zhengzhi 從貴林之死看辛壬之際的種族與政治 [Ethnicity and Politics during the Xinhai Revolution, from the Perspective of Guilin's Death]." *Shi lin* 史林 4 (2013): 89–98.

Shen, Shuzhen 沈淑貞. "Hushang nishe jinü xuexiao lun 滬上擬設妓女學校論 [Proposal of Establishing Schools for Prostitutes in Shanghai]." *Funü shibao* 7 (1912): 45–47.

Shen, Weizhen 沈維楨. "Lun xiaobanbi yu nüzi tiyu 論小半臂與女子體育 [On Brest Binding and Women's Physical Education]." *Funü zazhi* 1 (1915): 1–2.

Shen, Weizhen. "Lun xiaobanbi zhi hai yu nüzi tiyu 論小半臂之害與女子體育 [On the Harm of Breast Binding and Women's Physical Education]." *Funü shibao* 16 (February 1915): 9–11.

Shen, Ying 沈瑛. "Zhongguo nüxuehui zhi houguan xue nüshi shaohui shu 中國女學會致侯官薛女史紹徽書 [To Woman Historian Xue Shaohui of Houguan from the Women's Study Society]." *Zhixin bao* 知新報 59 (1898): 8–9.

Shen, Ying. "Zhongguo nüxue ni zengshe baoguan gaobai 中國女學擬增設報館告白 [Announcement of the Proposal of Establishing a Journal Affiliated with the Chinese Girls' School]." *Zhixin bao* 知新報 55 (June 9, 1898): 26b.

Shepherd, John R. *Footbinding as Fashion: Ethnicity, Labor, and Status in Traditional China.* Seattle: University of Washington Press, 2018.

Shepherd, John R. "The Qing, the Manchus, and Footbinding: Sources and Assumptions under Scrutiny." *Frontiers of History in China* 11, no. 2 (2016): 279–322.

Shu Zi 叔子. "Furen zhi weisheng 婦人之衛生 [Women's Hygiene]." *Funü zazhi* 8 (1915): 6–8.

Sievers, Sharon L. *Flowers in Salt: The Beginnings of Feminist Consciousness in Modern Japan.* Stanford: Stanford University Press, 1983.

Song, Butian 宋補天. "Jiating weisheng lun (yi) 家庭衛生論 (一) [On Family Hygiene (1)]." *Funü shibao* 10 (1913): 6–10.

Song, Suhong 宋素紅. *Nüxing meijie: lishi yu chuantong* 女性媒介：歷史與傳統 [*Women's Media: History and Tradition*]. Beijing: Zhongguo chuanmei daxue chubanshe, 2006.

Stevens, Sarah E. "Figuring Modernity: The New Woman and the Modern Girl in Republican China." *NWSA Journal* 15, no. 3 (2003): 82–103.

Sudo, Mizuyo. "Concepts of Women's Rights in Modern China." In *Translating Feminisms in China,* ed. Dorothy Ko and Wang Zheng, 13–34. Oxford: Blackwell, 2007.

Tan, Sheying 談社英, ed. *Zhongguo funü yundong tongshi* 中國婦女運動通史 [*A General History of the Chinese Women's Movement*]. Nanjing: Funü gongming she, 1936.

Tan, Sitong 譚嗣同. "Baozhang wenti shuo 報章文體說 [On Newspaper Styles]." *Shiwu bao* 時務報 29–30 (June 6–21, 1897).

Tang, Xiaobing. *Global Space and the Nationalist Discourse of Modernity: The Historical Thinking of Liang Qichao.* Stanford: Stanford University Press, 1996.

Tang, Xuezhen 湯雪珍. "Nüjie geming 女界革命 [Women's Revolution]." *Nüzi shiji* 4 (1904): 13–17.

Theiss, Janet. *Disgraceful Matters: The Politics of Chastity in Eighteenth-Century China.* Berkeley: University of California Press, 2004.

Theiss, Janet. "Managing Martyrdom: Female Suicide and Statecraft in Mid-Qing China." *Nan Nü: Men, Women and Gender in China* 3 (2001): 47–76.

Tianzuisheng 天醉生. "Jing gao yiban nüzi 敬告一般女子[Respectfully Exhort the General Women]." *Nüzi shiji* 1 (1904): 9–12.

Tsu, Jing. *Failure, Nationalism, and Literature: The Making of Modern Chinese Identity, 1895–1937.* Stanford: Stanford University Press, 2005.

Wan, Shiguo 萬仕國, ed. *Liu Shenshu yishu buyi* 劉申叔遺書補遺 [*Supplement to the Posthumous Works by Liu Shipei*]. Yangzhou: Guangling Press, 2008.

Wan, Xiu 晚秀. "Xianmu liangqi zhuyi yu jiuguo wenti 賢母良妻主義與救國問題 [The Ideology of 'Wise Mothers and Good Wives' and National Salvation]." *Funü shibao* 18 (1916): 1–4.

Wang, Changlin 王長林, and Tang Ying 唐瑩, ed. *Zhongguo jinxiandai nüxing qikan huibian* 中國近現代女性期刊匯編 [*Compilation of Women's Journals in Modern China*]. Beijing: Xianzhuang shuju, 2008.

Wang Chuanying 王傳英. "Xin dasheng pian 新達生篇 [A New Treatise on Easy Childbirth]." *Funü zazhi* 2 (1918): 1–4; 6 (1918): 4–8.

Wang, Jiajian 王家儉. "Minchu de nüzi canzheng yundong 民初的女子參政運動 [Women's Suffrage Movement in Early Republican China]." *Shida lishi xuebao* 師大歷史學報 11 (June 1983): 149–171.

Wang, Jieliang 汪傑樑. "Lixiang de jiating mofan 理想的家庭模範 [[Ideal Family Model]." *Funü shibao* 5 (1912): 1–7.

Wang, Jieliang. "Xiao'er baoyu fa 小兒保育法 [How to Take Care of Young Children]." *Funü shibao* 2 (1911): 35–40.

Wang, Jieliang. "Xiao'er jibing kanhu fa 小兒疾病看護法 [How to Care for Sick Children]." *Funü shibao* 3 (1911): 35–39.

Wang, San 王三. "Funü zhi tianzhi 婦女之天職 [Women's Natural Duty]." *Funü zazhi* 2 (1915): 1–4.

Wang, San. "Jinggao quanguo nüxuexiao 敬告全國女學校 [Respectfully Addressing All the Girls' Schools in China]." *Funü zazhi* 9 (1915): 1–3.

Wei, Hongzhu 魏宏珠. "Duiyu nü xuesheng zhi zhiyan 對於女學生之卮言 [Suggestions for Girl Students]." *Funü shibao* 5 (1911): 10–14.

Weinbaum, Alys Eve, Lynn M. Thomas, Priti Ramamurthy, Uta G. Poiger, Madeleine Yue Dong, and Tani E. Barlow, ed. *The Modern Girl around the World: Consumption, Modernity, and Globalization.* Durham: Duke University Press, 2008.

Widmer, Ellen. "The Epistolary World of Female Talent in Seventeenth-Century China," *Late Imperial China* 10 (December 1989): 1–43.

Widmer, Ellen. "The Rhetoric of Retrospection: May Fourth Literary History and the Ming-Qing Woman Writer." In *The Appropriation of Cultural Capital: China's May*

Fourth Project, ed. Milena Doleželová-Velingerová and Oldřich Král, 193–226. Cambridge: Harvard University Asia Center, 2001.

Widmer, Ellen, and Kang-i Sun Chang, ed. *Writing Women in Late Imperial China*. Stanford: Stanford University Press, 1997.

Wu, Bingyun 吳秉筠. "Nüxue yi zhuzhong fengren pengtiao lun 女學宜注重縫紉烹調論 [The Education for Women Should Emphasize Sewing and Cooking]." *Funü zazhi* 4 (1915): 9–10.

Wu, Shengqing. *Modern Archaics: Continuity and Innovation in the Chinese Lyric Tradition, 1900–1937*. Cambridge: Harvard University Asia Center, 2013.

Wu, Yi-li. *Reproducing Women: Medicine, Metaphor, and Childbirth in Late Imperial China*. Berkeley: University of California Press, 2010.

Xia, Xiaohong 夏曉虹. "He Zhen de wu zhengfu zhuyi 'nüjie geming' lun 何震的無政府主義 "女界革命" 論 [He Zhen's Anarchist Thought on 'Women's Revolution']." *Zhonghua wenshi lun cong* 中華文史論叢 83 (2006): 311–350.

Xia, Xiaohong. "Jiu xitai shang de wenmingxi: Tian Jiyun yu Bejing Funü kuangxuehui 舊戲台上的文明戲：田際雲與北京 "婦女匡學會" [The Civilized Drama on the Old Stage: Tian Jiyuan and the Women's Association of Rectifying Learning in Beijing]." In *Beijing: dushi xiangxiang yu wenhua jiyi* 北京：都市想像與文化記憶 [*Beijing: Urban Imaginations and Cultural Memories*], ed. Chen Pingyuan 陳平原 and Wang Dewei 王德威, 94–120. Beijing: Peking University Press, 2005.

Xia, Xiaohong. "Qiu Jin wenxue xingxiang de shidai fengmao: cong Xia Yan de huaju dao Xie Jin de dianying 秋瑾文學形象的時代風貌——從夏衍的話劇到謝晉的電影 [Historical Changes in Qiu Jin's Literary Imagery: From Xia Yan's Play to Xie Jin's Movie]." *Zhongguo xiandai wenxue congkan* 中國現代文學叢刊 4 (2009): 49–65.

Xia, Xiaohong. "Qiu Jin yu Guilin 秋瑾與貴林 [Qiu Jin and Guilin]." *Dushu* 讀書 9 (2007): 62–68.

Xia, Xiaohong. *Wan-Qing baihua wen yu qimeng duwu* 晚清白話文與啟蒙讀物 [*Late Qing Vernacular Writings and Reading Materials for Enlightenment*]. Hong Kong: Sanlian shudian, 2015.

Xia, Xiaohong. "Wan-Qing de nüzi tuanti 晚清的女子團體 [Women's Organizations in the Late Qing]." *Hangzhou shifan xueyuan xuebao* 杭州師範學院學報 1 (1996): 13–18.

Xia, Xiaohong. "Wan Qing nübao zhong de Xifang nüjie—mingzhi 'furen lizhi' duwu de Zhongguo zhi lü 晚清女報中的西方女傑：明治 "婦人立志" 讀物的中國之旅 [Western Heroines in Late-Qing Women's Journals: The Voyage to China of Meiji-Era Writings on Women's 'Self-Help']." *Wen shi zhe* 文史哲 4 (2012): 20–34.

Xia, Xiaohong. *Wan-Qing nüxing yu jindai Zhongguo* 晚清女性與近代中國 [*Late Qing Women and Modern China*]. Beijing: Peking University Press, 2004.

Xia, Xiaohong. *Wan-Qing shehui yu wenhua* 晚清社會與文化 [*Late Qing Society and Culture*]. Wuhan: Hubei jiaoyu chubanshe, 2000.

Xia, Zhen 遐珍. "Yu zhi zhonggao yu nü xuesheng 余之忠告於女學生 [My Advice for Girl Students]." *Funü zazhi* 4 (1915): 4–5.

Xiao, Yun 笑芸. "Nüzi fenmian hou zhi kanhu 女子分娩後之看護 [Care for Women Who have Given Birth]." *Funü shibao* 18 (1916): 52–55.

Xinghua 興華. "Pinglun yanshuo 評論演說 [Commentary and Speech]." *Huixing nüxue bao* 5 (September 10, 1908): 8.

Xingyong 興永. "Yanshuo nüxuesheng zhi zeren 演說女學生之責任 [A Public Speech on Female Students' Responsibilities]." *Huixing nüxue bao* 7 (November 8, 1908): 7.

Xingyong. "Yanshuo nüzi zhi waixiang 演說女子之外相 [Speech on Women's External Appearance]." *Huixing nüxue bao* 15 (July 2, 1909): 9–10.

Xiu, Zhen 秀珍. "Yindu nüxuetang zhu nüshi shuaicheng sijue 因讀女學堂諸女士詩率成四絕 [Verses Composed after Reading the Poems by the Ladies at the Chinese Girls' School]." *Xinwen bao* 新聞報 (July 4, 1898).

Xu, Chuying 徐楚影, and Jiao Lizhi 焦立芝. "Zhongguo jindai funü qikan jianjie, 1898–1918 中國近代婦女期刊簡介（一八九八——一九一八年）[An Introduction to the Early Chinese Women's Periodical Press, 1898–1918]." In *Xinhai geming shiqi qikan jieshao* 辛亥革命時期期刊介紹第四集 [*An Introduction to the Periodicals during the Xinhai Revolution, Volume Four*], ed. Ding Shouhe 丁守和, 680–693. Beijing: Renmin chubanshe, 1982.

Xu, Qing 許清. "Jinggao nü xuesheng 敬告女學生 [Respectfully Exhort Female Students]." *Zhonghua funüjie* 1, no. 7 (1915): 1–5.

Xu, Yibing 徐一冰. "Lixiang zhong de xin jiating 理想中的新家庭 [The Ideal New Family]." *Funü shibao* 4 (1911): 29–30.

Xue, Shaohui 薛紹徽. "Chuangshe nü xuetang tiaoyi bing xu 創設女學堂條議並敘 [Suggestions for Establishing the Girls' School, with a Preface]." *Qiushi bao* 求是報 9 (1897): 6a–7b.

Xue, Shaohui. "*Nü xuebao* xu 女學報序 [Preface to *Nü xuebao*]." *Nü xuebao* 1 (July 24, 1898): 2b–3a.

Ya Lu 亞盧 [Liu Yazi 柳亞子]. "Ai nüjie 哀女界 [Lamenting on Women/Women's World]." *Nüzi shiji* 9 (1904): 1–9.

Ya Te 亞特 [Liu Yazi]. "Lun zhuzao guomin mu 論鑄造國民母 [On Forging Mothers of Citizens]." *Nüzi shijie* 7 (1904): 1–7.

Yan, Fu 嚴復. "Lun Hushang chuangxing nüxuetang 論滬上創興女學堂 [On the Development of Girls' Schools in Shanghai]." In *Wan-Qing wenxuan* 晚清文選 [*Collected Works in the Late Qing*], ed. Zheng Zhenduo 鄭振鐸, 695. Shanghai: Shanghai shenghuo shuju, 1937.

Yang, Binbin. "Guardians of Family Health in Qing China: From the Exemplary Wife to the Reformer." *Modern China* 40, no. 4 (2014): 1–33.

Yang, Binbin. *Heroines of the Qing: Exemplary Women Tell Their Stories.* Seattle: University of Washington Press, 2016.

Yeh, Catherine Vance. *Shanghai Love: Courtesans, Intellectuals, and Entertainment Culture, 1850–1910.* Seattle: University of Washington Press, 2006.

"Yingguo xiaoshuojia Ailiatuo nüshi zhuan 英國小說家愛里阿脫女士傳 [Biography of the English Novelist Ms. George Eliot]." *Zhongguo xin nüjie zazhi* 4 (1907): 51–55.

Yip, Ka-che. *Health and National Reconstruction in Nationalist China: The Development of Modern Health Services, 1928–1937.* Ann Arbor, MI: Association of Asian Studies, 1995.

You, Jianming 游鑑明. *Yundongchang nei wai: jin dai Hua dong diqu de nüzi tiyu 1895–1937* 運動場內外: 近代華東地區的女子體育（1895–1937） [*On and Off the Playing Fields: A Modern History of Physical Education for Girls in Eastern China 1895–1937*]. Taipei: Zhongyang yanjiuyuan jindaishi yanjiusuo, 2009.

Yu, Jimmy. *Sanctity and Self-Inflicted Violence in Chinese Religions, 1500–1700* Oxford: Oxford University Press, 2012.

Yu, Lifen 余麗芬. "Kang Tongwei nüzi jiaoyu sixiang shuping 康同薇女子教育思想述評 [A Review of Kang Tongwei's Thought on Women's Education]." *Zhejiang shehui kexue* 浙江社會科學 4 (1995): 110–113.

Yu, Tiansui 余天遂. "Yu zhi nüzi jiaoyu guan 余之女子教育觀 [My Views on Women's Education]." *Funü zazhi* 2 (1915): 1–3.

Yu, Xingmin 于醒民, and Tang Jiwu 唐繼無. *Shanghai: jindaihua de zaochan er* 上海：近代化的早產兒 [*Shanghai: A Premature Child of Modernization*]. Taipei: Jiuda wenhua, 1992.

Zamperini, Paola. "Clothes That Matter: Fashioning Modernity in Late Qing Novels." *Fashion Theory: The Journal of Dress, Body & Culture* 5, no. 2 (2001): 195–214.

Zamperini, Paola. "Untamed Hearts: Eros and Suicide in Late Imperial Chinese Fiction." *Nan Nü: Men, Women and Gender in China* 3, no. 1 (2001): 77–104.

Zarrow, Peter. "He Zhen and Anarcho-Feminism in China." *Journal of Asian Studies* 47 (1988): 796–813.

Zarrow, Peter. "Historical Trauma: Anti-Manchuism and Memories of Atrocity in Late Qing China." *History and Memory* 16, no. 2 (2004): 67–107.

Zeng, Pu 曾樸. *Niehai hua* 孽海花 [*Flower in a Sea of Retribution*] (Taipei: Wenhua tushu gongsi, 1990).

Zhang, Hongsheng 張宏生, and Shi Min 石旻. "Fulu: Gudai wenxue funü de yanjiu qidian jiqi tuozhan: Hu Wenkai *Lidai funü zhuzuo kao* de jiazhi he yiyi 附錄：古代文學婦女研究的現代起點及其拓展——胡文楷《歷代婦女著作考》的價值和意義 [Appendix: The Modern Starting Point and Developments on Studies of Women in Traditional Chinese Literature—the Value and Meaning of Hu Wenkai's *Research on Women's Works from All Dynasties*]." In *Lidai funü zhuzuo kao*

歷代婦女著作考 [*Research on Women's Works from All Dynasties*], ed. Hu Wenkai 胡文楷, 1199–1224. Shanghai: Shanghai guji chubanshe, 2008.

Zhang, Yun. "The Emerging Modern Woman: Representations of the 'Girl Student' in Early Twentieth Century Urban China." *Harvard Asia Quarterly* 16, no. 3 (2014): 50–59.

Zhang, Yun. "Feminism in the Vernacular: *Baihua* Writing, Gender, and Identity in Late Qing China." *Twentieth-Century China* 45, no. 1 (2020): 85–104.

Zhang-Zhu, Hanfen 張朱瀚芬. "Lun Shanghai nü xuesheng zhi zhuangshu 論上海女學生之裝束 [On Shanghai Female Students' Clothing]." *Funü shibao* 1, no. 11 (1913): 11–13.

Zhao, Erxun 趙尔巽 et al. *Qing shi gao* 清史稿 [*Draft History of the Qing*] Beijing: Zhonghua shuju, 1977.

Zhao, Yuan 趙媛. "Jiating jiaoyu lu 家庭教育論 [On Family Education]." *Funü shibao* 1 (1911): 6–11.

"Zhi Tongjian xuexiao xuesheng banyan Huixing nüshi xinxi 誌通鑑學校學生扮演惠興女士新戲 [A New Play of Ms. Huixing Performed by Students at the Tongjian School]." *Huixing nüxue bao* 4 (1908): 6–7.

"*Zhonghua funüjie* guanggao 中華婦女界廣告 [Announcement from *Chung Hwa Women's Magazine*]." *Zhonghua funüjie* 1 (January 1915).

Zhong, Xinzhi 鐘欣志. "Yuejie yu manyou: xunmi xiandai guanzhong de 'Zhongsheng xinju' 越界與漫遊：尋覓現代觀眾的"鐘聲新劇" [Boundary Crossing and Wandering: In Search of Modern Audience in Wang Zhongsheng's New Drama]." *Xiju xuekan* 戲劇學刊 14 (2010): 111–151.

Zhou, Gang. *Placing the Modern Chinese Vernacular in Transnational Literature.* New York: Palgrave Macmillan, 2011.

Zhou, Xuqi 周敘琪. *1910–20 niandai duhui xin funü shenghuo fengmao: yi Funü zazhi wei fenxi shili* 一九一〇~一九二〇年代都會新婦女生活風貌——以《婦女雜誌》為分析實例 [*Aspects in the Life of Urban New Women in the 1910s and 1920s: Taking* Funü zazhi *as An Example*]. Taipei: National Taiwan University, 1996.

Zhou, Xuqi. "Yuedu yu shenghuo: Yun Daiying de jiating shenghuo yu *Funü zazhi* zhi guanxi 閱讀與生活——惲代英的家庭生活與《婦女雜誌》之關係 [Reading and Life: The Relationship between Yun Daiying's Family Life and *Funü shibao*]." *Si yu yan* 思與言 43, no. 3 (2005): 107–190.

Zhu, Hu 朱滸, ed. *Zhongguo jindai sixiangjia wenku: Jing Yuanshan juan* 中國近代思想家文庫·經元善卷 [*Works by Modern Chinese Thinkers, the Volume on Jing Yuanshan*]. Beijing: Zhongguo renmin daxue chubanshe, 2014.

Zhu, Youhuan 朱有瓛, ed. *Zhongguo jindai xuezhi shiliao* (di'er ji) 中國近代學制史料（第二輯） [*Historical Materials on China's Modern Education System*, the Second Collection], vols. 1 & 2. Shanghai: Huadong shifan daxue chubanshe, 1987.

Zhu, Yun. *Imagining Sisterhood in Modern Chinese Texts, 1890–1937*. Lanham, MD: Lexington Books, 2017.

Zhu-Zhou, Guozhen 朱周國真. "Nü xuesheng zixiu yongshu zhi yanjiu 女學生自修用書之研究 [Books for the Self-Cultivation of Girl Students]." *Funü zazhi* 5 (1915): 1–4.

Zhuan, Kun 轉坤. "Furen daiyu lun 婦人待遇論 [On Women's Conditions]." *Zhongguo xin nüjie zazhi* 1–5 (1907).

Zhuo, Hua 灼華. "Da yanshuojia Lifuma nüshi zhuan 大演說家黎佛瑪女史傳 [Biography of Ms. Mary Livermore, A Great Orator]." *Zhongguo xin nüjie zazhi* 4 (1907): 41–49.

Zhuzhuang 竹莊 [Jiang Weiqiao 蔣維喬]. "Nüquan shuo 女權說 [On Women's Rights]." *Nüzi shijie* 5 (1904): 1–5.

"Ziyou tan: Shimao pai 自由談：時髦派 [Free Talk: Fashion Clique]." *Shenbao* (January 6, 1912).

Index

www.ingramcontent.com/pod-product-compliance
Lightning Source LLC
LaVergne TN
LVHW020000031026
849161LV00021B/723

* 9 7 8 9 0 0 4 4 3 8 5 3 8 *